LION IN THE
BAY

LION IN THE BAY

The British Invasion of the Chesapeake, 1813–14

STANLEY L. QUICK WITH CHIPP REID

Naval Institute Press
Annapolis, Maryland

This book has been brought to publication with the generous
assistance of Marguerite and Gerry Lenfest.

Naval Institute Press
291 Wood Road
Annapolis, MD 21402

Library of Congress Cataloging-in-Publication Data
Quick, Stanley L.
  Lion in the bay : the British invasion of the Chesapeake, 1813–14 / Stanley L. Quick;
edited by Chipp Reid.
     pages cm
  Includes bibliographical references and index.
  ISBN 978-1-61251-236-5 (alk. paper)
  1. United States—History—War of 1812—Campaigns. 2. Chesapeake Bay Region
(Md. and Va.)—History, Military—19th century. I. Reid, Chipp, editor. II. Title.
  E355.1.C485Q53 2015
  973.5'2—dc23
                                                                    2015016039

♾ Print editions meet the requirements of ANSI/NISO z39.48-1992 (Permanence of
Paper).
Printed in the United States of America.

22 21 20 19 18 17 16 15 14   9 8 7 6 5 4 3 2 1
First printing

CONTENTS

Illustrations and Maps

ILLUSTRATIONS

MAPS

FOREWORD

STANLEY L. QUICK was born on May 14, 1923, in New York City. He graduated from Hempstead High School in 1940, from the Webb Institute of Naval Architecture and Marine Engineering in Glen Cove, New York, in 1944, and received his commission in the U.S. Navy. He earned a PhD in applied mechanics from Brooklyn Polytechnic in 1962. From 1944 to 1957 Stan served in the U.S. Navy, first as the assistant hull superintendent of the Portsmouth Navy Yard in New Hampshire and then as technical adviser on fabric acoustics for minesweeping and test engineer at the David Taylor Model Basin in Annapolis, Maryland. On his return to civilian life he acted as a design and development engineer for several companies, participating in and directing all phases of military and commercial endeavors. He was an active member of the Society of Naval Architects and Marine Engineers and of the Maryland Society of Professional Engineers. He died on November 7, 2008, in Chestertown, Maryland, at the age of eighty-five.

Stan and Marian, his wife of forty years, were boating enthusiasts who wanted a historic home on the Chesapeake Bay waterfront where they could enjoy retirement and keep their boat. In 1985, after much searching, they found Carvill Hall on Fairlee Creek in Kent County on Maryland's Eastern Shore. But Stan's retirement was short lived. With his keen interest in history, Stan quickly became immersed in learning more about his old house and the surrounding area. After learning that the British had attacked Fairlee Creek in the summer of 1814, Stan became engrossed in the War of 1812. As his interest expanded to the battle in nearby Caulk's Field, he delivered lectures and wrote "The Battle of Caulk's Field," a project that grew into this book—a comprehensive account of the War of 1812 in the Chesapeake.

Stan was a product of the old school who neither typed nor used a computer. He produced his manuscript the old-fashioned way: he handwrote every word. Beginning in 1985, when he was satisfied with a chapter he sent it out to be typed by Linda R. Coyle. The two became a cohesive team. Linda would return the typed chapters in hard copy, which Stan would alter as his research progressed. It was not uncommon for him to awaken in the middle of the night and go to his office to write down an idea that had come to him in his sleep.

Stan was determined and thorough in his pursuit of history. Expense did not deter him. Retained receipts show that he spent a small fortune accumulating maps, charts, books, manuscripts, illustrations, and anything else that would aid him in his research. Although the detail and breadth of this book would suggest that he was a veteran historian, this is actually the first book-length historical publication he had ever attempted.

Stan's methodology was interesting. Before reading other scholars' conclusions he would assemble the primary documents and write his own version of what had happened; only then would he read what other historians had to say. Sometimes his conclusions differed from theirs, largely because he often found sources they had not seen or used. For example, while snippets of Royal Navy ships' logs had been published or copied here and there, to our knowledge no one had ever gathered in one place the logs of nearly every British warship that participated in the Chesapeake campaigns of 1813 and 1814. Stan hired individuals (principally John Weiss) to make copies of each ship's log from the National Archives United Kingdom, London (formerly called the Public Records Office), and placed each in a three-ring binder. At the front of each binder he put his handwritten summary of what each log recorded on every day it was located in the Chesapeake. Information includes weather, stage of the moon, disciplinary measures, provisioning, watering details, fleet movements, debarkation and reembarkation of forces, deployment of tenders, and more. With these resources Stan could understand the total disposition of the British forces on the Chesapeake Bay and look at any engagement date and determine which vessels participated and in what manner.

He overlooked no detail. Using his knowledge as a naval architect to his advantage, he determined the draft of various ships and compared those with contemporary charts of the day. He compared the ships' logs with daily events. He knew where every ship was located during the campaigns of 1813 and 1814. His files included a calendar for those years on which he circled the date of the full moon for each month. In examining the actions on Fairlee Creek he accumulated the most comprehensive collection of land deeds for the area ever compiled, filling one file box and two map tubes.

This extensive research enabled him to locate the positions of three houses the British attacked over a three-day period. He made a sketch showing the Fairlee Creek area and the angle of each house in relation to the other two. Presumably, he did this to determine where the frigate HMS *Menelaus* would have been anchored when it bombarded the Waller house. Stan engaged Mark Myers to create a painting of this event, which appropriately graces the dust cover of this book, that is accurate down to the last detail, including the second-story window over the Waller house's front door.

Stan's dedicated wife, Marian, assisted him in his endeavors. Several books in his War of 1812 library were Christmas presents from Marian. His efforts were cut short in 2005 when he began to suffer the effects of a brain lesion, but his passion did not wane. When he regained consciousness after a successful operation, with the family present, the doctor asked Stan three questions to assess his mental state: What is your name? What year is it? Who is president? Stan replied, "Stanley Quick." "Eighteen-fourteen." "James Madison." While the doctor was initially puzzled and concerned by these replies, the family smiled; they knew he was fine because he lived in the War of 1812.

Eventually the meningioma reached a point at which Stan began making changes to his manuscript that appeared to alter his original intent. Family and colleagues worried about its prospects for completion. One day Marian announced that Stan wanted his research notes to go to Ralph Eshelman, with whom he had formed a close and respectful friendship based on shared questions and information about the War of 1812. Eventually, Marian gave Stan's entire collection to Ralph and asked if he could complete the book. Because Stan had been a U.S. Navy man and his book was a naval story, Ralph approached Richard Russell, the director of the Naval Institute Press, about publication. The press agreed, but because the software used was outdated, the entire manuscript had to be rekeyed. Chipp Reid, an up-and-coming naval historian, agreed to write the final chapters of the book on the Battle of Bladensburg and the Battle of Baltimore. These difficulties having been bridged, it seems fitting that a book by Stanley L. Quick, a Navy veteran and a professional naval architect, is to be published by the Naval Institute Press.

With the agreement of Marian, Ralph donated the Stanley L. Quick Collection to the Maryland State Archives, where it will be preserved and made available to future scholars studying the War of 1812 in the Chesapeake. Thanks to Dr. Edward Papenfuse, state archivist, much of Stan's research has been digitized and is now available to the public online. Stan would be pleased. This book and his collection are fitting tributes to a man who was not only a scholar himself but also met the world with a smile and was kind and generous in sharing his research.

—*Marian Quick, Chestertown, Maryland;*
Ralph Eshelman, Lusby, Maryland;
and John Weiss, London, England
February 2014

Editor's Preface

A CHANCE ENCOUNTER with a plumbing problem was the catalyst for this book. In 1985 Stanley and Marian Quick moved into a house on the Eastern Shore of Maryland near a small town called Rock Hall. Carvill Hall, built in 1695, once belonged to a prominent regional family, the Carvills. When Stanley and Marian moved into the house, it had already been through at least two major renovations. The first occurred sometime during or immediately after the War of 1812. The second came along much later when the owners added electrical service.

It was that first renovation that caught Stanley's attention. He noticed what he called "scars" on some of the bricks and stones he thought the original renovation had caused. Nevertheless, it was clear the Carvills had tried to preserve and reuse the materials from the original house. They had enlarged the house, but the old foundation and the signature of the first chimney were apparent.

Soon after Stanley and Marian moved in, a pipe burst in the ceiling, ruining plaster and wall boards in the original part of the home. The Quicks took on a fourteen-week remodel job, and it was then when Stanley had his eureka moment. "One night, sitting alone amidst the mess, it suddenly occurred to me that the Carvill renovation could not have been a voluntary undertaking to modernize the interior and styling," Stanley recalled. "Like us, they had to do it."

This realization set Stanley off on a quest to find out the story behind his new home. The search took him to libraries in London and Washington, and to historical societies all around the Eastern Shore. He soon learned that his home had been a focal point of a small, sharply contested British raid during the War of 1812, that the local militia had defended the place, and battle damage was the reason for the first renovation. All of this intrigued Stanley, although at first he confined his research to his home before broadening it to include the raid and the nearby Battle of Caulk's Field. He then decided to tackle the entire British campaign in the Chesapeake. His research was meticulous and all encompassing, and he packed as much detail as he possibly could into his manuscript. Stanley spent twenty-three years on his manuscript, but unfortunately he never had the chance to finish it. He passed away in 2008. Luckily, his manuscript found its way to the Naval Institute Press, where my editor, Adam Kane, believed it was a project that an old rewrite editor could sink his teeth into.

My usual area of expertise is biographies; while I was a journalist I often had the assignment of conducting the "big interview." Add in my other areas of interest—old sailboats, cannons, and Marines—and this appeared to be an easy match. It was, up to a point. I found it difficult at times to maintain Stanley's sentence structure and syntax—his voice—as I attempted to focus his sweeping narrative. Stanley passed away before he could write his chapters on the seminal events of 1814—the attacks on Washington, D.C., and Baltimore—so those also fell to me to complete. All told, what we thought would be a quick six-month edit became an eighteen-month odyssey filled with frustration, discovery, and a great deal of learning. I wish I could have met Stanley, because his passion for the history of the Eastern Shore was both unmatched and contagious.

There are a great many people I could thank for their help in this project, but I don't think it is my place to do so. This book is Stanley's, not mine. I am just the closer, the Mariano Rivera to his Andy Pettitte; and yes, I can make a Yankees reference because Stanley, like me, hailed from the New York City metro area. If I could be presumptuous for a moment, I would like to express my deepest thanks to the officers and Marines at 8th and I, Marine Barracks Washington. Their great interest in my research into the Marines' actions in the Chesapeake served as an inspiration on those days when I would have rather been sailing than sitting in a library. I would also like to thank the reviewers Adam lined up—the setup guys who are the unheralded part of any book. As always, the Naval Institute Press did a first-rate job in ensuring the story Stanley and, to a small extent, I tell is an accurate one.

I hope I have done justice to Stanley's passion and that this book will ensure the endurance of the story of Carvill Hall and the dark days of the British invasion—and the bright days of American valor.

—Chipp Reid
Annapolis, Maryland
June 2014

CHAPTER 1

Irreconcilable Differences

*T*HE WAR OF 1812 was the result of a complicated mixture of politics, expansionism, economics, and idealism. At its root, the United States declared war on England because of constant violations of American rights at sea and English efforts to thwart American expansion to the Mississippi River. For the people living along the Chesapeake Bay in Maryland and Virginia, freedom of the seas resonated much more than did outcries over British actions in the west. From Baltimore to Norfolk, the sea was the lifeblood of the economy, and many families protested the loss of loved ones to British impressment.

As early as 1792, just nine years after the end of the Revolutionary War, American diplomats protested to their English counterparts about British impressment gangs seizing American seamen while they were in English ports.[1] British warships were also stopping American merchantmen on the high seas and forcibly removing alleged Royal Navy deserters.[2] Even U.S. warships were not immune to British impressment. U.S. Navy commanders complained bitterly about British efforts to entice American crewmen to desert when Yankee frigates arrived in British ports such as Gibraltar and Malta, and there were reports of British press gangs waiting by the docks to snatch American bluejackets.[3]

England earned even more enmity from America in 1807 when it adopted a European-wide blockade. Napoleon, who controlled most of the continent, had declared he would seize as a blockade-runner any vessel trading in English ports or with English allies or colonies. England, in a tit-for-tat economic move, adopted Orders in Council essentially declaring all of continental Europe off-limits to neutral shipping. The British began seizing American merchant vessels that ventured into European waters, selling the boats and cargo to help pay for the war and impressing the seamen into the Royal Navy.[4]

The United States viewed the Orders in Council as a direct attack on its economy, although enough American merchants did business with England to offset some of the losses. The British economic sanctions hit the merchants and shipowners of Baltimore particularly hard.

Hundreds of schooners, brigs, and ships sailed from Baltimore for the West Indies, South America, and the Mediterranean, and they often had to sneak past British ships blockading ports under French control. Italian ports were especially confusing as they changed hands between Austria (a British ally), Spain (first a French ally, then a British ally), France, and England. The American merchants who stocked the ships with raw materials and other goods coveted in Europe did not care who controlled the ports as long as their ship masters could land those goods, sell them, and then buy clothing, porcelain, spices, and other items in demand back home, which guaranteed a profit. Britain's policies slowly put a stranglehold on business, however, and cost merchants and shipowners thousands of dollars in lost revenue. Many Americans blamed both the British and the French for their economic problems, with much of the blame falling on the British.[5]

President Thomas Jefferson answered the French and British actions with the Embargo Act of 1807, which outlawed foreign trade and further stifled the American economy. Exports plummeted from $108 million in 1807 to just $22 million in 1808. Imports plunged from $138 million to just $57 million over the same span. The only saving grace for the economy came from the coastal trade and the often-winked-at smuggling trade that quickly cropped up. American merchant vessels would find themselves "blown off course" and, in desperation, would seek shelter in a Caribbean port, where the locals just happened to want to buy the ship's cargo.[6] The Embargo Act lasted just two years, but its repeal did not provide the economic bounce-back newly elected president James Madison and his backers expected. Trade with England did rebound to nearly pre-1807 levels, but trade with France remained stagnant.[7]

Impressment, however, caused far more anger among Americans than did economic policies. Part of the dispute stemmed from how the United States and Great Britain viewed citizenship. American shipowners believed anyone who enrolled in the crew, no matter where he was born, could become an American by taking an oath of citizenship. Britain refused to recognize the legitimacy of a British citizen's oath to another country and claimed the right to seize any British man serving on board vessels flying a flag other than the Union Jack. The British also claimed the right to remove Danes, Swedes, Portuguese, Spanish, or French sailors from neutral vessels on the grounds that they, at varying times, were enemies of the Crown and therefore legitimate prisoners of war.[8]

It was a policy that would not change as long as Great Britain remained locked in its life-or-death struggle with France, and it was this attitude that rankled Americans. Secretary of State Timothy Pickering, in a 1796 letter to the U.S. minister to London, Rufus King, expressed the frustration many Americans felt when he claimed:

The injustice of the British claim and the cruelty of the British practice, have tested, for a series of years, the pride and patience of the American government.... The claim of Great Britain, in its theory, was limited to the right of seeking and impressing its own subjects, on board of the merchant vessels of the United States, although, in fatal experience, it has been extended (as already appears) to the seizure of the subjects of every other power, sailing under a voluntary contract with the American merchant; to the seizure of the naturalized citizens of the United States, sailing, also, under voluntary contracts, which every foreigner, independent of any act of naturalization, is at liberty to form in every country; and even to the seizure of the native citizens of the United States, sailing on board the ships of their own nation, in the prosecution of a lawful commerce.[9]

A decade later the situation had only grown worse. War nearly broke out in 1807 after the frigate HMS *Leopard* attacked the U.S. frigate *Chesapeake* on the grounds that the American warship had numerous British deserters among her crew. After winning the presidency in 1808, Madison began making a case for war with England. In addition to what he called British transgressions at sea, Madison pointed out that Great Britain had yet to abide by the Treaty of Paris of 1783, which granted America its independence. Britain was supposed to abandon its forts along the Ohio River and in the Northwest Territory—Ohio, Indiana, Illinois, and Michigan—but instead kept many of its garrisons in place to forestall the westward growth of the United States. England also armed the Native Americans who resisted the American settlers as they pushed into new territories.[10]

The anger built in states such as Maryland, where commerce was the lifeblood of the local economy, and by 1811 had finally reached a boiling point. The Maryland state legislature, on November 26, 1811, issued a resolution condemning Great Britain and lauding President Madison, and sent it to the U.S. Congress:

Whereas, It is highly important at this eventful crisis in our foreign relations, that the opinions and feelings of every section of the union should be fairly and fully expressed; Therefore, we the legislature of Maryland do Resolve, That in the opinion of this legislature, the measures of the administration with respect to Great Britain have been honorable, impartial and just; that in their negotiations they have evinced every disposition to terminate our differences on terms not incompatible with our national honor, and that they deserve the confidence and support of the nation;

Resolved, That the measures of Great Britain have been, and still are destructive of our best and dearest rights, and being inconsistent with justice, with reason and with law, can be supported only by force; therefore if persisted in, by force should be resisted.[11]

Just six months later, fifty of the most prominent prowar businessmen in the state gathered at the Fountain Inn in Baltimore to adopt a resolution calling for war with England that was sent to the president: "The time has at length arrived when we must determine whether by tameness and submission we shall sink ourselves below the rank of an independent nation," said businessman Joseph H. Nicholson, "or whether by a glorious or manly effort we shall permanently secure that independence which our forefathers handed down to us as the price of their blood and their treasure."[12] They got their wish on June 18, 1812, when James Madison became the first American president to ask Congress for—and to receive—a formal declaration of war on a foreign nation. The declaration divided the nation into pro- and antiwar camps.

Maryland, like much of the country, had a sizable antiwar population, but the most strident opposition came from New England, where ship and business owners feared a war with Britain would wreck the still-recovering economy. The Non-Intercourse Act of 1809, which had replaced the Embargo Act, allowed American merchants to conduct trade with any country except England or France but only slightly eased the pressure on the U.S. economy. Merchants, especially in New England, lobbied for complete freedom to resume their profitable trade with England.

The port town of Salem, Massachusetts, was one of the centers of New England antiwar sentiment. For the merchants of Salem, trade with England meant money not only for themselves but also for the country. Salem alone contributed more than $7 million of the $25 million in import duties the federal government collected in Massachusetts from 1801 to 1810.[13] One ship from Salem, the 233-ton brig *Leander,* landed cargo from China that paid more than $179,000 in duties.[14] Wealthy merchants in Philadelphia, Baltimore, and Charleston opposed the coming conflict for the same reasons as their New England counterparts.

The antiwar opposition was also highly politicized. Two parties dominated early American politics: the Democratic-Republicans, the party of Thomas Jefferson and Madison, and the Federalists. Aside from fundamental differences over what role the government should play in Americans' daily lives, the two parties differed greatly on economic and diplomatic matters.

Federalist newspapers and members of Congress quickly presented a solid antiwar front. The tenor of the Federalists' opposition was so strident that Democratic politicians threatened to treat opponents of the war as traitors.

Robert Wright, for example, governor of Maryland from 1806 to 1808 and a U.S. representative in 1812, said in a speech prior to the declaration of war that if "the signs of treason and civil war discover themselves in any quarter of the American Empire the evil [will] soon be radically cured, by hemp and confiscation."[15]

In Maryland, Federalist sentiment ran high among the residents of the Eastern Shore—the mostly agrarian part of the state between the Chesapeake Bay and Delaware—as well as in the state capital, Annapolis, and the farm country along the Patuxent and Potomac Rivers. There was also a small but extremely vocal Federalist minority in the radically Democratic city of Baltimore. The third largest city in the United States, after New York and Philadelphia, Baltimore had a large and unruly anti-British working class. City officials actually condoned periodic riots against the British and Federalists. Wright, as governor, once pardoned several people convicted of tarring and feathering a British shoemaker.[16]

The situation in Baltimore, with pro- and antiwar supporters clashing in the newspapers and sometimes on the streets, was something of a microcosm of the nation as a whole. The prowar supporters, in many cases, had very personal reasons for wanting war, whether it was trade, new land, or "sailors' rights." The antiwar supporters, who also loathed the practice of impressment, viewed war on a more national scale.[17] If two men embodied these divisive forces in Maryland, they were Capt. Charles Gordon of the U.S. Navy and newspaper editor and lawyer Alexander C. Hanson.

There were likely few people in Baltimore as happy about the onset of the war as Gordon, who had a very personal grudge against England. Although he was a capable and well-respected naval officer, Gordon had not had an easy life, and he blamed his misfortunes on the British. Born in Chestertown, Maryland, in 1778, Gordon was one of the six children of Charles Gordon Sr., an English-born lawyer who immigrated to America in 1750. The elder Gordon married into the powerful Nicholson family of Maryland, but not even the Nicholsons could help their son-in-law when he expressed his unabashed support for England at the start of the Revolution. His Loyalist views were greatly at odds with those of the patriots of the Eastern Shore, and in 1780 the governor of Maryland ordered his arrest. The Nicholsons, staunch patriots, intervened, and the governor ordered Gordon's exile. He left America, never to return.[18]

Gordon was two when his father left. Within two years of his father's exile the Gordons had gone from being relatively wealthy to destitute. The state confiscated the family's home and assets, forcing his mother to appeal to relatives for help. Gordon went to live with the Samuel Chew family in Chestertown.

As he grew up, he had numerous fights with boys—his age and older—who accused him of being a Loyalist like his father. When his mother died in 1786, Gordon became a ward of the state.[19] How he lived for the next thirteen years is a mystery, although he apparently received a better-than-average education, probably thanks to his powerful family connections. By the mid-1790s Gordon was a crewman on a merchant ship out of Baltimore, an experience that instilled in him a love of the sea. In 1794 a war scare with Algiers, one of the infamous Barbary States, goaded Congress into authorizing the creation of the U.S. Navy. Although another three years would pass before a single ship slid down the ways, Gordon applied for a warrant in the new force.

His connections to the Nicholson family helped Gordon secure an appointment as a midshipman in 1799, just in time to serve in the Quasi-War against France. He served first on the *Insurgente*, a captured French frigate, and then transferred to the frigate *Constellation*. Although he saw little combat action, Gordon impressed his superiors with his skill as a navigator and his seamanship. He earned a promotion to lieutenant within a year. Despite his lack of combat experience, Gordon was among the thirty-six lieutenants retained under the Peace Establishment Act that greatly reduced the size of the Navy at the end of the conflict with France.[20]

Gordon held a variety of posts over the next two years, serving on the frigates *New York* and *Chesapeake* in the first two years of the conflict with Tripoli that broke out in 1801. In 1803 he became the first lieutenant on the U.S. frigate *Constitution* and served in the squadron Edward Preble commanded. Gordon shined under Preble, earning the commodore's commendation for his handling of the flagship and for bravery when Preble put him in command of a gunboat.

The campaign against Tripoli was the crucible that molded many young officers in the new navy. Gordon fought alongside Stephen Decatur, Charles Stewart, Isaac Hull, James Lawrence, Oliver Hazard Perry, Thomas Macdonough, and Richard Somers, and earned the respect of his peers. For perhaps the first time in his life, Gordon felt among equals. Like many of his brother officers he was from the Mid-Atlantic region, and he learned that no one cared about his father's politics. All that mattered were his actions. He quickly won promotion to lieutenant commandant and then to master commandant.

In 1807 Gordon took command of the *Chesapeake*, then fitting out at Hampton Roads, Virginia, for a cruise to the Mediterranean.[21] Although he commanded the frigate, Gordon found himself relegated to little more than a figurehead when Commodore James Barron claimed the *Chesapeake* as his flagship. Barron, not Gordon, would command the ship if she saw combat.

The *Chesapeake* was ill prepared for the cruise. Gordon took command of the frigate in April, and by June he was still working frantically to ready her for sea. The *Chesapeake* had been in ordinary—in mothballs—since 1805, and whole parts of the ship required reconstruction. Although the work was incomplete when Barron arrived in Norfolk in June, Gordon told the commodore the *Chesapeake* was ready for action. Barron, after a cursory inspection, agreed.[22]

Gordon also had the responsibility of recruiting the *Chesapeake*'s crew. Many Americans eagerly joined when offered an advance of a month's pay but then promptly disappeared. Gordon believed he had no choice but to enlist men he knew were British. He likely tried to hide his misgivings about the crew as the *Chesapeake* pulled away from the dock on June 22, knowing the 50-gun *Leopard* was lurking off the coast. That ship's commander, Capt. Salisbury Pryce Humphreys, had declared publicly he believed the *Chesapeake* had British subjects—including Royal Navy deserters— among her crew and had vowed to stop the American warship to retrieve them.

The two ships "met"—Humphreys was on the hunt for the Yankee frigate—off the Virginia coast. Humphreys ordered the *Chesapeake* to stop to allow a British boarding party to search her for British subjects. Barron, who outranked Gordon and held command of the *Chesapeake*, refused. The *Leopard* then fired four broadsides into the *Chesapeake*, killing three men and wounding eighteen (one died later from his wounds), and completely unnerving Barron. The commodore ordered the *Chesapeake*'s flag hauled down and offered to surrender. Humphreys refused. A British party boarded the *Chesapeake* and removed four crewmen—three of whom were in fact Americans.[23]

The incident touched off a firestorm of indignation in the United States. Citizens marched in the streets calling for war with England. The American people also demanded to know how one of their frigates could be so ill prepared for combat. Secretary of the Navy Robert Smith was just as incensed and ordered the court-martial of Gordon, Barron, and two other *Chesapeake* officers. Gordon faced charges of neglect of duty for not properly training (or "exercising") his crew and for reporting the *Chesapeake* ready for sea when she was unfit for battle.[24]

In his defense, Gordon deflected the responsibility for the fiasco. He admitted the *Chesapeake* was poorly prepared for battle when he left the dock that June morning. Her guns were not fitted properly and he had not exercised the crew much prior to leaving Hampton Roads, but none of those problems was his fault, Gordon said. He had not exercised his crew on the guns because until June 19 the *Chesapeake* had only twelve cannon mounted. Moreover, he did not have his full battery until the very morning the frigate sailed. Lastly, the final decision on whether to sail was Commodore Barron's, not his, Gordon said, and the commodore should have easily seen the poor state of readiness on the vessel.[25] "Yes, gentlemen," said Gordon,

> if I had detained the ship but one second after she was able to cross the Atlantic, and have so reported, I should have been called to a severe account for it. My accuser would then have

said, all this work was not the business of half an hour and might as well be done as you were crossing the Atlantic with but little else to do. Thus I am placed between Scylla and Charybdis. For reporting the ship ready, I am censured; for detaining her longer when she was ready I certainly should have been censured. The alternative I adopted in this situation, while it disproves the charge [of negligence], was that alone which I could safely adopt.[26]

The trial could have cost Gordon his career. Instead, the brunt of the blame fell on Barron. The court found Gordon guilty of negligence for not having the *Chesapeake* ready for battle but sentenced him only to a private reprimand.[27]

The incident did little to sidetrack Gordon's career. If anything, it made him more attentive to detail than ever before. It also further ingrained in him a hatred of everything English. For the second time in his life, an authority figure, this time Commodore Barron, had let him down and left him open to ridicule. Just as it had been with his father, he saw the British as the root cause.

Following his court-martial Gordon received command of the brig *Syren* with orders to transport a diplomat to France on a "special mission." On the warship's arrival, the French, borrowing a page from the British, demanded to board her to search for alleged deserters. Gordon refused and ordered his crew to clear the brig for action. The French backed down.[28] Paul Hamilton, the new secretary of the Navy, "fully approved" of Gordon's actions and tagged him for higher command, saying Gordon had helped restore public faith in the Navy by standing up to the French.[29] Gordon's hatred of the English and his propensity to blame them for any setback, however, continued to shape his life.

Three months after the *Chesapeake* incident, in November 1807, Gordon resorted to pistols to gainsay the claim he had unfairly jettisoned the blame for the disaster onto James Barron. The duel was against a distant cousin of Barron's, a Dr. Stark. Under the terms of the duel, if either man fired before the other, the other duelist and his second could return fire. After four missed shots, Stark fired early on his fifth, missing Gordon. Gordon's second, Lt. William Crane, immediately fired, hitting Stark in the arm. Stark's second then stepped in and challenged Gordon and winged him in the arm. The wound had no effect on Gordon's service; nor was it the last time Gordon would fight to defend his actions on the *Chesapeake*.

Politically, Alexander Hanson was Gordon's opposite—passionately against war with Britain. Hanson was born on February 27, 1786, in Annapolis, the grandson of John Hanson, the first president of the Continental Congress. He graduated from St. John's College in Annapolis in 1802 with a law degree and

The Conspiracy against Baltimore, or The War Dance at Montgomery Court House, a contemporary engraving satirizing antiwar Federalists. The bad blood between prowar and antiwar parties sparked riots and vicious attacks in local newspapers.
MARYLAND HISTORICAL SOCIETY, BALTIMORE

practiced as an attorney for six years. His political views were well known in the state capital, and he soon became a leading voice among Maryland's Federalists.

In 1808 he began publishing the *Federalist Republican*, a highly partisan newspaper that quickly drew the attention and ire of federal officials. In one of its first issues Hanson wrote a biting editorial condemning the Embargo Act. A year later he again drew fire when he wrote a series of articles called "Reflections" in which he accused President Madison of ignoring Britain's attempts at reconciliation, a common theme among Federalists. Britain, Hanson said, did not want a second war, nor could it afford to lose access to American raw materials. It had offered—and paid—reparations for the attack on the *Chesapeake* and had begun looking at ways to either modify or repeal the Orders in Council to answer America's demand for access to European ports. The British also knew of land-hungry Americans' designs on Canada as well as the strong antiwar movement in New England. Although England did not see America as a powerful enemy, any conflict that would divert resources from its war against Napoleon was something Britain wanted to avoid.

Federalists were quick to point out Britain's willingness to negotiate. They were just as quick to blast Madison and congressional "war hawks" for their increasingly belligerent tone. On January 1, 1810, Hanson penned an editorial about the *Chesapeake-Leopard* incident in which he ridiculed the administration, and Democrats in general, for their anti-British stance and their refusal—as Federalists saw it—to see reality: "Shall we go to war with England because she protests . . . and refuses to sanction *our encouragement of British seamen to desert* . . . these men, if we recollect right, were encouraged to desert from their ships . . . were paraded about the streets of Norfolk in defiance of and in the presence of their own officers, and *their* existence on board the *Chesapeake* was formally and officially denied."[30]

The deep division in Maryland politics continued right up to the declaration of war. When Madison sent his declaration to Congress, six of Maryland's nine representatives, all Democrats, voted in favor. The state's two senators were divided. Samuel Smith of Baltimore, the former secretary of the Navy, voted for war; Philip Reed of the Maryland Eastern Shore, a Federalist, voted against it.[31]

Two days after the declaration of war, on June 20, 1812, Hanson wrote a scathing editorial condemning the war and laying out the roadmap for Federalist opposition.

> Thou hast done a deed whereat valor shall weep. . . . As the consequences will soon be felt, there is no need in pointing them out to the few who have not the sagacity to apprehend them. Instead of employing our pen in this dreadful detail, we think it more apposite to delineate the course we are determined to pursue as long as the war shall last. We mean to represent in as strong colors as we are capable, that it is unnecessary, inexpedient and entered into in partial, personal and as we believe motives bearing upon their front marks of undisguised foreign influence, which cannot be mistaken. We mean to use every constitutional argument and legal means to render as odious and suspicious to the American people, as they deserve to be, patrons and contrivers of this highly impolitic and destructive war, in the fullest persuasion that we shall be supported and ultimately applauded by nine-tenths of our countrymen, and that our silence would be treason to them. We detest and abhor the attempts by faction to create civil contest through the pretext of a foreign war it has rashly and premeditatedly commenced and we shall be ready cheerfully to hazard everything most dear, to frustrate anything leading to the prostration of civil rights, and the establishment of a system of terror and proscription announced in the Government paper at Washington as the inevitable consequence of the measure now proclaimed. We shall cling to the rights of freemen, both in act and opinion, till we sink with the liberties of our country or we sink alone. . . . We are avowedly hostile to the presidency of James Madison, and never will breathe under the dominion, direct or derivative, of Bonaparte, let it be acknowledged when it may.

Let those who cannot openly adopt this confession abandon us; and those who can, we shall cherish as friends and patriots worthy of the name.[32]

The editorial was the match that touched off a three-day firestorm in Baltimore as mobs took the debate over the war into the streets.

The *Federalist Republican* was based in downtown Baltimore. Two days after Hanson's editorial appeared, a mob of Democrats gathered outside the newspaper's office. Shouts of indignation quickly escalated to rock throwing. The mob smashed the windows, broke down the doors, and rushed in to destroy the printing press and set the building on fire. Local officials who responded to the disturbance did nothing to stop them.[33]

Hanson arrived at the ruins of his office the next day. Far from silencing the Federalist mouthpiece, the mob attack emboldened Hanson. He moved his newspaper office to Georgetown, in Washington, D.C., and made plans to start publishing once more. It took him roughly a month to get everything he needed, during which time anti-Federalist sentiment grew ever stronger in Baltimore.

Hanson opened a new office in Baltimore on July 26 in the Charles Street home of Jacob Wagner, one of his partners and a leading Baltimore Federalist. Wagner had vacated his house soon after the mob sacked the newspaper office, leaving his furniture behind, and agreed to lease the house and its contents to Hanson.[34]

The day he opened his office, Hanson released his first newspaper issue since June. He once more attacked the Democrats, blaming them for the destruction of his first office. He also railed against rival newspapers for fomenting the attack and heaped insults on the city officials who had done nothing to stop the mob on June 22, a group that he said included Mayor Edward Johnson, the city's chief magistrate, and the police chief. He also slammed the mob that attacked his office, calling the rioters mindless tools of Democratic politicians.

The inflammatory editorial elicited an immediate response. A mob

Newspaper owner and Federalist firebrand Alexander Contee Hanson, author of the editorials that sparked the infamous Baltimore riots in June 1812. Engraving by an unknown artist. MARYLAND HISTORICAL SOCIETY, BALTIMORE

formed in Fells Point, on the city's waterfront, and marched to Charles Street. They arrived at the Wagner house around 11 p.m. to find that Hanson was not alone; he had enlisted the help of several other Federalists to protect his new office. At first there were nine men, including former Continental Army generals James M. Lingham and the famed Henry "Light Horse Harry" Lee. Others included militia captain Richard Crabb, Dr. P. Warfield, Charles J. Kilgour, Otho Sprig, Ephraim Gaither, and John Howard Payne. According to those in the house, "Several others were to have gone, but were prevented; and on the night of the attack, the party was joined by three other volunteers from the county, who were not fully apprised by Mr. Hanson, of his determination, but received their information in confidence from others—Major Mesgrove, Henry G. Gaither, and William Gaither. On the evening of the attack, they were joined by about twenty gentlemen living in Baltimore, one or two only of whom were invited to the house by Mr. Hanson."[35] The defenders were determined to "meet force with force. . . . Reliance upon the civil authority they early perceived to be fruitless, for on application to the Mayor by the owner of the house, he peremptorily declined all interference and left town, as it was understood, to prevent his repose from being disturbed."[36]

As the mob converged on the house, Hanson and his supporters brandished firearms. The mob responded with a fusillade of rocks. Subsequently, "an attempt was made to break down the street door, which was at length actually broken and burst open. All these acts of violence were accompanied by loud and reiterated declarations by the mob of a determination to force the house, and expel, or kill all those who were engaged in its defense."[37]

Hanson and the others built a barricade of chairs and other furniture and prepared for the worst. Retreating to the second floor, they fired a volley over the heads of the rioters that sent them scurrying. The mob soon returned, however, with a Dr. Gale at its head. Gale exhorted the crowd to attack the house once more. With Gale in the lead, a number of rioters charged. The moment they crossed the threshold, Hanson and his men opened fire, killing Gale. The rioters returned fire and Ephraim Gaither dropped to the floor with a severe wound.

Just as the mob was about to charge again Mayor Johnson arrived with a group of militia. The mayor attempted—halfheartedly—to convince the mob to retire, but his words met with a chorus of boos and jeers. Johnson then asked Hanson and his men to surrender into his custody, promising he would protect them and remove them to a place of safety. By then it was 6 a.m. on July 27, and the standoff had gone on for nearly seven hours. Hanson and the others agreed to Johnson's plan. They left the house under escort and walked to the jail.[38]

Later that day, the Democratic *Baltimore Whig* printed a caustic attack on Hanson in which it called him and the others in the house "murderous traitors" who should have been put to death. The editorial sparked off more rioting, and a mob headed for the prison. The party of militia Mayor Johnson had left to guard the jail was no longer on duty because the local commander had ordered the armed men to return to their homes. "The dismissal of the militia was instantly made known to the mob at the jail . . . and they regarded it, as was natural, as the signal for attack." The mob stormed the jail and began battering down the doors to the cells that housed Hanson and his supporters. It took the rioters fifteen minutes to either knock down the doors or convince the jailor to unlock them—no one is quite sure which. Once they gained access to Hanson and his men, the mob dragged the Federalists outside and began to beat them. Hanson suffered a number of broken bones while Lee, a hero of the Revolutionary War, suffered so many blows that he remained an invalid until his death in 1818. James Lingham died of multiple stab wounds. In all, the mob beat a dozen Federalists, killing one and maiming the others.[39]

Federalists in Baltimore likened the riots to the worst excesses of the French Revolution, but Baltimore juries refused to convict any of the rioters. City authorities, however, indicted Hanson for manslaughter in the death of Dr. Gale, claiming Hanson had provoked the riots and he and his followers deserved the treatment they received. Hanson's lawyer had the trial moved to the Federalist stronghold of Annapolis, where a jury acquitted Hanson of any wrongdoing.[40] The "Baltimore Riots," as newspapers dubbed the street battles between Hanson and the mob, shocked many in Maryland and deepened the rift between Federalists and Democrats in the state.

The rift the riots caused lingered throughout the war and had lasting effects on both Gordon and Hanson. The two met face-to-face just once—in a duel. Two years before the riot, Hanson, in his "Recollections" editorials, had claimed Barron and Gordon were directly to blame for what in 1810 seemed like an inevitable war with England. The two officers had willfully ignored the fact that the crew of the *Chesapeake* included many British nationals, hoping to precipitate an attack. The article incensed Gordon, who immediately challenged Hanson to a duel. The two met January 10, 1810, at the dueling grounds in Bladensburg, Maryland.

Hanson was a crack shot and, as a result of his vitriolic writings, an experienced duelist. Gordon had fought a duel only once before—back in 1807, when he missed his opponent four times. Hanson had the better aim and shot Gordon in the abdomen; Gordon's shot missed Hanson altogether. The wound nearly killed Gordon. He was bedridden for more than a year, and only in March 1812 was he able to move around again, although he never completely recovered.[41] Nevertheless, he assumed command of a small, ad hoc naval force somewhat grandly called the "Baltimore Squadron" in May 1812, just a month before the declaration of war.

When the news of the declaration reached Baltimore, Gordon wrote to his friend John Bullus about his burning desire to finally get back at the British and "send in a few large British prizes this summer." Above all, Gordon told Bullus, he wanted to join with Stephen Decatur, Isaac Hull, and his close friend James Lawrence in commanding a frigate. "To be among them is the most ardent desire of my soul," he said.[42] He never would, and although he was frequently near the scene of battle, Gordon never engaged an English warship. He finally got to sea just as the war came to an end. His wound continued to plague him, and he died while on station in the Mediterranean on September 6, 1816.[43]

Hanson lived only slightly longer. He won election to the U.S. House of Representatives as a wave of Federalist sympathy swept through Maryland and served in the House from 1813 to 1816 and then in the Senate from 1816 to 1819. He never fully recovered from the injuries he suffered in the Baltimore Riot, and he died in 1819 at the age of thirty-three.[44]

Ultimately, the reasons behind the conflict that had brought the two men together mattered little. The gulf between Federalists and Democrats would continue to plague Maryland, and to a lesser extent Virginia, when the war entered the Chesapeake.

CHAPTER 2

A Very Exposed Coast

THE UNITED STATES was woefully unprepared for war with Great Britain in June 1812. The Regular Army had an authorized strength of 9,160 privates and noncommissioned officers and more than 500 officers. Had that force gathered in one place, it would have mustered barely enough men to equal the single division the British army had fighting in Spain under Wellington. The authorized strength of an infantry company was 106 privates and noncommissioned officers and 4 officers. Each regiment had 10 companies, giving an infantry regiment an authorized strength of 1,060 soldiers and 40 officers, plus the regimental command.[1] The infantry alone, then, should have had at least 7,420 privates and noncommissioned officers. The Army's lone artillery regiment was set up as an infantry regiment—it had the same authorized size, but with officers and enlisted men also assigned to cannon, which decreased the overall company strength.[2] The regiment of cavalry, or light dragoons, had an authorized strength of 10 companies of 68 privates and noncommissioned officers.[3]

The actual strength of the U.S. Army in January 1812, however, was just 6,686 officers and men split into 7 infantry regiments, an artillery regiment, and a regiment of light dragoons.[4] None of the units authorized by Congress was at full strength. In January 1812 Congress authorized the expansion of the Army to 35,600 officers and men divided into 18 regiments of infantry, 2 of artillery, 1 of dragoons, and 1 of riflemen. More than 15,000 of these troops, however, were to enlist for just 18 months. The short-term enlistments allowed members of Congress opposed to a large standing army to justify the increase but did little to immediately augment the nation's land forces.[5] Despite the authorized increase, the actual strength of the Army never approached its allowed maximum. In June 1812, when Congress declared war, the Army numbered 11,744 officers and men, about 3,000 of whom were new recruits.[6]

The Regular Army also did not operate as an army. There was no general staff, and the senior commander, Maj. Gen. James Wilkinson, and the secretary of war, William Eustis, owed their positions to politics, not competence.[7] The Army's regiments rarely operated above a company level. Units garrisoned a series of forts along the Canadian border from Fort Michilimackinac, on the strait between Lake Michigan and Lake Huron, to Fort Dearborn, on the site of what is now Chicago, and Fort Detroit and Fort Niagara, at the mouth of the Niagara River on Lake Ontario. Other companies garrisoned forts that protected major cities on the East Coast. Some units guarded the routes pioneers used to move west into the new territories. Companies from the same regiment often never saw one another for months at a time.[8] No unit commander then in the Army had experience leading more than a few companies of Regulars supplemented with local militia in battle. As war grew more and more certain, the lack of preparations, coupled with the small number of Regulars available and readily assembled and the dearth of experience among the officers in leading large bodies of soldiers, placed the United States at a distinct disadvantage.[9]

Although spread out, the companies of the Regular Army did have combat experience from the ongoing wars with Native American tribes. One of the major reasons prowar politicians used to defend the conflict was Britain's support of Indian raids in the new territories of Michigan, Indiana, Illinois, and Louisiana. It was the hard-marching Regulars, often in company with local militia, who fought off the native tribes and attempted to wrest control of the still untamed Northwest Territory from their hands.

The situation was a little better at sea. The U.S. Navy had fifteen ships ready for war in January 1812.[10] Five of the vessels were battle-tested frigates: the 44-gun warships *Constitution, United States*, and *President*; the 36-gun *Congress*; and the 32-gun *Essex*. The Navy also had three sloops—ship-rigged vessels smaller than a frigate: the 20-gun *John Adams* and a pair of 18-gun vessels, the *Hornet* and the *Wasp*. Finally, there were seven brigs ranging in size from 16 to 10 guns: the *Argus, Syren, Nautilus, Vixen, Enterprise, Oneida*, and *Viper*. Four other frigates were in ordinary.[11]

More important, the officer corps of the Navy was nearly unparalleled. Their names are legendary in the pantheon of U.S. naval heroes—Stephen Decatur Jr., Charles Stewart, Isaac Hull, James Lawrence, William Bainbridge, Oliver Hazard Perry, and Thomas Macdonough. All were veterans of Commodore Edward Preble's 1803–4 campaign against the Barbary pirates, and all except Bainbridge had grown into command under Preble.[12]

Despite their skills as sailors, however, none of the officers could overcome the financial constraints a penny-pinching Congress continued to use to shackle the military. Both the House of Representatives and the Senate continually cut appropriations for the Navy. In his 1809 appropriations request to Congress, Navy secretary Paul Hamilton reported the service needed at least $180,000 more per year just to maintain the Navy's current strength of nineteen ships and its fleet of gunboats.[13] The brainchild of President Thomas Jefferson, the U.S. Navy's gunboats were probably among the worst ideas ever forced on the military. Jefferson became enamored with gunboats in 1805 after reading the reports of Edward Preble's success against the Barbary Pirates in Tripoli, when Preble borrowed a half-dozen gunboats and two mortar boats from the Kingdom of Naples and carried his assault literally to the walls of Tripoli castle.[14]

Jefferson and his political allies viewed gunboats as a cost-effective means of national defense; the Navy could build and stockpile gunboats for times of emergency while using small groups of them for harbor patrol. There would be no need for the larger, much more costly to maintain frigates, which the Navy could place in ordinary until a need for them arose. Jefferson pointed out that the cost of building one gunboat at five thousand dollars was eight times less than the cost of maintaining a 44-gun frigate for one year.[15]

The Navy built and launched its first gunboat at the Washington Navy Yard in 1805. Capt. John Rodgers oversaw the construction of the vessel, dubbed gunboat *No. 1*. The gunboats ranged in size from 60 to 71 feet and varied in rig. Some had a lateen rig, others a schooner rig, and others a sloop or Bermuda rig. Their armament also varied; some carried 32-pound cannon and small swivel guns, others two long guns, and others a mix of long guns and carronades. The differences in the boats were the result of the opinions of their captains and the shipwrights who built them.[16] Even Jefferson offered design tips.[17] What the gunboats had in common was their poor performance in open water. Lt. James Lawrence had the unenviable task of taking gunboat *No. 6* to the Mediterranean as part of a flotilla of gunboats going to Syracuse on the island of Sicily. Lawrence, who reported to *No. 6* in New York in May 1805, later admitted he did not believe the frail craft would ever reach the Mediterranean, or anywhere else.[18]

Much to Lawrence's surprise, all but one of the gunboats survived the journey. Only gunboat *No. 7* failed to reach Syracuse. It sank somewhere on its voyage. When Lawrence arrived off Gibraltar after a harrowing Atlantic crossing, he reported that the British frigate *Lapwing* offered *No. 6* assistance, believing the little boat to be a wreck.[19]

When gunboat *No. 1* swamped in a storm and washed ashore on a coastal farm, it was a source of amusement from Charleston to Boston. One newspaper ran an editorial advising, "Let her rest there and she will grow into a ship of the line"; while a popular toast immediately after the mishap was, "To gunboat *No. 1*: If our gunboats are of no use on the water, may they be best on land."[20] The gunboats, however, remained in service. By January 1, 1812, the Navy had 170 gunboats, all in varying states of readiness. In his annual report to Congress, Navy secretary Hamilton noted that fewer than 20 of the vessels were in fact combat ready.[21]

One of the reasons the gunboat policy remained in force was its resonance with politicians and citizens who shared Jefferson's belief in the third arm of national defense—the militia. Nothing could fire imaginations like the legendary picture of the patriotic farmer dropping his plow, picking up his musket, and chasing the British redcoats from America's shores. Jefferson argued that the gunboats could form the backbone of a naval militia. The port towns the gunboats were to defend had ample seamen who could man the vessels, meaning each boat would require just a handful of artillerists, which the land militia could provide.[22]

The belief in militia was ingrained in the American psyche. Although somewhat better prepared in 1812 than in 1775, America's militia remained a poor substitute for Regulars. Training, discipline, equipment, and uniforms all varied widely from state to state and unit to unit. It was up to each state to oversee the readiness of its own militia, and although Congress, in 1807 and 1809, debated adopting national standards for militia, the local forces remained largely unprepared for war.

The military situation along the Chesapeake Bay largely mirrored that of the country. A handful of Regulars manned forts in Baltimore and Norfolk while a mix of Marines and Army troops garrisoned the national capital at Washington, D.C. All other defense rested on the unsteady soldiers of the militia.

Governor Levin Winder, a Federalist, commanded the Maryland militia. Winder had been elected in 1812 before the war began. A veteran of the Revolutionary War and a native of Somerset County on the Eastern Shore, Winder personally commanded the 2nd Division, which encompassed all of the Eastern Shore as well as Cecil and Harford Counties, which wrapped around the bay to Baltimore County. Although opposed to the conflict, he nevertheless began preparing his state's troops for battle.[23]

The task was daunting. The Chesapeake Bay covers an area of 3,237 square miles. From its mouth at Norfolk, Virginia, the bay runs 195 miles north, past Annapolis and Baltimore, to its terminus at Elkton. The bay is an estuary formed mainly by three rivers—the Susquehanna, Potomac, and James—but the Severn, Patapsco, Patuxent, Anacostia, and Chester Rivers all flow into the Chesapeake as well. In all, 419 creeks and rivers feed the bay, creating a total of 4,600 miles of shoreline. Winder had to defend this vast area with only his militia.

On paper, the Maryland militia consisted of three divisions. Each division comprised four to five brigades, and each brigade had four regiments of two battalions. An infantry regiment had an authorized strength of eight hundred men, but few managed to reach that number. Only in Baltimore city and in the state's 3rd Division, under Maj. Gen. Samuel Smith, did units approach their authorized strength.[24]

In addition to the three infantry divisions, the Maryland militia had—on paper—eleven cavalry regiments that reported to the infantry brigade commanders. Normally, each infantry regiment in a brigade was assigned a troop

Map 1. Chesapeake Bay

THE NAVAL WAR OF 1812: A DOCUMENTARY HISTORY, VOL. 3: *1814–1815 CHESAPEAKE BAY, NORTH-ERN LAKES, AND PACIFIC OCEAN*, PT. 2 OF 7, NAVAL HISTORICAL CENTER, DEPARTMENT OF THE NAVY, WASHINGTON, D.C. 2002

of cavalry to act as scouts and couriers. Cavalry was neither trained nor used to provide battlefield support. Artillery was also a brigade function, with one company usually assigned to each regiment, although some regiments appear to have had additional volunteer artillery companies that were recruited locally.[25]

The Maryland militia was in a real sense a resident army of volunteers. They were the sons, brothers, cousins, and friends of their officers, who were landowners, businessmen, and public servants within the territories they protected. Any commander who needlessly imperiled his men knew his friends and neighbors would hold him accountable. Cowardice and bravery were equally exposed to community view.

Only a few militia companies had regulation uniforms, and the British moving into the Chesapeake often took these properly attired units for Regulars—at least until the shooting started. Members of Regular Army units wore a single-breasted blue coat with a high choker collar; facings of white, red, or buff denoted infantry, artillery, and cavalry, respectively. White trousers, leather leggings over black shoes, crossed white shoulder belts that held cartridge boxes and equipment bags, and a black leather shako completed the uniform. Regulation uniforms for field officers of the cavalry were dark blue with silver epaulettes and a red sash, in addition to a cape trimmed with silver braid, yellow gloves, calf-length boots with silver spurs, and a black cap with a long white plume in front held in place by a silver eagle. Cavalry carried swords and pistols for arms.[26]

Militia units rarely had such elaborate uniforms. Most men wore a round hat cocked on one side and a homemade greenish smock known as a rifleman's shirt. The smock had small capes over the shoulders and red fringe trim. Some units also wore white overalls and black shakos.[27]

The lack of uniforms often entertained the well-dressed British forces moving into the Chesapeake. "Persons in England . . . find it difficult to consider as soldiers, men neither embodied nor dressed in regimentals. . . . The fact is, everyman is a militiaman . . . to be drilled or trained. He had always in his possession either a musket or a rifle-barrel piece . . . and with it . . . could do as much execution in a smock frock or plain coat as if he wore the most splendid uniform."[28]

On the other hand, when three visiting American officers from Virginia's Eastern Shore appeared in imaginative homemade uniforms, their British hosts found them ludicrous. "They were in regimentals," recalled Lt. James Scott, "but certainly the fashion and cut of them rendered their exact rank and calling somewhat dubious. The trio sported red coats, silver epaulettes, and silver-mounted side arms, white linen waistcoats, and trousers of the same material, Hessian [knee-length] boots which claim no knowledge of acquaintance [with shoe polish], old fashioned French cocked hats, with feathers that might, from their towering height, have served as sky-scraper, completed their attire."[29]

Weapons varied as much as uniforms. The standard-issue musket of the day was the .69-caliber Springfield pattern 1795 musket. A copy of the French infantry weapon, the Springfield was a smoothbore musket that used a flintlock to fire. The weapon took its name from the Springfield Armory in Springfield, Massachusetts, although the armory at Harpers Ferry, Virginia, also produced the Springfield. Notoriously inaccurate, muskets were usually employed en masse, with long lines of troops blasting away at one another until one side or the other got close enough to use bayonets.

American militia also carried rifles—some of them homemade, others military grade. The typical rifle fired a .40-caliber round ball. Although far more accurate than muskets, rifles could not carry bayonets because the muzzle was too wide. Rifles also took slightly longer to load than muskets because more force was required to push the ball down the barrel, which had rifling grooves. Once a rifleman fired, he was essentially helpless to defend himself if an enemy charged with bayonets.[30]

Militarily, Talbot County on Maryland's Eastern Shore, under the command of Brig. Gen. Perry Benson, was one of the better-organized and -equipped areas. Benson had several uniformed infantry companies in his command, units that had distinctive names such the "Light Infantry Blue," "Easton Fencibles" (named for the town of Easton, Md.), "Mechanic Volunteers," "St. Michaels Patriotic Blues," and "Hearts of Oak." Even in Talbot County, however, poorly trained officers, many of them ignorant of infantry tactics, trained the militia. Arms were so scarce that muskets were transferred from company to company depending on the need. Even the best-equipped units often had to use "wooden snappers"—fake guns—to drill. Benson, sensing the danger the poorly defended coast presented, begged for more arms, ammunition, and at least some Regulars to defend the new armory the government had recently built in Easton. Governor Winder replied that he could not "give to the inhabitants of that place further security," while Secretary of War John Armstrong said, "In this case it might be well to remove the armory."[31]

Complicating the situation for Winder and his militia commanders was the omnipresent specter of politics. The backlash over the Baltimore riots in June had created a surge of Federalist sentiment in Maryland, which President James Madison greatly resented. As the British gathered off the Chesapeake, Winder begged Washington for Regular Army reinforcements, but Madison's government pretended not to hear the pleas and allocated troops to Virginia rather than Maryland. Federalists lambasted Madison with charges of favoritism: "Virginia has but to ask and she receives; but Maryland, for her political disobedience, is denied."[32] Winder would eventually have to convene a special session in May 1813 to raise money to pay the state's militia.[33]

At sea, the defense of the Chesapeake rested on whatever vessels were at the bay's two principal ports, Norfolk and Baltimore. The frigate *Constellation* was fitting out in Norfolk for an Atlantic cruise, and Madison's government moved quickly to protect her. Capt. Charles Stewart, who commanded the frigate, proceeded to upgrade the defenses around Norfolk, erecting batteries while trying to get the port's handful of the hated gunboats seaworthy enough for action.

Baltimore's defenses were even worse. Fort McHenry, manned by a small group of Regular Army engineers and artillerymen, stood as the lone guardian of the port city. There were a few gunboats, but they were not ready for action, nor did they have crews. To help organize the sea defenses, Navy secretary Hamilton ordered Capt. Charles Gordon to take command of the "Baltimore Squadron."

Gordon, still recovering from the wound he suffered two years earlier in his duel with Hanson, did not have much to organize. His "squadron" consisted of four privateers—two brigs and two schooners—he had managed to borrow from their owners, with the caveat that he would release the boats on request so they could plunder British shipping. He also had a few Navy gunboats.[34]

Chesapeake Bay was an obvious target for the British. In addition to being home to Baltimore, which the British knew was a hotbed of prowar sentiment, the bay offered the most direct route to the nation's capital. The Chesapeake watershed was an important supply area, sending poultry, grain, iron ore, and fish to other parts of the country. At first, however, the English took a defensive stance. Already embroiled in a titanic struggle with Napoleonic France, the last thing Britain wanted to do was detract from that effort. Britain's North Atlantic Squadron, which had responsibility for the waters from Nova Scotia to the Caribbean, consisted of just six ships of the line, thirty-one frigates, and thirty-three smaller vessels.[35] Rather than become bogged down in a land campaign, the British decided to blockade selected areas—New York, the Delaware River (and Philadelphia), and the Chesapeake. Although it took nearly six months to assemble a blockade force, by the time the Royal Navy arrived off Norfolk in February 1813, it had another reason for being there—to stop American privateers.

Two weeks after declaring war on England, Congress approved "An Act concerning Letters of Marque, Prizes and Prize Goods." The law allowed any shipowner who received a letter of marque to legally attack and capture British merchant vessels. For the shipowners of Baltimore, languishing under the British Orders in Council and the U.S. Embargo Act, the law allowing

The Baltimore privateer *Patapsco* making good her escape from pursuing British ships. The *Patapsco* was one of more than 150 privateers that set out from Baltimore to prey on British merchant ships during the War of 1812. MARYLAND HISTORICAL SOCIETY, BALTIMORE

privateers was a godsend. Hundreds of owners lined up for letters of marque, seeing privateering as a way to recoup the financial losses they suffered under the English and American laws. Captured vessels and their cargoes were sold, with the bulk of the proceeds going to captain and crew, although the government also took a cut.

Brigs, sloops, and above all schooners—the famed Baltimore clippers—fanned out from the Chesapeake across the Atlantic Ocean searching for prey. They had no trouble finding it. Joshua Barney in the privateer *Rossie*, among the first captains to set out from Baltimore, cleared Fells Point on July 11 and returned on October 22 after capturing 18 vessels worth $1.5 million and taking 217 prisoners.[36]

Richard Moon, another privateer captain who set out in July 1812, exemplified the spirit of the fiery Baltimore watermen. In August, Moon, commanding the privateer *Sarah Ann*, fell in with the British ship *Elizabeth* off the Bahamas. Moon's vessel carried just one cannon—a long 9-pounder mounted on a swivel. The *Elizabeth* carried ten 12-pound carronades. Although completely outgunned, Moon chased the *Elizabeth* for three hours before closing and boarding the ship, taking her at a cost of just two wounded. He sailed into Savannah, Georgia, with his prize laden with coffee and sugar.[37]

All told, 126 shipowners in Baltimore snapped up letters of marque or commissioned privateers, capturing or destroying 556 British merchantmen by the war's end.[38] Shipping insurance rates at Lloyd's of London skyrocketed.[39] Unsurprisingly, the success of Baltimore's armed vessels played a major role in Britain's decision to send forces into the Chesapeake.

CHAPTER 3

The Gathering Storm

C APT. CHARLES STEWART had a problem. The commander of the 36-gun U.S. frigate *Constellation* was off Hampton Roads waiting to enter the yard at Norfolk, Virginia, to complete repairs to his ship before slipping out to sea. Situated across the James River from Norfolk, Hampton Roads was the gateway to the Atlantic Ocean from the Chesapeake Bay and an obvious target for the British. Stewart was fighting the calendar. On December 26, 1812, Britain declared the entire Chesapeake Bay under blockade. As yet Stewart had no reports of any Royal Navy ships off the bay, but he knew it was simply a matter of time.

The thirty-four-year-old Stewart arrived in Washington in October 1812 to take command of the *Constellation*, one of three U.S. warships lying in ordinary at the Washington Navy Yard. Stewart expected to find the vessel at least somewhat ready for action. Instead, he discovered he would have to almost completely refurbish her. The 36-gun frigate *New York* and the 32-gun frigate *Boston*, also in ordinary, were in even worse condition than the *Constellation*.

At the same time, Stewart became embroiled in the debate over expanding the Navy. After the declaration of war against England, some lawmakers favored building a true blue-water force that included 74-gun ships of the line. Many others opposed the plan, but Stewart, one of the leading intellects in the Navy, became part of the lobbying effort for the expansion.[1] Stewart spent two months refitting his vessel and pushing Congress to augment the Navy. When Congress finally approved the legislation on December 8, 1812, Stewart began preparations to leave the yard.

Stewart slipped down the Potomac on December 26, 1812. He had orders from William Jones, the new secretary of the Navy, to sail for Annapolis, where he was to test the effectiveness of the gunpowder he had taken on in Washington. Stewart battled ice all the way, arriving in Annapolis after three difficult days. He remained there until January 23, 1813, when he pointed the *Constellation* toward the Atlantic. The long layover revealed several deficiencies in the job the workers in Washington had done, especially with the rigging. He needed the facilities at Norfolk to complete the repairs so he could get to sea, but he also expected to see the masts of the British fleet at any moment.[2]

The *Constellation* arrived off Hampton Roads on February 2, 1813. Stewart anchored for the night and planned to enter Norfolk the next day. At sunrise on February 3, however, Stewart received crushing news. A harbor pilot reported seeing numerous masts off Cape Henry. For Stewart, the game was up. Figuring he would not be able to reach the Atlantic, he turned his frigate toward the safety of Norfolk, only to find the tide and current against him. "We discovered . . . the enemy working up between the Middle Ground and Horse Shoe for the Roads," Stewart reported to Secretary Jones. "It being calm we hove up and kedged the ship to the flats, where the tide having fallen, the ship took the ground and lay until the evening flood."[3]

Despite grounding, Stewart never panicked. The *Constellation*'s sailing master, Benjamin Bryan, wrote in the ship's log that she struck ground around 2 p.m. and noted Stewart hired four schooners to remove provisions, equipment, and water to lighten the frigate. Four hours later, as the tide came in, the *Constellation* floated free.[4] Stewart brought his ship into Norfolk around 11 p.m. and anchored under the protective guns of Fort Norfolk. He incorrectly believed the British had targeted him, writing to Jones: "The object of the Enemy appeared to be this ship, as they got under way (from information) on the evening's flood with a leading breeze and run up to the roads. Finding we were gone they went down again and anchored at Lynnhaven Bay [near Virginia Beach]."[5] While he had saved the ship, Stewart believed the only American frigate on the bay was now officially bottled up in the blockade. The British actually had no idea where he was.

The Royal Navy arrived in force off the Chesapeake Bay on February 4, 1813. The squadron consisted of a pair of 74-gun ships of the line, the *San Domingo* and *Dragon*; the frigates *Junon*, *Statira*, *Maidstone*, and *Belvidera*; the 22-gun sloop *Laurestinus*; and the brigs *Sophie* and *Syron*, all under the command of Adm. Sir John Borlase Warren. The Royal Navy squadron quickly announced its presence by capturing a pair of small schooners. Warren found the mouth of the bay to be a busy place. Many of the merchant ships he encountered were destined for Portugal, illegally carrying supplies for the British army fighting the French. Warren issued those vessels passes and allowed them to proceed but seized all others not destined for Portugal.[6]

Warren received intelligence from one of the squadron's prizes about the movements of the *Constellation* and headed toward Hampton Roads. The American frigate was a primary British target. The same light winds and ebb tide that had grounded the American warship, however, foiled Warren's movements. He turned toward Lynnhaven Bay on the Atlantic coast of Vir ginia, where he could keep an eye on Norfolk.

Admiral Warren was an anomaly among British naval officers of the Napoleonic era.[7] While most officers received their education at sea, Warren had a master's degree in divinity from Cambridge University and for a time had considered answering a calling higher than the sea.[8] Warren was very much like many of his peers, however, in that he owed his position to powerful friends in the Admiralty and at court who helped him progress rapidly through the ranks.

Warren entered the Royal Navy as a midshipman in 1777. He made lieutenant a year later; by 1779 he had command of his own ship, and by 1793 he was a squadron commander. He earned a knighthood when his squadron attacked and captured a squadron of French frigates. In 1795 Warren commanded a Royal Navy flotilla that supported a force of French royalist troops attempting to overthrow the French Republic. When the monarchist force suffered a brutal defeat at the hands of the French Republicans, Warren successfully evacuated 3,500 soldiers. In 1798 he commanded a squadron that intercepted a French squadron that was planning to land soldiers in Ireland to support an uprising. His victory earned him the thanks of Parliament, and in 1810 he achieved promotion to admiral.[9]

His fellow officers considered Warren brave, active, and personable but somewhat lacking in practical seamanship. Some detested the fact that powerful interests aided his career; others saw him as an aging commander bereft of zeal. One captain called him a "superannuated admiral." The criticism had little impact on Warren's career. In August 1812 the Admiralty appointed him commander of North American operations.[10]

To create Warren's command, the Royal Navy combined the Halifax and Caribbean Squadrons, giving Warren a force of six ships of the line, thirty-one frigates, and thirty-three smaller vessels. His orders were simple: induce the Americans to agree to a quick peace and protect British shipping from American privateers. When President Madison brusquely refused to negotiate unless Britain renounced the policy of impressment, the Royal Navy moved to blockade the Chesapeake Bay, Delaware River, and New York Harbor.[11]

It took Warren time to gather his forces because they were spread out from Canada to Columbia; it was time the American commanders used to get to sea. Navy warships and privateers quickly scored several headline-grabbing victories, boosting morale among Americans but doing little to affect the nation's overall fortunes against the British. Following the victories of the American frigates *Constitution* over the *Guerriere* and *Java*, and the *United States* over the *Macedonian*, as well as the victories of the sloops *Wasp* and *Hornet*, the Royal Navy ordered its captains to avoid one-on-one combat with "the larger class of American ships; which though they may be called frigates, are of a size, complement and weight of metal much beyond that class, and more resembling line of battle ships."[12]

Warren used the defeats to squeeze reinforcements out of the Admiralty, receiving four more ships of the line, thirteen frigates, and seventeen smaller ships.[13] The Admiralty also promised to send Warren two battalions of Royal Marines that had been recalled from Europe after Napoleon was defeated in Russia. The improving situation on the continent also put England in a position to exact its share of blood from the United States so England could preserve "the character and interests of the country."[14]

Two days after arriving off Cape Henry, Warren decided to head toward Bermuda, leaving the *Maidstone* to watch the *Constellation*. The American frigate was safely anchored under the guns of the forts that guarded the harbor, and Warren had orders to look out for a French frigate squadron supposedly on its way to help the Americans. He took the two 74-gun ships—the *San Domingo* and *Dragon*—with him along with the brig *Syron*, leaving Capt. George Burdett of the *Maidstone* in command of the flotilla off the bay. Upon reaching Bermuda, he ordered Adm. George Cockburn to command the blockade of the Middle Atlantic, the area from the Delaware Capes south to the Virginia Capes.[15]

It was a fateful choice. No British officer would earn more enmity from Marylanders than Cockburn. Almost as soon as he arrived off the Chesapeake, Cockburn instituted a form of warfare Americans had not yet experienced. He burned, pillaged, threatened, and plundered his way up and down the bay, very nearly knocking Maryland completely out of the war. Cockburn was in essence a modern warrior in an age when at least the appearance of chivalry was important. He relentlessly exploited British strengths in the bay and just as ruthlessly took advantage of American weaknesses. He pioneered amphibious combined-arms operations, although many of his innovations would be largely forgotten.

The second son of a Scottish baronet, Cockburn went to sea at age fourteen. His father secured for him the patronage of the admirals Lord Samuel Hood and Sir Joshua Rowley, who saw to it that young Cockburn served his apprenticeship under an outstanding captain. At age seventeen Cockburn sailed for the East Indies on a mission to survey harbors and shores, giving him experience that would later prove invaluable on the Chesapeake, which lacked buoys and markers. At the onset of the war with France in 1793, Hood transferred Cockburn, by then a lieutenant, to his flagship, the 100-gun *Victory*. The need for officers quickly depleted Hood's staff, and he was able to promote Cockburn from tenth to first lieutenant in less than half a year. In rapid succession Hood gave Cockburn command of a brig, and then, when Cockburn's aggressive command of that vessel earned him promotion to post-captain, the frigate *Meleager*. The ensuing fifteen years of diverse combat service hardened the young captain into a bold practitioner of amphibious warfare, a skillful negotiator, and an unbending disciplinarian.[16]

One of the accomplishments of which Cockburn was most proud was his colonelcy in the Royal Marines, an honor he earned while leading an attack on the French-held island of Martinique. In a combination of sheer will and manpower, Cockburn managed to get a heavy 13-inch naval howitzer to the top of a hill overlooking the fort guarding Port Royal, the main city on Martinique. Getting it there took more than three hours, but once it was in place Cockburn's gun could rake the French fortifications. Three hours after Cockburn opened fire, the French surrendered. Lt. James Scott, who served under Cockburn for six years, said the seamen and marines celebrated Cockburn's accomplishment. "I should almost be afraid to specify the quantity of swizzle [rum punch] individually made away with during the six-and-thirty hours we were thus employed."[17]

Cockburn's star continued to rise. In 1811 he commanded the defenses of Cádiz, Spain. His insistence on strict discipline earned him a reputation among seamen for harshness, especially those whose lapses earned them a date with the cat-o'-nine-tails. Others, however, saw in Cockburn the model officer. His natural aggressiveness and superb ship-handling abilities appealed to sailors, but Cockburn's genuine concern for the welfare of his men appealed even more. Cockburn saw to it that his crews always had proper food and gave them leave whenever possible. He also groomed a generation of young officers, including Lieutenant Scott and Lt. George Augustus Westphal, both of whom would lead British raids on the Chesapeake in the coming months. "It is almost impossible to depict my boyish feelings and transport when . . . I gazed for the first time in my life, on the features of that undaunted seaman," said one midshipman who fell under Cockburn's spell. "With his sunburnt visage, and his rusty gold-laced hat—an officer who never spared himself, either night or day, but shares on every occasion, the same toil, danger and privation of the foremost man under his command."[18]

Cockburn was still in Cádiz in November 1812 when he received orders to "lose not a moment" in proceeding to Bermuda in his flagship, the 74-gun *Marlborough*. He arrived in mid-January to find that Warren had already left Bermuda for the U.S. coast. Cockburn settled in to wait for Warren's return, watching with growing anticipation as "the continual arrival of captured vessels . . . showed . . . the rich harvest to be gathered by only putting in our sickle."[19]

Cockburn left Bermuda on February 18, 1813. In addition to the four ships of the line with which he had arrived—the *Marlborough*, *Poictiers*, *Victorious*, and *Dragon*—he had the newly arrived 74-gun *Ramilles* and the 40-gun frigate

Rear Adm. George Cockburn, tactical commander of the 1813 and 1814 British campaigns in the Chesapeake. NATIONAL MARITIME MUSEUM, GREENWICH, LONDON

Acasta. The passage from Bermuda to the Virginia Capes was brutal as storms lashed the English flotilla. One man on the *Marlborough* was lost overboard, and an outbreak of "anguish colds" debilitated the crews on every ship.[20]

Cockburn arrived off the Chesapeake on March 3 and began peeling off ships to cover his blockade area. He sent the *Dragon* and the frigate *Belvidera* to patrol off Sandy Hook and Egg Harbor, New Jersey, and ordered Sir John Beresford in *Poictiers* with the sloops *Narcissus* and *Paz* to cover Delaware Bay. The admiral used his remaining ships to blockade the Chesapeake. Warren had left orders for Cockburn to reconnoiter the defenses of Washington and Norfolk to determine whether those cities were susceptible to attack as well as to capture or destroy the frigate *Constellation*. Included in the orders was a somewhat bizarre instruction to minimize contact between British seamen and Americans, in order "to avoid corruption, seduction or the seeds of sedition being sown."[21]

Far more worrisome—at least to Americans—was Warren's directive that Cockburn could enlist black men as pilots. Some Americans believed that order was aimed directly at slaveholders and might foment a slave uprising. What Marylanders and Virginians really should have worried about was the increasing use by the British of small boats acting as auxiliary warships.

Every ship of the line, frigate, brig, and even schooner carried small boats. The larger vessels carried barges—25- to 32-foot-long boats equipped with sails and oars. The boats were strong enough to mount a cannon—usually a carronade—in the front and made effective fighting platforms. Ships also carried cutters, which used sails or oars depending on the situation, and other rowboats. Gigs, depending on their size, could accept a swivel gun or a small naval howitzer and also came equipped with sails. The Royal Navy also snatched up as many small bay craft it could to augment its ships' boats. These boats were formidable when packed full of sailors and marines, and they gave the British a high degree of mobility in the shallow waters of the Chesapeake where deep-draft ships of the line and frigates could have problems operating.

The British gave the Americans a taste of how well they could deploy their small boats even before Cockburn arrived. On February 8, 1813, Burdett, whom Warren had left in command of the blockade, spotted a heavily armed schooner approaching from the northwest. Burdett ordered the ship's barges, cutters, and other small boats from the *Maidstone*, *Belvidera*, and *Statira* to intercept the schooner. Nine boats carrying 240 sailors and marines set out in pursuit.[22]

The schooner was the privateer *Lottery*, under the command of Capt. John Southcomb and bound for Bordeaux, France. She carried a crew of thirty men and was armed with six 9-pound cannon. Southcomb reversed course when he saw the boats full of red-coated Royal Marines and sailors chasing his ship. The *Lottery* struggled in a light breeze and could not pull away from the British. After a chase of three hours, the wind died and Lt. Kelly Nazer of the *Maidstone*, commanding the small boats, moved in for the kill. The Americans opened fire, sending broadside after broadside of grapeshot and canister at the approaching boats, but failed to stop them. Nazer's tars and marines surrounded and then boarded the schooner. The small American crew put up a ferocious fight, suffering nineteen casualties, including Southcomb, who was mortally wounded.[23] Capt. Richard Byron of the *Belvidera* took Southcomb on board his frigate, where the American officer died. The British sent his body ashore "with every mark of respect," reflecting the mixture of honor and satisfaction the British held toward an enemy who would stand, fight, and if necessary die when attacked by a superior force.[24]

The *Lottery* was a handsome prize for Burdett and the British. She weighed 225 tons, had a coppered bottom and copper fastenings, and by all accounts was a fast and nimble ship. The British certainly believed so. After Burdett sent the *Lottery* to Bermuda as a prize, Warren had her condemned and purchased her for the Royal Navy. Rechristened the *Canso*, the schooner would return to the Chesapeake as part of the blockading force.[25]

The Royal Navy used its small boats to telling effect throughout February 1813, capturing more than two dozen prizes by the end of the month. One of the prizes was the *Cora*, a Baltimore-based schooner reputed to be the fastest ship to come from that city. Under the command of Joseph Gould, she was on her way back from France with a load of brandy, wine, silk, and flints when she stumbled on the blockade off Cape Henry.

The British used a captured pilot schooner to lure the *Cora* inshore, at which point three small boats rushed toward her. A militia unit appeared on the shore looking to cover the *Cora* as her crew tried to ground her. The wind, however, had died and the *Cora* sat helpless in the water. The British attacked, and after a half-hour battle in which two of the *Cora*'s crew were killed, Gould struck his colors. Burdett joyfully sent the 258-ton schooner, which carried six long 9-pounder cannon and a pair of 12-pound carronades, off to Bermuda.[26]

Despite the early effectiveness of the blockade, Maryland and Virginia shipowners continued to fit out vessels as privateers for the same reason the Royal Navy was eager to snap them up—money. Prize money was a strong incentive for sailors on both sides. The more ships an American privateer could take, the more money the owners and crew would split. Shipowners paid the U.S. government a bond of either $5,000 or $10,000 for a letter of marque; the amount was determined by the size of the ship and her crew. Owners, captain, and crew shared unequally in the proceeds of a successful capture. Captains placed prize crews on board captured vessels to bring them to the nearest safe port. Once docked, the crew would initiate a prize case, called a "libel," with an admiralty court. If the court found the seizure lawful, it would "condemn" the prize, awarding it to the captors. After judgment, the ship and goods were sold at market price. The proceeds went to the privateer's owner, who received a 50 percent share; the remainder was distributed to captain, officers, and crew in accordance with an agreement all had signed before the voyage.[27]

The Royal Navy took a different tack when it came to prizes. A change in maritime law in 1808 gave the entire value of a prize to the crew—less a small fee to the Crown. The admiral in charge of the station received 12.5 percent of the proceeds. The captain who took the prize received 25 percent of the remainder, the senior ship's officers received 12.5 percent, and the midshipmen and crew split what was left. Some Royal Navy officers amassed fortunes in this way. Capture of a ship worth £50,000 could provide a captain with prize money that could exceed thirty years' pay. Prize money was a major reason why some senior English officers resented Warren's command in North America. They knew he stood to earn thousands, as did his captains and crews.[28]

The lure of prize money would keep the Chesapeake a major theater of operations as long as the hostilities lasted.

CHAPTER 4

Lighting the Fuse

REAR ADM. GEORGE COCKBURN had a pair of objectives in mind when he took command of the Chesapeake blockade. First and foremost, he wanted to capture or destroy the American frigate *Constellation*, which was blockaded in Norfolk, seemingly ripe for the picking. His second objective was somewhat less concrete. Cockburn had orders not only to reconnoiter local defenses but also to establish a safe place to supply the squadron and to enlist the help of local pilots in charting the treacherous inlets and coves up and down the Chesapeake.

He decided to tackle both problems at once. On March 3, 1813, Cockburn ordered Capt. George Burdett with the frigate *Maidstone* and the sloops *Laurestinus* and *Fantome* "to proceed up the Chesapeake for the annoyance of the enemy." Burdett's job was twofold. First, he was to sink or capture any privateers he met. Second, and of more importance, Burdett was to find supplies for the British squadron. Cockburn, meanwhile, set his sights on Norfolk and the *Constellation*.

Charles Stewart was well aware the *Constellation* was a major prize. The Philadelphia native was a close friend of Stephen Decatur and Richard Somers in his youth and remained close to Decatur after Somers' gallant and tragic death in 1804 during the First Barbary War. Stewart knew the British wanted not only his ship but Norfolk as well. The strategic port controlled one of the exits of the Chesapeake and would give them a major base at which they could resupply and repair damaged vessels.

Almost as soon as Stewart got the *Constellation* into Norfolk on February 4, he began to build up the defenses around the vessel. He had the help of Virginia's governor, James Barbour, who ordered the 54th Regiment of Virginia militia to march to Norfolk. Barbour also ordered rifleman, artillery, and cavalry companies to the city from as far away as Richmond and Petersburg.[1] The governor placed Brig. Gen. Robert B. Taylor in command of the city's defenses. A noted lawyer, Taylor had acted as Commodore James Barron's defense counsel during his court-martial following the *Chesapeake-Leopard* incident.

Taylor's second in command was Littleton W. Tazewell, the judge advocate general at the court-martial.

Within a week Taylor had mustered a force of 1,500 men to defend Norfolk. He received still more reinforcements when a company of Regulars from the U.S. Army 7th Infantry Regiment arrived to garrison Fort Nelson. Taylor ordered Norfolk's militia to man Fort Norfolk, the other of the two forts that guarded the entrance to the Elizabeth River, Portsmouth, and the Gosport Navy Yard in Norfolk. Militia also took up positions on Craney Island, a low sandbank at the mouth of the river. Although much of Taylor's force was composed of new draftees subject only to a three-month tour of duty, their presence convinced Cockburn to delay any assault.[2]

By the beginning of March, however, the British admiral had decided it was time to attack. On March 9 Stewart moved the *Constellation* from the navy yard to a spot off Craney Island and joined forces with a squadron of the gunboats stationed there to protect the engineers who were strengthening the island's fortifications.[3] Cockburn learned about the move and on March 10 arrived off Hampton Roads with the *Marlborough, Dragon, Victorious, Acasta,* and *Junon*. He took up a position about four miles north of the *Constellation* and waited. Also waiting at the roads was a Portuguese vessel, the brig *Princeza*, which had spent a week at the mouth of the Chesapeake at the end of February after stumbling on the British blockade. Now outbound for Lisbon from Baltimore, the *Princeza* was once more delayed as the British prepared to attack Norfolk. Portugal was a British ally, and Cockburn put a party of sailors on the brig as lookouts to sound the alarm should the *Constellation* try to break out. An American passenger on the *Princeza*, on overhearing the British sailors talking about the American frigate, managed to slip away and warn Stewart that Cockburn planned a night attack. The attack, however, fizzled as a result of fog and drizzle.[4]

The next day the captain of the *Princeza* visited Stewart. The British had allowed the Portuguese brig into Norfolk to offload her cargo, but the captain, incensed at being stopped twice by the Royal Navy, told Stewart that Cockburn still planned a night raid to capture the *Constellation* and would come that night. Forewarned, Stewart alerted Taylor and prepared his defenses, which included boarding nets outstretched over the gunwales so they could be dropped down to trap British boats and sailors that approached the frigate.[5]

At 10 p.m. on March 11, Cockburn ordered his ships' boats under the command of George Westphal, the first lieutenant on the *Marlborough*, to head toward the *Constellation*. The attack was to take place at ebb tide, when the current would swing the frigate's stern toward the oncoming British ships and open a gap between the *Constellation* and the screen of gunboats protecting her. The two lead boats, fitted with Congreve rockets, were to fire the weapons into the American frigate's stern, and a boarding party would storm on board during the uproar and confusion of the rocket attack. A separate detachment of boats was to attack the gunboats. Just as the British launched their boats, a strong southerly wind sprang up and slowed their advance. The wind and a strong tide combined to separate the British boats. Westphal tried to regroup, but the wind proved too strong; at daybreak he ordered the boats back to the squadron.[6]

The *Constellation* remained off Craney Island until March 17, when Stewart returned to Norfolk with the frigate and the gunboats and anchored under the guns of Fort Nelson and Fort Norfolk. Stewart scuttled four vessels to block the channel at Lambert Point, the way in to the *Constellation*'s anchorage. That move all but ended the threat of a seaborne attempt to take the *Constellation*, but it also bottled up one of America's primary warships for the rest of the war.[7] It did not, however, prevent either side from engaging on the water.

On March 20 Stewart decided to attack the *Junon* after the 36-gun frigate had moved away from the main British squadron to guard boats heading up the James River and had become becalmed. Stewart ordered nine gunboats to the attack, but the British reacted quickly at their approach and sent out a swarm of boats to take the *Junon* under tow. The British tars successfully pulled the *Junon* back under the protective guns of Cockburn's flotilla. Cockburn quickly struck back. That night the admiral ordered a force of six hundred sailors and marines to attack the gunboats that had tried to attack the *Junon*. Finding the gunboats anchored out of reach and with low tide approaching, however, the force gave up and rowed back to the flotilla.[8]

Burdett, meanwhile, had found a way to get the supplies Cockburn needed by capturing local merchant ships. The same day Cockburn made his first effort to capture the *Constellation*, Burdett captured three ships off Mobjack Bay, on the Virginia side of the bay opposite Cape Charles. One of the vessels carried more than six hundred tons of beef and pork, which Burdett sent on to the squadron.

Captures, however, were only part of the supply equation. Cockburn was willing to pay market price for food and other supplies, and he believed—rightly as it turned out—that Federalist and antiwar sentiment was high enough in Maryland's Eastern Shore that he could buy what he needed locally. Cockburn apparently already had at least one sympathizer among the local population. On March 13 he wrote to Warren, "I am not without hope that the squadron may be furnished . . . from the upper part of the Chesapeake with supplies of cattle and vegetables, a person having been engaged to send me such but whether he will . . . elude the great vigilance of the American government is extremely doubtful."[9]

From the speed with which he made the arrangement, it appears Cockburn was in contact with at least some antiwar residents prior to his arrival in the Chesapeake. He alluded to this in secret orders he sent to his captains that "vessels coming down the Chesapeake, which, on approaching any of His Majesty's Ships, hoist a white flag, instead of an ensign, will be loaded with supplies of cattle and vegetables for this squadron." Cockburn also went to great pains to protect his local suppliers, telling his officers, "Care is to be taken to prevent as much as possible any particular remark or observation towards them from the shore and no part of their cargoes is on any account to be taken out of them during daylight."[10]

It was the start of what would come to characterize Cockburn's campaign in the Chesapeake. The wily British admiral tried to stoke antiwar sentiment on both sides of the bay, essentially attempting to foment a civil war of sorts among the populace. He made clear he would destroy any war materiel he found but promised to leave unmolested the farms and livestock of those who helped the British. He also offered rewards for information and promised to pay full market price for any supplies his troops confiscated. Individuals or towns that resisted the British, however, faced a different fate. Cockburn promised to classify any community that refused to cooperate as a fortified post and its men as soldiers. As such, the admiral said, he would raze the towns and take all the males as prisoners in addition to confiscating all supplies.[11]

Cockburn made the war even more of a personal affair for slaveholders up and down the bay. Slaveholders in Maryland and Virginia might attempt to portray slavery as a benevolent institution, but they lived always in fear of a slave rebellion. Although the British had explicit orders not to incite a slave revolt, which England believed would be counterproductive, Cockburn could and did offer incentives to slaves to flee their masters, including freedom to any who managed to reach the British. Cockburn had orders to transport runaway slaves to Canada or Bermuda; or they could enlist in special black regiments.[12]

Both the Americans and the British underestimated the power of that offer. Slaveholders seemingly had forgotten the response to a similar offer Sir Henry Clinton made during the Revolutionary War, when nearly 100,000 slaves flocked to British colors, although the British made no effort to end the practice of slavery. Whether because they remembered or simply responded to the opportunity, the slaves' response to the British offer of freedom was dramatic. Charles Ball, himself a runaway slave who served with American forces, reported that one plantation owner lost a hundred slaves in one night. "In the morning when the overseer arose, and went to call his hands to the field, he found only empty cabins."[13]

Slaveholders quickly attempted to reach an accord with Cockburn. They sent emissaries to the British asking for the return of their "property," which the British had unjustly confiscated. Cockburn's response was to take a jab at both the war hawks and the practice of slavery, telling slaveholders they were welcome to ask their slaves to return to bondage, adding, "I fear that they are not likely to succeed."[14] The British did allow representatives of slaveholders to meet with the runaways. It was usually the same scene. The white men would speak to the Africans "in softened accents about the cause of their desertion," to which the now former slaves would give "some quaint and home spun reply."[15] The white men almost always left empty-handed because the former slaves had "their heads filled with notions of liberty and happiness" on some island in the West Indies.[16]

Adm. Sir John Warren returned to take command of the British squadron in late March, bringing with him the *San Domingo, Ramilles, Statira, Orpheus,* the brig *Mohawk,* and the captured American privateer schooner *Highflyer.* With the augmented squadron he initiated his plan to take the war into the northern part of the Chesapeake while maintaining a strong blockade of the bay.

The activities of both blockade-runners and blockaders were predictable. Anytime a northerly breeze sprang up, dozens of American ships tried to run the gauntlet of British ships. Many made it past the blockade, and many did not. From February 18 to March 22, 1813, the British grabbed thirty-five prizes trying to break out of the Chesapeake while also sharpening their skills in making small-boat attacks.

Warren ordered the squadron north on April 2. He planned a two-pronged effort, keeping his 74-gun ships of the line in the deeper water in the center of the bay, flanked by the frigates, while his growing flotilla of brigs and schooners—most captured from the Americans—worked inshore. The large warships were the first prong. They would deny the Americans the open water of the Chesapeake. The small boats were the second prong. These boats and their crews would operate inshore as well as up and down the many creeks, inlets, and bays, taking the war to the interior country of Maryland and Virginia. When the British came to New Point Comfort near the mouth of the Rappahannock River on the Virginia side of the bay, the Royal Navy gave the Americans an example of what Warren expected to accomplish.

New Point Comfort was a natural harbor that provided some protection from the occasionally capricious winds on the lower bay. On April 2, four American privateer schooners ducked into the anchorage for the night. Then Warren's squadron appeared. The American captains attempted to escape up the Rappahannock almost the instant they saw the masts of the British ships. Warren ordered the *Mohawk, Fantome, Highflyer,* and fourteen boats from the squadron to pursue the four schooners.

Apparently unaware of how adept the British sailors and marines had become at handling their small boats, the Americans anchored for the night across from the mouth of the Corrotoman River, eight miles from the mouth of the Rappahannock. The British boatmen rowed through the night, covering the eight miles by daybreak. Both sides could now see each other in the increasing light. The privateer captains used sweeps to move their ships into a line, presenting their broadsides to the British.

The defensive alignment failed to deter Lt. James Scott and Lt. George Urmston, who led the British force. "Our enemies were drawn up in battle array," Scott recalled. "The Stars and Stripes were floating proudly at their peaks . . . their guns were run out, and all prepared to receive us."[17] The two lieutenants had the barge from the *Marlborough*, armed with a 12-pound carronade, along with 4 other boats and 105 men under their immediate command. They feinted toward the center of the line of schooners before they bored in on the rearmost, signaling the other boat crews to pick their own targets.[18]

The four schooners—the *Arab*, *Lynx*, *Racer*, and *Dolphin*—loosed broadsides at Scott's and Urmston's boats but missed. The captain of the *Arab*, Daniel Fitch, ordered his crew to roll-tack the schooner and bring her other broadside to bear on the oncoming British boats. The maneuver opened a gap between the *Arab* and the *Lynx*, the next boat in line, and the *Arab* then shuddered to a halt as she grounded on a shoal.[19]

Scott and Urmston immediately came alongside, and British sailors and marines swarmed onto the *Arab*'s deck with cutlasses, pistols, and pikes. Fitch and his crew put up no fight, diving overboard to avoid capture and leaving the British in command of the *Arab*.

The capture of the *Arab* put the other three privateer schooners at a severe disadvantage because it removed one of the anchor ships of the battle line. A general melee ensued as the remaining British boats launched their own attacks. Lt. James Polkinghorne of the *San Domingo* led a boatful of sailors and Royal Marines straight for the 6-gun privateer *Lynx*. The red-coated marines maintained steady musket fire while the sailors pulled for the schooner. The *Lynx*'s crew of thirty-five men under Capt. Elisha Taylor returned fire with grape and canister, but once more the American gunners missed their target, allowing the British to come alongside. Even before Polkinghorne could lead his men onto the deck of the *Lynx*, Taylor hauled down his flag and surrendered.[20]

Polkinghorne next attacked the 6-gun privateer *Racer*, the third ship in the line. His men rushed onto the deck and overwhelmed the twenty-eight-man crew, forcing Capt. Daniel Chayton to surrender. The British then turned to the last American ship, the 12-gun privateer *Dolphin*.[21] Polkinghorne had his sailors man three of the *Racer*'s cannon and turn them on the *Dolphin* to cover the approach of Lt. George Bishop with twenty-two men from the *Statira* and Lt. Matthew Liddon of the *Maidstone* with twenty men. The cannon fire from the *Racer* distracted the *Dolphin*'s ninety-eight-man crew long enough to allow Bishop and Liddon to come up on her starboard side and board her. The privateers outnumbered the British two to one and fought desperately to keep their ship. Bishop and Liddon led multiple charges across the deck only to have the Americans push them back. Despite their superior numbers, the privateers could not stand up to the sustained assaults from the British professionals, however, and they began to waver. The Americans finally surrendered after a spent 12-pound shot from the *Racer* ricocheted off a bulwark and knocked their captain, William Stafford, unconscious. Six Americans and two Englishmen died in the fight.[22]

The entire engagement lasted slightly more than four hours. The British reported two dead and eleven wounded, including Polkinghorne and Royal Marine lieutenant William Brand.[23] The surgeon on the *Dolphin*, however, claimed the British lost upward of fifty men and asserted American cannon fire had sunk two of the British boats. Warren's report made no mention of losing boats. The Americans reported six dead, ten wounded, and more than fifty captured.[24] The British took the four privateers into service as tenders, commissioning the *Lynx* and *Racer* as the *Mosquitobit* and *Shelbourne* respectively.

On April 6 the British used their new vessels to trap seven schooners and two brigs at the mouth of the Rappahannock. The four captured schooners, all flying American flags, entered the small bay in which they had been captured four days earlier and found more vessels lying at anchor. A local pilot recognized the *Racer* as a Baltimore ship and hailed her, asking whether her captain had seen the British. "Yes," Lieutenant Scott answered, "they are coming up the bay." Scott sent the *Shelbourne* (formerly *Racer*) to starboard of the Americans, the *Mosquitobit* (formerly *Lynx*) to port, and kept the *Arab* and *Dolphin* in the center. When the American ships were surrounded, the British raised the royal ensign and opened fire, unnerving the American crews, who abandoned their vessels. The British took fifteen ships as prizes that day, but a nasty gale blew in that night and drove five of them aground. The British burned the remainder of the boats and continued their journey north.[25]

Admiral Warren followed a brutally simple strategy as he moved his squadron up the Chesapeake, using his flotilla of captured vessels to drive every American ship from the lower and middle parts of the bay. Any captain who resisted found himself under attack by boats full of Royal Navy sailors and marines. Warren's advance spread panic among residents living on the shoreline and near the mouths of rivers. Farmers removed their livestock, crops, and personal property to prevent the British from confiscating it. Home guard units sprang up all along the bay, devising a system of emergency alarms for common defense.[26]

The farther north the British moved, the more personal the war became for both inhabitants and invaders. The British boat crews often operated miles away from the main force and engaged local militia in short skirmishes. In an exchange on April 12, Lt. George Hutchinson's boat crew from the *Dolphin* captured a schooner carrying oak planks in the Choptank River, northeast of Cambridge on Maryland's Eastern Shore. Local militia attacked the British while they were unloading the prize. Hutchison lost the schooner but killed four militiamen in the battle.[27]

Inhabitants who failed to adhere to Cockburn's strict terms suffered the consequences. When the British anchored off Sharps Island on April 12, for example, Jacob Gibson, a prosperous farmer and politician who lived on the island, decided to defy Warren's edict. Gibson fled up the Miles River to St. Michaels on the Maryland Eastern Shore and raised the alarm, but later returned to his farm to remove as much of his property as he could. When he arrived home, he found the British already in possession. Gibson told the British he had no involvement with the militia or local defenses, and the invaders took only half of his livestock. In a letter to Secretary of State James Monroe, Gibson complained that although the British gave him a small cash payment for what they took, it was not enough to cover his losses. "I was treated by all the officers, but particularly by the admiral (Warren) with marked politeness and delicacy," he wrote to Monroe. "The purser of the admiral's ship left on the island $54.00 in specie and informed me he should leave bills on his government for the balance of the stock taken."

Gibson managed to hide the fact that he had warned St. Michaels of the presence of Warren's fleet, but when he presented a pair of 6-pounder cannon to the local militia regiment, the British got word of his double-dealing. After leaving the island on April 13, he returned several weeks later to find his farm completely stripped. Although the British left another $40 in cash and a government bill for $133, Gibson estimated his losses at more than $1,200.[28]

As Warren replenished his provisions by raiding farms, Cockburn arrived off Annapolis on April 15 with the *Marlborough* and a flotilla of smaller vessels, throwing the city into an uproar. Only two small forts guarded the entrance to the harbor of the Maryland state capital, with garrisons of at most thirty Regulars. Cockburn first anchored near Kent Island but soon dispatched his boats to sound the harbor and reconnoiter the defenses. He sent the *Fantome* up the Severn River, and she anchored above Annapolis, blocking the river.

The arrival of the British force off his capital shocked Governor Winder. He called out the militia and sent crucial state papers inland to Upper Marlboro before writing to President Madison and Secretary of War John Armstrong pleading for help. In a strongly worded letter, Winder told Monroe and Armstrong it was their constitutional duty to protect the states from foreign invasion. He said Annapolis was essentially defenseless and demanded the federal government send a regiment of Regular Army troops as well as fourteen cannon to bolster the defenses of the two forts that protected the city.

Winder never received a reply—reinforcing the belief, at least in Maryland, that Madison's government would not aid Federalists.[29]

Cockburn had no intention of attacking Annapolis, at least not yet. Instead, he continued pushing north, planning to test the defenses around Baltimore. The city remained a thorn in the side of the British. Despite the blockade, privateers continued to outfit at Baltimore and sneak into the Atlantic, where they wreaked havoc with British convoys. In addition, the British viewed the city as the principal locale on the upper bay capable of building ships that could potentially challenge the Royal Navy. With the *Constellation* bottled up in Norfolk, Cockburn wanted to keep the Chesapeake clear of enemy warships.

The British squadron arrived off the mouth of the Patapsco River on April 17. Cockburn spotted a group of ten small schooners anchored upriver and a lone gunboat under the guns of Fort McHenry. Cockburn ordered the *Marlborough*, *Maidstone*, and *Statira* to send their boats to attack the schooners. The American captains raised anchor and sails when they saw the cutters and barges approaching, but the adept British crews, along with a contrary wind and strong current, foiled their escape attempt. The British captured all ten of the vessels, which were loaded with firewood. Cockburn's men eagerly snapped up the firewood, which was running low in the squadron.[30]

Cockburn spent four days reconnoitering the defenses around Baltimore, which appeared open to attack. He established a watering point at Poole's Island, which would remain unmolested until the end of the war, and pushed as far up the Patapsco as he dared, charting the coastline and taking soundings. The more he saw, the more certain he became that his force could easily take Baltimore. When Admiral Warren arrived on April 21, Cockburn urged his commander to attack the city. Warren, however, refused. In a letter to the Admiralty, Warren said he was "convinced of the impossibility of the frigates of the squadron approaching the town and shipping, without the forts and batteries upon the river being carried by a corps of troops . . . and being of the opinion that it would be an unwise measure to risk the ships of the line . . . I stood down." Although he decided against an immediate attack, Warren told his superiors, "From every observation it has been in my power to make . . . I never saw any country so vulnerable, so open to attack or that affords the means to support [supply] an enemy's force."

Cockburn was decidedly unhappy with his commander's decision. Indeed, had Warren known the actual state of Baltimore's defenses he might have allowed Cockburn to attack. The entire garrison in the city amounted to a handful of Regulars manning Fort McHenry and two thousand untrained militiamen in the city proper. Warren had orders from the Admiralty to avoid a major land battle to prevent the British from suffering a Yorktown-like defeat. The most likely reason for Warren's decision not to attack, however, was that he saw no need to mount a major land assault. His squadron was taking many prizes, and Warren did not want to divert any resources from that important—and lucrative—aspect of his campaign. He did not bother to inform the Admiralty of his decision not to attack Baltimore until he returned to Bermuda in May. His letter did not reach London until July 8.[31]

Frustrated in his desire to attack Baltimore, Cockburn pressed north with his flotilla. As his ships neared Havre de Grace at the mouth of the Susquehanna River, he began to run into more and more resistance. The tenders from the *Mohawk* and *Fantome* engaged militia units assembled along the shore to fire on the barges and cutters full of Royal Navy sailors and Royal Marines that preceded the larger vessels. Cockburn sailed south from Havre de Grace and entered the Elk River, on the east side of the bay. Frenchtown, an important supply point about thirteen miles up the Elk, was an obvious target.

Lt. George Westphal of the *Marlborough* led a group of 150 marines in barges toward the hamlet. Militiamen fired several small cannon at the barges but failed to hit them. When the barges, armed with 12-pound carronades, returned fire, the militia fled toward Elkton, about two miles north. On entering Frenchtown the marines found a tavern, two storehouses, and stables. The "town" was little more than a waypoint—albeit a strategic one—on the road from Baltimore to Philadelphia. It had become even more important as the British blockade forced more and more goods to move overland. One of the storehouses was stuffed with Army uniforms, cavalry saddles, bridles, military equipment, flour, and general merchandise. Westphal ordered his men to confiscate everything they could carry; then the British burned the storehouses along with a pair of schooners anchored at a small wharf. The inhabitants never rebuilt the town.

Westphal's men reembarked and pulled upriver toward Elkton. Three forts—Fort Defiance, Fort Frederick, and Fort Hollingsworth—defended the approaches. As the British rowed into view, they spotted the well-defended lower two forts (Defiance and Frederick), and Westphal wisely withdrew back down the river. He reported his activities and the presence of militia to Cockburn. The admiral noted the activity and decided to reprovision his squadron before his next foray. Cockburn had learned of a large amount of livestock on Spesutie Island, on the western side of the bay below Havre de Grace, and he landed a force of six hundred sailors and Royal Marines that scooped up everything with feathers or four legs. The presence of the British on the island brought out the bravado of the local defenders, who fired on the British barges from a newly built battery at Havre de Grace. Cockburn decided if the town was worth defending, it was also worth attacking.[32]

Command of the expedition to attack Havre de Grace fell to Westphal, whose force of five hundred sailors and marines shoved off in their barges and cutters around midnight on May 2 from the northern bank of the

Susquehanna. Westphal armed one of the barges with Congreve rockets and used it as the lead vessel. Although notoriously inaccurate, the rockets were potent psychological weapons because they made an eerie screeching sound as they flew from their launching ramps. Each rocket carried a 12-pound charge, and although they were not particularly effective when fired at individual guns or bodies of troops, they were excellent anti-materiel weapons that could set wooden buildings on fire.

Defending the town were elements of the 42nd Maryland Regiment of militia, comprised mostly of men from Harford County. Two companies—one of ninety-eight men under the command of Capt. Thomas Courtney, the other of seventy-one men under Capt. William Whiteford—had hastily erected a small battery on the Susquehanna side of the town. As Westphal approached the south shore of the river, his rocket barge came under heavy fire from the battery.

The British immediately opened up with rockets and carronades and chased off the militia. Once his boat touched shore, Westphal leaped onto the bank with a handful of marines and chased the fleeing militia. Finding the cannon abandoned, he turned the guns on their former owners. Pressing forward, Westphal captured a militia private and took his horse, using it to chase down John O'Neill, the last man to leave the battery, who was busy trying to rally the fleeing militia, crying, "Damn it men, return! We can certainly beat the rascals off!"[33]

When Westphal rode up to O'Neill on the captured horse, the American was confused and asked whether Westphal was English or American. The Royal Navy officer yelled, "An Englishman you Yankee rascals!" Westphal drew his pistol and demanded O'Neill's surrender. When the American refused, Westphal pulled the trigger, but his pistol misfired. O'Neill managed to get off a shot from his musket that hit Westphal in one hand, but the Royal Navy officer drew his sword with his good hand and took O'Neill prisoner.[34] O'Neill would later receive plaudits as the only militiaman who actually stood up to the British during the battle.[35]

Westphal and his force entered Havre de Grace and began setting fire to nearly every building they saw. The stately tavern of Richard Mansfield was the first to go up in flames, followed by the home of Roxana Moore, a widow. Moore at first refused to leave her house, telling Westphal she would not make her children homeless. Westphal replied he would burn the house down with her in it if she preferred. Moore left, but she and her neighbors were able to snuff out the flames each time the British tried to torch her home. The British finally gave up trying and moved on to burn the rest of the town.[36]

Exactly what occurred on May 3 in Havre de Grace remains a point of contention. Admiral Cockburn, in his official report, said that after the defending militia fled to the woods outside the town, his force set "fire to some of the

Contemporary engraving of the destruction of Havre de Grace, Maryland, in 1813. Cockburn burned the town in retaliation for opposition the local militia mounted against his forces. MARYLAND HISTORICAL SOCIETY, BALTIMORE

houses to cause the proprietors (who had deserted them and formed part of the militia who had fled into the woods) to understand and feel what they were liable to bring upon themselves by building batteries and acting toward us with so much useless rancor. I embarked in the boats the guns from the battery . . . having also destroyed 130 stand of arms."[37]

Americans, however, claimed the British looted and pillaged everything of value, from clothing, hats, and furniture to plates and silverware. Jared Sparks, a local historian who was in Havre de Grace the day of the attack, blasted the invaders in his account:

> The conduct of the sailors while on shore was exceedingly rude and wanton. The officers gave such of the inhabitants as remained behind the liberty to carry out such articles of furniture as they chose, while the sailors were plundering their houses, but the sailors, not content with pillaging and burning, broke and defaced these also, as they were standing in the streets. . . . Little can be said, indeed, in favor of the officers' conduct in this particular. They selected tables and bureaus for their private use, and after writing their names on them, placed them on board the barges. . . . But the most distressing part of

the scene was at the close of day, when those who fled in the
morning returned to witness the desolation of their homes and
the ruin of all their possessions.[38]

No matter which account is the more correct, the British clearly took out
their wrath on Havre de Grace and burned most of it to the ground. They fired
Congreve rockets at buildings apparently solely for the joy of watching the
rockets slam into buildings and set them on fire. They also took everything of
value they could find, stripping the town bare.

The work complete, Cockburn pushed up the Northeast River and
destroyed the Principio Foundry—one of the few in the United States capable of casting cannon—and then wrecked the casting machinery and disabled
the five 24-pounder guns that protected the foundry, along with twenty-eight
32-pounders ready for shipment and eight cannon and four carronades that
were in various stages of manufacture. The British finally withdrew from the
area around 10 p.m., leaving behind a scorched district and a population itching for revenge.[39]

CHAPTER 5

By Land and by Sea

*T*HE DESTRUCTION OF HAVRE DE GRACE marked a new phase in the British campaign in the Chesapeake, and in the war as a whole. For more than a year America had enjoyed almost unlimited success at sea. American frigates had scored impressive, morale-boosting victories in one-on-one fights with British warships while American privateers bedeviled British merchant shipping. On the Great Lakes, Master Commandant Oliver Hazard Perry worked to build a squadron to control Lake Erie while Capt. Isaac Chauncey attempted to build another to fight for Lake Ontario. Both lakes would be the scenes of future campaigns. On land, however, the war had been disastrous for America.

The United States launched four invasions of Canada, all of which ended in failure. The latest defeat came almost the same day Admiral Cockburn burned Havre de Grace. Henry Dearborn, an aging veteran of the Revolutionary War, led an army over Lake Ontario in a bid to capture the crucial city of Kingston, which would give America control of the lake. Dearborn assembled a force of 1,700 Regulars and volunteers that embarked and sailed up Lake Ontario without incident, arriving off York (present-day Toronto) before daybreak on April 27. After a nasty battle in which the American tactical commander, Brig. Gen. Zebulon Pike, the explorer of the American Southwest, was killed, the Americans managed to take the city. The losses were heavy on both sides—almost 20 percent of each army. With General Pike dead, the American troops got out of hand and looted and burned the public buildings and destroyed the provincial records, something the British never forgot. The success was short lived because the British soon pushed Dearborn's force out of the town.[1]

In the west, a relatively small British army, in concert with Native American tribes under the incomparable leader Tecumseh, had taken the strategic town of Detroit and systematically chased the Yankees back to the Indiana border. President Madison sacked Gen. William Hull, who had surrendered Detroit, and replaced him with Indian Wars hero William Henry Harrison. The change in command at first did little to improve the fortunes of the Army of the West. Harrison could do nothing more than read incoming reports in horror from his base in Ohio after Indians wiped out a unit of Kentucky militia that surrendered at Frenchtown in Michigan Territory, an act that both frightened and enraged Americans living in the west. "Remember the River Raisin," became a rallying cry for the U.S. units that fought to retake the Northwest Territory. The massacre at Frenchtown, combined with other defeats, forced Harrison to retreat into Ohio and Indiana. He established a supply base at Sandusky, Ohio, while pinning his defense on Fort Meigs on the Maumee River, near present-day Perrysburg, Ohio.[2]

The continued reverses forced Madison finally to realize that the conflict was a real, knockdown war. He fired bumbling Secretary of War William Eustis and replaced him with John Armstrong, a Revolutionary War veteran who kept his eyes firmly fixed on the north and west, much to the chagrin of Governor Levin Winder of Maryland.

The burning of Havre de Grace, the poor showing of the state militia, and the destruction of an important foundry capable of forging artillery convinced Winder he had to do something—anything—to bolster the defenses of Maryland. The British blockade had all but completely closed the Chesapeake to trade, preventing much-needed arms shipments from arriving and also cutting off one of the state's main sources of income. Winder had turned to Washington for both arms and money, but the federal government, at least in the governor's eyes, did not care about Maryland.

At the beginning of May 1813 Winder told the Maryland legislature that federal armories had shipped only five hundred new muskets to the state since the outbreak of the war, which did not come close to meeting the needs and requests from regiments up and down the bay. "The United States refuses to aid us," Winder raged to Brig. Gen. Thomas Foreman, who commanded the militia from Harford and Cecil Counties. "The treasury is now empty."

Winder also had no answers for Brig. Gen. Caleb Hawkins of Charles County. After Hawkins wrote the governor explaining the poor state of readiness of his troops, Winder replied, "We understand a considerable part of your brigade is very miserably supplied. . . . The Arsenal is now empty." Winder told his subordinate that his ability to procure arms depended on his receiving authority to borrow money. To Hawkins and anyone else who would listen Winder described his position as "utterly impossible."[3]

Maryland had borne all of the costs for maintaining its militia—pay, subsistence, uniforms, camp equipment, arms, and ammunition—and the state had yet to receive its money's worth. The abysmal performance of the militia tasked with defending Havre de Grace was particularly galling to the governor. He told General Foreman, "The conduct of the officers to whom the defense of Havre de Grace was committed was in the highest degree culpable, and as such ought to subject them to a trial . . . ascertain upon what charges."[4]

Although the militia's performance infuriated the soldier in Winder, the politician knew his troops needed more support than his state could provide. The embattled governor sent a committee to Washington in May to take the state's case directly to President Madison. Winder ordered his delegation to confront the president personally and press the case for Maryland's dire need for money and arms. When the committee met with Madison and remonstrated with him over the lack of support, Madison pointed out that Virginia, where there was widespread support for the war, continued to send men and materiel to the war and to the Canadian frontier, and New York "was peculiarly exposed to the invasion of the enemy," and both also required federal resources.[5]

Winder's representatives pressed Madison for a written answer, but he shunted them to John Armstrong. The new secretary of war said he understood Winder's desire "to ascertain . . . what further protection will be afforded by the General Government against the common enemy," as well as to know "what provisions may be expected to liquidate the expenditures which have been or may be incurred in providing against their aggressions." However, he had only bad news for the governor. "I can but subjoin in assurance, that every attention to the special defense of Maryland, that may be compatible with the just claims of the other parts of the Union, shall be promptly and cordially given." As for financial help, Armstrong said, "As far as expenditures have arisen or shall arise for militia calls by the state, without the participation of the United States, no provision [for reimbursement] is found to exist under the present laws." In other words, so long as Maryland kept its militia at home for local defense, Washington would provide no help for its expenses.[6]

The news was devastating to Winder, who called a special session of the legislature to ask for permission to borrow money to fund the state's defense. Federalists controlled the House of Delegates, and they spent most of their time passing resolutions demanding an end to the war. Even the Federalists, however, could see the need to bolster the state's defenses, and they put their antiwar sentiments aside long enough to approve a measure that allowed Winder to borrow money from the state's banks so he could purchase weapons and pay the militia. True to form, though, they tacked on yet another call for the U.S. Congress to end the war. The state Senate also approved the measure, although its main focus was on passing a resolution laying the responsibility for continuation of the war on Britain. The House of Delegates rejected the Senate's resolution but passed one of its own demanding an end to the war by a 43 to 15 vote.[7]

That Governor Winder managed to keep the militia, especially units on the Eastern Shore, willing to serve Maryland and oppose the British is astonishing. The success had less to do with his position as the state militia's commander in chief than it did with the relationships he had built up while commander of the Eastern Shore–based 2nd Division. Winder could tug on the patriotic bonds between the various regimental and brigade commanders that had been forged while all were young lieutenants enduring the hardships and early defeats of the Revolutionary War. No matter how hard he tugged on those bonds, however, Winder could not ensure that his amateur state troops would stand up to Cockburn's hardened professionals, a fact that tortured the governor throughout the Chesapeake campaign.[8]

The lack of military support from Washington concerned the inhabitants of the upper and lower Chesapeake just as it did their elected leaders, but of even more concern in the Tidewater region of the bay was where the astoundingly nimble British sailors and Royal Marines would appear next. Cockburn's tactic of using ships' boats to screen the advance of his mosquito fleet of tenders, which in turn screened the main British force of frigates and 74-gun ships of the line, had proved wildly successful. The cutters and barges could operate just about anywhere, while the larger Royal Navy vessels prevented the Americans from mounting any type of seaborne defense. For the people of the Eastern Shore, shouts of sails on the horizon brought fear and panic.

The success of the British campaign in the spring of 1813 also had a profound impact on the slave population, who believed the British were already triumphant in the war. Desertions became more numerous and more frequent, and those who succeeded in reaching the British ships often returned ashore to enlist their friends. The fact that it was planting season encouraged the flow of runaway slaves, who came by the canoe load. One man whose master had badly mistreated him reached the British only to ask to go back to retrieve his wife. On returning to the house he found that the master had locked her in the same room in which he slept. The escaped slave waited two days before he succeeded in slipping his wife out of the house and then made his way successfully back to the British.[9]

The escaped slaves enhanced the British force's mobility because they could guide small boats through the labyrinth of creeks, rivers, inlets, bays, and marshes along the coast. They also proved adept at leading British raiding parties as much as ten miles inland, where they stole livestock, robbed postmen, and attacked isolated militia outposts.[10]

The next communities to experience the terror of Cockburn's seagoing marauders were Georgetown and Fredericktown, two small farming towns that sat on opposite sides of the Sassafras River along one of the main roads leading north to Elkton. Georgetown lay on the south bank of the Sassafras in Kent County, and Fredericktown was on the north bank in Cecil County. Georgetown was the larger of the two and contained a few dozen buildings. Fort Duffy on the Cecil County side of the river and entrenchments at Pearce Point on the Kent County side guarded the approaches. Cockburn, on May 5, "sent the boats and Marines of the squadron" to destroy the two towns.[11] Well aware of the psychological effects of the destruction of Havre de Grace, he sent a warning along with them.

The Sassafras is a long and tortuous river with sharp horseshoe bends blocked by long sandbars and many deceptive side channels. In the dark, without pilots, it took the British more than eight hours to row the eight-mile course. Capt. Henry Byng of the *Mohawk* led the expedition. He captured two mulatto men in a small boat about two miles south of the towns and ordered them to row ahead of the British force to "warn their countrymen against acting in the same rash manner as the people of Havre de Grace; assuring them, that if they did, their towns would inevitably meet a similar fate." Those who offered no resistance would suffer no harm.[12] The two men made their way to the towns and gave the militia commanders Cockburn's ultimatum, but the commander of the Georgetown garrison, Lt. Col. Thomas Veazy, nevertheless mustered four hundred men of the 49th Militia Regiment and prepared to engage the British.[13]

Almost as soon as the messengers gave Veazy the British ultimatum, Cockburn ordered his forces to advance up the river. John Thomas, an eyewitness, reported that fifteen barges and three smaller boats formed a column four abreast and several hundred yards long. The admiral's barge took the van, allowing those in the rear to close ranks. The red uniforms of the marines added a splendid touch in the bright sun.[14]

As the British approached Georgetown, Veazy readied his defenders. Although he did have one cannon, he had only one round for it. When he judged the distance to be right, he fired his lone round in a somewhat futile gesture. The British responded with a salvo of Congreve rockets and a volley of canister and grapeshot from their carronades. The Americans opened up with musket fire, which the British returned. The resulting din panicked half of the militiamen, who fled into the woods. Nearly all the rest of the defenders ran off as the British charged, leaving only Veazy and thirty-five men to defend the area.[15]

Cockburn and the marines pushed ashore north of the two militia defenses, isolating the towns. As the marines fixed bayonets, Veazy and his thirty-five stalwarts lost heart and also fled to the woods, leaving the towns wide open. A witness said, "Whether it was from their political aversion to the present war, their dislike of shedding blood or actually through fear, I cannot determine." Cockburn quipped that the militia's new position would allow the Americans to witness the destruction of their homes.[16]

In Fredericktown, Cockburn ordered his troops to search for the homes of the militiamen who had opposed him. As he questioned the inhabitants he became increasingly frustrated. Although everyone with whom he spoke knew the men, none seemed to be from in or around Fredericktown. Byng, leading thirty or forty men, tried to catch up with the fleeing militia. He managed to find the home of one militiaman, Cpl. Joshua Ward, and posted a guard in the hope Ward might try to sneak home after fleeing the battlefield. When he did not show, Byng's men sacked the house and the *Mohawk*'s captain himself set fire to the structure. It was the first of many fires that evening.[17]

Cockburn, meanwhile, had spoken with John Allen, a former sea captain who owned a house, warehouse, and large farm in Fredericktown. Allen gave Cockburn as much information as he had about the militia and told the admiral he had taken no part in the resistance, expecting the British officer to live up to his promise to spare the property of noncombatants. Cockburn countered by asking Allen how much poultry he had and what stores were in the warehouse. Allen replied that he had none at the moment, at which point Cockburn damned Allen and burned his house and granary. Turning to his officers as the rest of the town also went up in flames, Cockburn observed, "Well, my lads, this looks well," and ordered his force to return to the boats to cross the river to Georgetown.[18]

The British, whom *Niles' Weekly Register*, a Baltimore news magazine, dubbed the "Water Winnebagoes" after a fierce Indian tribe, then fell on Georgetown, which lay undefended. Dr. Edward Scott, who owned a farm in Galena, about two miles from Georgetown, saw the result of the British attack. "It was the order of the Admiral as acknowledged by his officers, to destroy every house, but some were spared at the entreaty of the women and aged, and the fire extinguished in some others after the enemy had abandoned them. . . . Georgetown contained a meeting house, tavern, one or two mechanic's shops, as many old store houses and granaries, with 30 dwellings. All of the buildings but the meeting house and 11 houses with their outhouses are reduced to ashes."[19]

Burning was only half the story. Scott reported the British went on an orgy of destruction. "Women and children and even blacks were plundered nearly to their all. Beds were cut open and the feathers scattered abroad. Desks, looking glasses, cupboards, tables, chairs, clocks, etc., were shivered to fragments. Even Bibles were taken off for the avowed purpose of making cartridges. With the honorable exception of a Capt. Byng and one or two others, Admiral Cockburn's officers behaved in the same inhuman, indecent style."[20]

At least one Georgetown resident gained folk hero status when she defied Cockburn's troops and single-handedly saved an elderly widow's home. Catharine "Kitty" Knight, thirty-eight, said she watched in horror as Royal Navy sailors began burning the town. She said she followed the British to the house of the widow and pleaded with Cockburn to spare the structure. Sailors had just set the house on fire when Cockburn ordered them to extinguish the blaze. However, the British did set fire to the home next to the widow's, and the wind blew the flames toward the old lady's house. Local legend claims Knight remained at the widow's home, bravely fighting and eventually extinguishing the wind-driven fire with her broom.[21]

The campaign in the northern Chesapeake cost the British very little: twelve men wounded and two deserters. It cost the Americans much more. The inhabitants of the upper bay, humiliated by their display of military ineptitude and cowardice, unsupported by the federal and state governments, and pillaged by the British, were ready to concede defeat. They believed they were being sacrificed to Madison's attempt to conquer Canada and were no longer willing to support the war. While he was still on the Sassafras, Cockburn received a delegation from Charlestown, a port town on the Northeast River of the Maryland Eastern Shore, who told him they had no intention of resisting the British or doing anything to aid the American war effort and would not allow any militia to garrison their town. The delegation also told Cockburn that most of the towns on the upper bay that the British had yet to attack had adopted similar resolutions. In the space of just ten days the British had completely shut down the entire Chesapeake.[22]

Cockburn earned the lasting hatred of many Marylanders, who saw his campaign as wanton destruction. *Niles' Weekly Register* railed against the British admiral, claiming, "This Cockburn is one of the vilest wretches in existence, even when a child he had all those propensities to rapine and plunder that so mark his existence. So says a respectable man in Baltimore, who was his school fellow." The newspaper also tried to turn the burned homes and plundered farms into a rallying cry, grandly but falsely claiming, "The villain deed has raised the honest indignation of every man—no one pretends to justify or excuse it. It has knit the people into a common bond for vengeance on the incendiaries. It has destroyed party; and, by a community of interest, effected what patriotism demanded in vain.... Federalist and Democrats have laid their little bickerings ... this is as it should be."[23]

Admiral Warren left for Bermuda on May 17 on his flagship, the *San Domingo*, taking with him forty of the best prizes his squadron had seized since he arrived in March. He sent another thirty prizes north to Halifax in convoy with the *Dragon*, *Belvidera*, and *Maidstone*. Those vessels were the only ships the British actually wanted. They destroyed just as many others during their assault up the Chesapeake.[24] The boat attacks continued unabated as the British attacked isolated militia posts, burned the homes of prowar residents, and stole livestock and crops. They also continued their haul of prize ships. On many days the boat crews captured or burned three or four vessels.[25]

The continual work took a toll on the Royal Navy crews. Cockburn stripped his larger vessels of crews to man the boats, leaving the ships of the line and frigates without the sailors necessary to even man the warships' cannon. Cockburn ordered some of his largest ships to remove cannon to reduce their draft and allow them to maneuver in the shallow waters of the Chesapeake. The constant work in the boats left the men exhausted, and although meat and poultry were there for the taking, the British tars had been unable to find the fresh vegetables and fruit they needed to remain healthy. They were in particularly dire need of the commodity that would give them their nickname—limes.

Sailors in the eighteenth and nineteenth centuries who embarked on long cruises required citrus juice to ward off scurvy, a disease resulting from a vitamin C deficiency. Since the 1790s the Royal Navy had made lime and, to a lesser extent, lemon juice part of the basic rations of its sailors. Scurvy caused apathy, weakness, easy bruising, skin blisters, bleeding gums, and swollen legs. By mid-May, Cockburn reported that many of the men in the squadron were showing these symptoms.[26]

Cockburn sent the *Fantome* to Delaware Bay in search of the frigate *Statira*. Her commander, Capt. Hassard Stackpoole, had requisitioned 126 gallons of lime juice from the supply vessel *Three Sisters*, which had arrived off the Chesapeake at the beginning of May. Cockburn ordered Stackpoole to send half the lime juice he had back to the squadron. The lime juice duly arrived, averting a potentially crippling outbreak of scurvy.[27]

Watching Cockburn's every move was Capt. Charles Gordon, commander of the Baltimore Squadron. Observing was about all Gordon could do; his small force stood no chance against the massive British fleet. Gordon had faced long odds almost from the day he took command in Baltimore. When he took office in January 1813, Navy secretary William Jones had reorganized the defenses of the bay, sending the bulk of the Jefferson-era gunboats—including those in Baltimore—to Norfolk before the British clamped down their blockade.

Jones correctly believed that when Cockburn and Warren pushed up the Chesapeake in the spring, their mission would be reconnaissance and raiding rather than a set-piece attack on either Baltimore or Annapolis. Jones thought the British were trying to wage a type of reverse economic war, and that their presence in the bay was intended to divert U.S. resources from Canada and the Northwest Territory as well as to clamp down on American privateers, which were a major threat to the British economy. The British knew that the United States could not send effective forces everywhere at once, and by stretching American resources to the breaking point were trying to protect their own economy while placing a huge financial burden for defense on America.[28]

Gordon probably knew little about Jones' theories. He did know he was in command of an important station that was essentially defenseless. The only vessel Gordon had in April that was even close to combat-ready was the mortar ketch *Spitfire*. He also had gunboat *No. 138*, but she needed repairs.[29] He received some good news on April 15 when Jones sent permission to hire and outfit local ships to form a makeshift squadron. Baltimore, Jones said, was home to many "schooners of a class and description suitable for the occasion." Despite the alarm Warren's fleet had raised up and down the bay, though, Jones told Gordon he could hire only four ships and warned him that he would have to return any borrowed vessels to the owners "in the same condition in all respects as they were delivered to you."[30]

Jones' orders contained one clause that increased the difficulty of Gordon's task. Seamen who remained with the hired vessels were to receive standard Navy wages, which were notoriously lower than those merchant seamen normally received.[31] That made it nearly impossible for Gordon to entice sailors to serve on his borrowed warships. "For not withstanding the great outcry in vessels and men in abundance . . . I find trouble and difficulty" in recruiting crews, he told Jones, because few merchant seamen were willing to leave the ships on which they served for poor Navy wages.[32]

It took the squadron commander more than a week to get his force together. The appearance of Cockburn's and Warren's combined squadron off Baltimore undoubtedly spurred recruitment of sailors and made shipowners more willing to lend their vessels. Gordon used a fairly persuasive argument to hire three of the best privateers in the city. He simply pointed out to the owners that with the British off the city and at the mouth of the bay, there was little chance of the privateers actually putting to sea. The owners could at least rent their vessels to the Navy. They would not earn what they could make from commerce raiding, but some money was better than none.[33]

By early May 1813 Gordon's squadron was coming together. His biggest ship was the *Revenge*, which carried fourteen 12-pounder carronades, a pair of long 12-pounders, and a long 18-pounder on a pivoting mount. Second was the schooner *Patapsco*, reputed to be one of the best sailing vessels on the bay. The *Patapsco* carried a dozen 12-pounder carronades and a pair of long 12-pounders. His third vessel was the *Comet*, which carried twelve 12-pounder carronades and two long 9-pounders.[34] For captains Gordon selected three of the more experienced sailors he could induce to accept Navy pay. Capt. Jacob Mull commanded the *Patapsco*, Thomas Boyle had the *Comet*, and Job West was captain of the *Revenge*.[35]

Gordon reported problems finding a fourth vessel suitable for the type of action he anticipated. The owners of the other large vessels in port were unwilling to rent their ships to the Navy while they still had cargoes on board. The blockade prevented the ships from bringing those cargoes to other American ports or friendly destinations in the Caribbean as much as it kept them from going out on privateering voyages. Gordon finally settled on the small schooner *Wasp*, which carried two 12-pounder carronades and a long 9-pounder on a swivel mount. He also had a single U.S. Navy gunboat, *No. 138*, with her 24-pounder long gun and a pair of 12-pounder carronades.[36]

His squadron set, Gordon sailed out of Baltimore on May 21 with orders to use his new flotilla to restrict the movement of enemy tenders and boats. If possible, he was to recapture some of "those fine schooners which have recently and unfortunately fallen into [enemy] hands."[37] He dutifully sailed south toward Annapolis, shadowing the British fleet, and spent nearly a month following Warren and Cockburn as they burned their way back down the Chesapeake. Although the British kept their tenders, schooners, barges, and cutters in constant use, the larger Royal Navy ships effectively covered the smaller vessels, a tactic that Gordon said "rendered any offensive operations on our part impractical."[38]

His water expended and the *Revenge* hampered by a sprung mainmast, Gordon returned to Baltimore. Although he had been unable to break the blockade or retake any of the dozens of ships the Royal Navy had captured, Gordon had maintained contact with Warren's force and reported accurately on the force's movements, especially as the ships moved south on the bay. As he turned his vessels toward Baltimore, Gordon reported that "after taking every opportunity to reconnoiter and observe the enemy," he believed their next target would be somewhere south of the Potomac River.[39] It was easy enough to guess what that target was.

CHAPTER 6

Target: Norfolk

AS SPRING TURNED TOWARD SUMMER in 1813, it was clear the Americans and British viewed the Chesapeake theater in very different ways. The Madison administration could not seem to grasp the strategic importance of the bay as a haven for privateers, as a source of supplies, and as the gateway to the nation's capital. The federal government remained fixated on the campaign against Canada and, increasingly, on defending the territories acquired in the Louisiana Purchase. Victories over British troops and their Indian allies near Detroit may have restored the prewar borders in the Michigan and Indiana territories, but control of the Great Lakes remained in doubt, and losses in Canada left the United States open to attack through New York State.

Madison also had to contend with the possible expansion of the war into Spanish Florida. Volunteers from Tennessee and Kentucky had assembled under cantankerous Gen. Andrew Jackson and prepared to seize the Spanish territory, but an uprising in the Alabama territories of the Creek Indians and their allies forced Jackson to shift his attention there. Still, an American force occupied undefended Spanish West Florida, including the city of Mobile, and prepared to head toward St. Augustine.

The open oceans also remained a major concern for both sides. America went to war with England ostensibly because of its belief in "free trade and sailors' rights." So far, at least at sea, the Americans continued to enjoy success. The brig *Argus* and the frigates *President* and *Chesapeake* made successful cruises, capturing or destroying numerous prizes while bringing the war to English home waters. Victories such as those, however, were becoming rare as the Royal Navy tightened its blockade. Privateers and some merchantmen still managed to slip out, but the Eastern Seaboard from Long Island Sound to Charleston was slowly being closed to American shipping.

Great Britain also saw Canada and the Great Lakes as major theaters of the war, but unlike the Americans, realized the importance of operations in the Chesapeake. The English recognized the strategic role of the bay as a supply base for the Americans as well as for their own navy. They also believed their early nineteenth-century form of total war would force the Americans to divert resources from Canada to the Chesapeake.

The most obvious place for the British to expand the Chesapeake campaign was at Norfolk—the gateway to the bay and the location of the *Constellation*. A victory at Norfolk could conceivably destroy morale and create a domino effect throughout the bay. At the very least, it would take one of the U.S. Navy's frigates out of the war. The Admiralty dispatched an expeditionary force of 2,300 men under Col. Sir Thomas Sidney Beckwith to Bermuda. From there, Admiral Warren, with the *San Domingo* and the *Plantagenet*, escorted the force to the mouth of the Chesapeake. The reinforced squadron arrived off Cape Henry at the mouth of the bay on June 5.

Beckwith's force arrived on seven transports. His orders from London gave him command over all of the British land forces, although Warren had the authority to pick Beckwith's targets. The Admiralty told both commanders their mission was to "harass the enemy by different attacks" without taking permanent possession of any particular target. They were to reembark their troops as soon as they accomplished the immediate objective of any attack and were to avoid a general action unless it was necessary to cover a retreat. Their orders authorized Warren and Beckwith to exact tribute from any community in return for refraining from destroying nonmilitary property. On no account, however, were they to encourage a slave rebellion, "which must be attended by atrocities inseparable from commotions of such a description." If individual blacks offered to assist the British and requested asylum, Warren could take them into one of the Colonial Marine Corps units that served in the West Indies. Nevertheless, since Warren was to free any slaves who offered help and to maintain them at public expense, London urged him to exercise discretion to ensure he could fulfill that commitment. Warren also received an admonition that "it will rarely, if ever, be necessary to advance so far into the country as to risk [your] power of returning."[1]

Beckwith's command comprised two battalions of Royal Marines; a detachment of the 102nd Infantry Regiment under his second in command, Lt. Col. Charles Napier; and two companies of the Regiment of Independent Foreigners, a unit made up of French prisoners of war. The two marine battalions each had a company of light artillery consisting of a pair of light 6-pound naval guns mounted on wheeled carriages, a 12-pound and a 24-pound howitzer on carriages, and a 10-inch mortar. In addition, Beckwith had the squadron's marines and sailors at his disposal, giving him another 688 marines and 1,286 small-arms-trained sailors on whom to draw.[2]

Land forces were only part of the equation for Beckwith. The colonel also had Warren's fleet to provide covering fire as well as the ships' barges and cutters, which carried Congreve rockets and carronades. On paper, at least, the veteran of the Peninsular Campaign had everything in place to attack and carry Norfolk—everything, that is, except landing craft.

The fleet's launches and barges were perfect craft for the type of warfare the British had employed so far—slashing raids in which rowers and marines alike exited the craft to attack a particular town or farm—but were ill suited for landing large bodies of troops. To send several thousand marines and soldiers ashore the British needed "flats," shoal-draft scows with ramped ends that were similar to the tobacco boats that plied the bay. Each flat could carry forty troops or two artillery pieces and twelve men, although they required a tow from either an oared or a sailing vessel. Warren put Cockburn to work on the boats. Cockburn stripped the crews of the *Barrosa* and *Narcissus* and set them ashore on Watts Island, where they cut twenty-five acres of forest to build fifty landing craft.[3] When combined with the ships' boats that would tow the flats into combat, Beckwith could put ashore 2,600 men in one sortie.[4]

The defenses of Norfolk had improved since the British first tried to rush up the Elizabeth River to capture the city and its navy yard. Brig. Gen. Robert Taylor remained in command and continued to pull in militia units from the surrounding area to reinforce his garrison. By June 5 Taylor had five militia infantry regiments and one regiment of artillery ready for action. He also had the Regulars stationed at Fort Norfolk under his command.[5]

Taylor was among the better militia commanders who would face the British in the Chesapeake region. He knew how to organize units and worked hard to make the militia more professional. He eliminated the colonial practice of electing field officers and grouped his disparate militia companies into sequentially numbered regiments, putting an experienced officer in command of each. Although none of his regiments had its authorized strength of one thousand officers and men, at least every militiaman had a weapon, and many had rifles.

Taylor also had a pair of naval officers who knew how to employ the fifteen ungainly gunboats then in Norfolk. Master Commandant John Cassin and Master Commandant Joseph Tarbell were both veterans of the U.S. campaign against Tripoli in 1803–4; Cassin was in command of the Gosport Navy Yard, and Tarbell had temporary command of the *Constellation* (Capt. Charles Stewart was on his way north to Boston to take command of the *Constitution*). Both officers understood the need for gunboats and had experience using them, and they prepared their little flotilla for action.[6]

The weak point at Norfolk remained Craney Island. More sandbar than actual island, the spit of land was about a half mile long and two hundred yards wide. The western tip of the island concealed a sandbar that was invisible

at high tide. Two narrow guts separated Craney Island from the mainland.
The first, called the Thoroughfare, was on the western side of island and was
about one hundred yards wide. The second, Craney Island Creek, at the south
end of the island, was four hundred yards wide, six feet deep, and had a footbridge across it. A third watercourse, Wise's Creek, bordered the island along
the north bank of the Elizabeth River and fed a swamp that faced Hampton
Roads and in turn drained into a series of mudflats that made any approach by
ship from that side of the island impossible.

Taylor was well aware of the importance of Craney Island to Norfolk's
defense. As he watched the British preparing to attack, he dashed off a note to
Secretary of War Armstrong on June 18, telling him, "Should the enemy . . .
attack Craney Island, it must fall unless we throw the greater part of our forces
there." Knowing he could not strip Norfolk of its defenders, Taylor told Armstrong he would resort to trickery if necessary to keep Cockburn off balance.[7]

The British could not have asked for a better pair of ground commanders than
Col. Sir Thomas Sidney Beckwith and Lt. Col. Charles Napier. Beckwith came
from a military family. His three brothers were all commissioned officers in
the British army; the oldest was a lieutenant general. Sir Sidney was already a
legend in the British army for his handling of light infantry troops in Spain
during the Peninsular War. At the Battle of Sabugal on April 3, 1811, Beckwith
commanded a brigade of light infantry of Wellington's army and led his men
into the thick of the action. Beckwith's horse was shot out from under him
and he was wounded in the action, but that did little to slow him down. He
remained with his command and fought just days later at the Battle of Fuentes
de Oñoro on May 3–6, 1811. In recognition of his gallantry, Beckwith received
a knighthood and became the quartermaster general of Lt. Gen. John C. Sher-
brooke's forces in Halifax. Later in his career he was promoted to lieutenant
general and made commander in chief of British forces in Bombay. His peers
called Beckwith "one of the ablest outpost generals and one of a few officers
that knew . . . how to make the most of small forces."[8]

Charles Napier was the oldest of four brothers, all of whom entered military service. His star was just on the rise as the Peninsular War came to a close.
Physically small and nearsighted, Napier possessed an amazingly sharp intel-
lect and seemed to know intuitively how to handle troops. He suffered a series
of wounds while serving in Spain and Portugal in 1809, including broken ribs,
a gunshot wound, and a bayonet wound. After he recovered from those injuries he returned to duty and was again in the middle of close combat. At the
Battle of Busaco on September 27, 1810, he led his command on a wild charge
that turned the French flank, during which a shot through his face broke his

Lt. Col. Charles Napier, British army, one of the senior ground commanders during the British Chesapeake campaign in 1813. He often found fault with the way his superior, Rear Adm. George Cockburn, conducted the campaign.
NATIONAL MARITIME MUSEUM, GREENWICH, ENGLAND

jaw. He nevertheless returned to take part in the Battles of Sabugal and Fuentes de Oñoro. Later in his career Napier would command part of the British army in India and would quell uprisings in several provinces as well as claim victories in Afghanistan. His spectacular series of successes earned him the nickname "Conqueror of Sind," and London's citizens erected a huge bronze statue of him in Trafalgar Square, paid for through popular subscription.[9]

Although confident of their own skills, the two infantry officers were less sanguine about those of their naval counterparts. Neither Napier nor Beckwith had worked with the Royal Navy prior to coming to the Chesapeake, and so far, at least, neither Warren nor Cockburn had impressed them. Cockburn, on the strength of his successes in the northern part of the bay, fancied himself an infantry tactician, while Warren, as overall commander, picked the targets. In addition, there was the order from London "to avoid the risk of a general action." Beckwith, according to Napier, seemed unable to deal with the complicated command situation. "Had either Sir John Warren, Sir Sidney Beckwith or Admiral Cockburn acted singly and without consultation, we should not have done such foolish things," Napier wrote. "Sir Sidney ran sulky when required to do what he deemed silly, which in my opinion made it more silly."[10]

Before leaving Bermuda, Warren and Beckwith had sent Cockburn a long list of questions concerning the approaches to Craney Island, Fort Norfolk, Fort Nelson, the Gosport Navy Yard, and the city of Norfolk. Warren was particularly interested in the approaches to Fort Norfolk from the east side of the Elizabeth River. Beckwith appeared more interested in landing a large force at the Nansemond River west of Norfolk and then proceeding east overland to Fort Nelson and Gosport before attacking Norfolk over the bridges from Gosport. Cockburn received Warren's and Cockburn's questions on June 12 and immediately set to work providing answers, albeit most of them reflected his own opinion. The rear admiral believed any attack from Gosport toward Norfolk would give the Americans too much time to draw in reserves. An attack from the Nansemond River would also force the Americans to concentrate their defenses around Norfolk, which in turn could bring on the "general action" the British were to avoid. Cockburn favored a two-pronged assault in which ground forces would strike Craney Island while also landing on the eastern side of the Elizabeth River. Cockburn believed this approach would prevent Taylor from bringing in reinforcements and open Fort Norfolk to attack. Once Beckwith's troops took Fort Norfolk, Fort Nelson would be untenable and the British would have complete control of the area on both sides of the river. It took Cockburn four days to compose answers to all the questions, and he never sent them because Warren arrived with Beckwith's troops on June 20.[11]

As part of his information gathering, Cockburn ordered Cdr. Frederick Hickey in the sloop *Atalante* to reconnoiter the areas around Craney Island

and Cape Henry to find suitable landing sites—preferably places near roads leading inland that would aid the invasion force. Hickey set off on June 14. He got something of an advance notice of the mood of the local inhabitants when he pulled up to what he called "Ragged Island Lake Plantation," an island with a small farm that had several houses, two corn mills, and fields well stocked with cattle. Hickey demanded the owner provide his ship with corn and other supplies, but the owner refused. Unsure what to make of the owner's stance, Hickey anchored the *Atalante* outside cannon range that night and returned in the morning. He ordered a landing party of sailors and marines to return to the farm and again demand supplies, and to warn the owner that if he refused, "Down goes your Mill." The owner replied by revealing the presence of a small group of militia, which immediately opened fire on the British landing party. A company of the 2nd Virginia militia under Maj. William Nimmo was also on the island, and he moved quickly toward the sound of the guns.

After repulsing the first group of British, the militia now faced nearly the entire crew of the *Atalante*, which Hickey sent ashore with orders to burn everything on the island. The militia drove the British landing party back to the *Atalante*. Hickey then opened fire with the ship's guns. He fired more than a hundred rounds and set one of the mills ablaze, but the militia stood its ground and extinguished the fire. The Virginians kept shooting until they expended all of their ammunition.[12]

If the unexpected defense of the small, unnamed island did not alarm Cockburn, the Americans' next move certainly did. On June 19 the U.S. Navy launched a surprise attack on the frigate *Junon*, which had become separated from the rest of Cockburn's squadron. The ship was short of crew because Cockburn had most of his seamen out in the small boats making charts and placing buoys in the areas near Craney Island.

Cassin ordered Tarbell to strip the *Constellation* of crew to man the fifteen gunboats still in Norfolk. The gunboats set off late in the evening of June 19, using rain squalls for cover as they moved downriver toward the British. Even with the crew from the *Constellation*, the gunboats were undermanned. The craft normally carried crews of between 35 and 40 men. The 150 sailors and 50 Marines Tarbell took off the *Constellation* and split up among the 15 gunboats gave each vessel a skeleton crew of just 13 men. The river current helped the boats move, but the few crewmen on board still had to man the sweeps as the gunboats advanced.

At 2:30 a.m. on June 20, Capt. James Sanders of the *Junon* caught a glimpse of the American gunboats heading toward him. *Junon* was the westernmost ship in the British anchorage and could not move because of a lack of wind. The neighboring frigates *Barrosa* and *Narcissus* faced the same the problem, but Tarbell was headed toward the *Junon*, not the other ships. At a range of about a half mile, Tarbell ordered his gunners to fire. The long 24-pounders

belched flames into the darkness, striking the *Junon* four times, killing one
sailor and wounding three. Just as the gunboats were ready to fire a second
salvo, however, the wind came up from out of the northeast and the three
British frigates got under way and moved toward the gunboats. Both the *Junon*
and the *Narcissus* were able to bring their 18-pounder main batteries to bear
on Tarbell's flotilla and began to pound the gunboats. Tarbell, directing the
action from a small tender, ordered the gunboats to retire at 6:30 a.m. American casualties were light. Master's Mate Thomas Allinson of the *Constellation*
was killed on gunboat *No. 139* when an 18-pounder cannon ball ripped him
in two, and two Marines suffered splinter wounds. All of the gunboats were
damaged. The attack amounted to very little—although Tarbell believed he
could have taken the *Junon* had the wind not changed—but it served to show
the British that the defenders of Norfolk were not the same as those of Havre
de Grace or Fredericktown. It also instilled a measure of respect in Cockburn
for the gunboats.[13]

The attention of the British next centered on Craney Island. Warren
arrived on June 22 with Beckwith, Napier, and the troop transports and found
Cockburn already preparing for an attack on the island. Warren was committed to making an overland attack on Fort Norfolk from the rear, which
required taking the sandy spit of land. Napier and Cockburn appeared to agree
with Warren's strategy, but Beckwith did not, although Beckwith's reluctance
to embrace the plan did not hinder the naval officers.

Warren assigned two separate forces to attack the island simultaneously:
a land force from the west under Beckwith and an equally strong amphibious
force under Capt. Samuel John Pechell of the *San Domingo* that would attack
from the north. Cockburn, with his group of frigates and sloops, was to coordinate and provide covering fire for the attack. His ships were also to serve as
the assembly point for both prongs of the assault.

Once they captured the island and cleared it of defenders, Warren planned
to reembark both forces and redeploy them to Tanners Creek, from which
they could hit Fort Norfolk. Warren ordered Cockburn to transfer his flag to
the frigate *Barrosa* and take command of the *Junon, Narcissus, Laurestinus,
Moselle, Atalante, Nemesis,* and *Mohawk* along with six tenders. Once Cockburn safely landed the assault force, he was to ascend the river with his new
squadron and destroy the gunboats. After Beckwith had reduced Fort Norfolk
and Fort Nelson, the combined force was to capture or destroy the *Constellation,* the navy yard, and any shipping present in Norfolk harbor.[14]

On paper, it was a good plan. The British apparently expected the Americans to put up no more than token resistance, as they had at Havre de Grace
and Fredericktown. They did not know that, unlike the Maryland state forces
on the upper bay, the Virginians guarding Norfolk wanted the British to
attack.

CHAPTER 7

The Battle of Norfolk

MAJ. JAMES FAULKNER of the Virginia militia had always wanted to be an army officer. For years before the war Faulkner had tried unsuccessfully to persuade the secretary of war or President Thomas Jefferson to grant him a commission in the Regular Army. His lack of success failed to deaden his ardor. In 1811, as war with Britain loomed, Faulkner raised his own volunteer artillery company, which was attached to the 67th Virginia militia out of Berkeley County. By 1813 Faulkner was a militia major with command of an artillery battalion.

Governor James Barbour of Virginia ordered Faulkner to bring his battalion to Richmond and then to Norfolk. Brigadier General Taylor, desperately short of field-grade artillery officers, on June 19 ordered Faulkner to take command of the artillery on Craney Island.[1] When he arrived on the island Faulkner reported to Lt. Col. Henry Beatty, commander of the 4th Virginia Infantry Regiment. Beatty was a veteran of the Revolutionary War who had commanded the state's 31st Regiment of Militia before he came to Norfolk. His second in command, Maj. Andrew Waggoner, had served with Faulkner in the 67th militia before moving to Norfolk.

Although its title suggested a unified command, Beatty's 4th Infantry was actually an amalgam of several disparate militia companies from all over Virginia. He had two companies of Waggoner's and Faulkner's 67th militia; three companies from Frederick County under three captains: Charles Brent, George Holliday, and Thomas Roberts; two companies from Jefferson County under Zachariah Buckmaster and Thomas B. Taws; one company from Fauquier County under Enoch Jeffries; a company from Loudon County under Thomas Gregg; and a company from Orange County under William Dulaney.[2]

Aside from the normal problems of integrating different units into a single command Beatty also had manpower problems; none of the ten companies was up to strength. The authorized size of a Virginia infantry regiment was 750 men, but Beatty had just 466, with another 46 on the sick list. Faulkner, meanwhile, took command of the two independent companies of

light artillery on the island, which totaled another ninety-one men and four
6-pounder field guns.³

After watching Rear Adm. George Cockburn scout the island on June
20, Taylor asked Capt. Joseph Tarbell if he could spare any sailors to man a
battery of naval guns on the island. Tarbell stripped the *Constellation* of her
remaining crew, leaving just a master and twelve men on the frigate, and sent
one hundred sailors under the command of Lt. B. J. Neale and fifty Marines
under the command of Lt. Henry Breckenridge. The naval force took charge of
three 24-pounder guns. Tarbell positioned the shorthanded *Constellation* in
between Fort Norfolk and Fort Nelson with springs on her anchors, making
it appear the frigate could enfilade the channel from Craney Island. Tarbell
positioned his fifteen gunboats between Craney Island and Lamberts Point,
covering the entire span of the Elizabeth River.⁴ Taylor also managed to scrape
up another sixty men to send Beatty—thirty Regulars under Capt. Richard
Pollard and thirty volunteer riflemen. All told, 767 men now held Craney
Island. They dug in behind log-and-sand breastworks and waited for the British to attack.⁵

Admiral Warren made his move at midnight on June 21. A group of thirty
ships' boats and fifteen flats under the command of Capt. John Martin Hanchett of the *Diadem* embarked Colonel Beckwith's 1,500-man landing force,
which comprised Napier's 102nd Regiment, a company of the Independent
Foreigners, the Second Battalion of Royal Marines, and a contingent of sailors under Lieutenant Westphal. Napier, in a letter to his sister, described the
passage:

> We have two or three miles to row, the boats tied together and
> moving slowly . . . filled with armed men gliding in silence over
> the smooth water, arms glittering in the moonshine, oars just
> breaking the stillness of the night, the dark shade of woods we
> are pushing for combining with the expectation of danger to
> affect the mind. Suddenly Cast off! is heard, and the rapid dash
> of oars begins, with the quick hurrah! hurrah! hurrah! as the
> sailors pull to shore. Then the soldiers rush into and through
> the water. I forbid all noise until they can rush on the enemy;
> then they have leave to give a deadly screech and away! away!⁶

Beckwith's troops landed on the beach east of Hoffleur's Creek near Pig
Point at the mouth of the Nansemond River. The colonel had his 1,500 troops
assembled by daybreak, and they set out through the woods toward Craney
Island. The force ran into problems almost immediately because Beckwith

had used French prisoners of war from the Independent Foreigners as an advance guard. The French, sensing an opportunity, bolted almost at once, and twenty-five men disappeared into the woods.[7]

The island's defenders quickly spotted the large force of Royal Marines and soldiers toiling through the woods. William Schutte, a militiaman posted at Hoffleur's Creek, ran down to the Thoroughfare and called across the creek to Faulkner, reporting the enemy's movements.[8] Faulkner could see the British forming on the beach to enter the forest along the shore that led to the farm of Capt. George Wise, a militia officer. Realizing that his battery of four 6-pounders would be no match for the British, Faulkner decided to transfer the Navy's two 18-pounders and two 24-pounders from the unfinished fort to the west end of the island. He and Thomas Rourk, master of a blockaded ship and a former member of a militia artillery unit from Portsmouth, Virginia, organized a working party that dragged the 5,000-pound guns off their platform in the unfinished fort and up the length of the island in an hour.[9]

Faulkner maneuvered all seven cannon onto a rise forty feet behind a previously prepared low, U-shaped breastwork facing Wise's farm and Hampton Roads. He placed the four 6-pounders on the right while Rourk commanded the two 18-pounders on the left along with the two 24-pounders under a Captain Emmerson, commander of the Portsmouth militia's artillery unit. Beatty posted his infantry along the breastwork under his deputy, Maj. Andrew Waggoner. The mixed bag of militia and Regulars erected a flagpole and nailed the colors to it. As the American defenders settled into their new position, Lt. William Shubrick and Lt. James Saunders from the *Constellation* arrived with a supply of shot and gunpowder. The naval officers had stripped the supplies from the frigate and the gunboats and, lacking draft horses, had moved the heavy shot and powder by foot and boat, using the sailors already on the island to do the bulk of the work.[10]

Beckwith planned his attack to occur at low tide. When he reached the Thoroughfare at 7 a.m., however, he found an uncharted seven-foot-deep channel running through the center of the tidal channel. A man in "colored clothes" who claimed he was a deserter offered to show the British a way around Wise's farm to the wooden bridge over Craney Island Creek. Beckwith followed the man until he grew dubious of the "deserter's" intentions, then turned back and returned to his troops. He ordered Capt. Robert Russell of the Royal Marine Artillery to take the rocket unit and create a diversion to draw attention from the amphibious assault. The marines fired about a half-dozen rockets, and Rourk responded with a barrage of grape and canister that pummeled the British position. The gunfire was so intense and rapid that it put one of the 18-pounders and one of the 6-pounders out of commission for the rest of the battle. Gunboat *No. 67* of Tarbell's flotilla also joined in the cannonade, the only direct participation of the flotilla that day.[11]

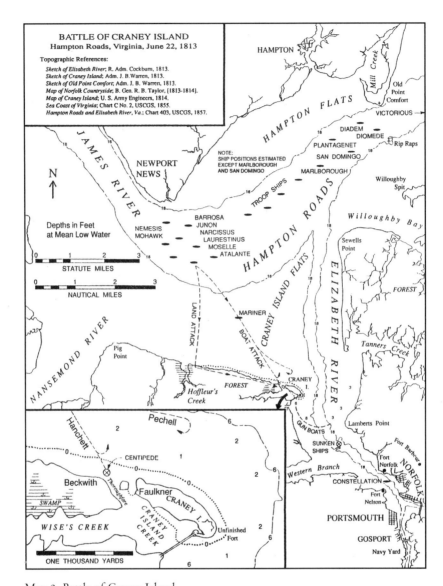

Map 2. Battle of Craney Island
TAKEN FROM AN ORIGINAL DRAWING BY STANLEY QUICK

The opening salvo from the American battery killed a sergeant standing next to Lieutenant Colonel Napier, who ordered the rest of his men to take cover in the woods. The 102nd executed the order promptly, but the marines reacted more slowly and remained under fire. Three more American salvos struck the marines before they scrambled to safety, killing three and wounding eight.

Some of the British troops tried to hide behind the Wise farm's slave quarters, but American gunfire tore the roof off the building and knocked down the chimneys. The marines dashed to the woods for safety. As they did, Napier heard an officer yelling to the men in the woods but could not make out what the man was saying. The continuous din from the American cannon fire drowned out almost every other noise. The man was a courier Beckwith had sent to Napier with orders to withdraw. Beckwith, seeing Napier's force was caught in a cul-de-sac and facing unexpectedly heavy artillery fire, wanted to pull back. The courier, however, refused to move to Napier's position. He shouted from a safe distance, "You are to retire! You are to retreat!" Napier scornfully replied, "Come up and tell us so!" and began to pull his men back to the beach. It would prove to be a major mistake. Both Napier and Beckwith, however, blamed the fiasco on Cockburn, believing the admiral had failed to properly ascertain the depth of the Thoroughfare. No matter who was to blame, the main prong of the British attack on Craney Island was out of the fight without even reaching the island.[12]

By 8 a.m. the sun was high, the sky cloudless, and the weather sultry. The defenders of the island had no shelter and no source of freshwater. They collected rainwater by digging holes and straining the water from the mud. Sweat coursed down the bodies of the gunners and drenched their clothing. Only Major Faulkner, Lieutenant Breckenridge, Captain Pollard, and the thirty Regulars wore uniforms. The rest of the Americans, either preferring comfort or because they were militia and unused to wearing uniforms, had stripped down to shirtsleeves. Out in the river they could see the rocket vessel *Mariner* moving into position just out of range of their long guns; landing craft laden with troops clustered around her. A boat moved out from the *Mariner*, the crew searching for the shoal Lieutenant Westphal had found during his reconnaissance. As the boat moved closer to the island, the naval gunners opened fire, driving the British boat back to the *Mariner*. Two more boats pushed off from the *Mariner*, each armed with rockets. The boats attempted to engage the American artillery but never moved into range, all of their shots falling short. The gun battle served as cover for the landing craft, which joined the two rocket boats, forming a pair of parallel columns. One veered to the north, outside the shoal as if heading toward the line of American gunboats, while the other pushed straight toward the beach.[13]

Capt. Samuel Pechell of the ship of the line *San Domingo* led the assault, taking the front boat in the column feinting toward the gunboats. He led a force of some two hundred soldiers, sailors, and Royal Marines arrayed in twenty boats and flats. Capt. John Martin Hanchett led the column heading straight for the beach, using Admiral Warren's personal 24-oar gig as his attack craft. The 50-foot-long boat was packed with sailors, marines, and thirty Independent Foreigners; another five hundred soldiers, sailors, and marines followed in nineteen boats and sixteen flats.[14]

Neither of the British officers was happy with his assignment. The assault was supposed begin at high tide, but by 8 a.m. the tide was already ebbing. More ominously, the plan for a two-pronged encirclement of the defenders on Craney Island had already fallen apart when Beckwith decided not to push ahead with his attack at the Thoroughfare. Now the British attack would be a straight frontal assault. Hanchett and two other officers spoke out heatedly against proceeding, but Pechell, believing it was his duty to support Beckwith, ordered the troops to attack.[15]

Faulkner watched as Hanchett's column of British troops headed straight toward the artillery position. The major ordered his gunners to hold their fire, allowing the British boats to approach so close that the Americans could clearly tell the officers from the enlisted men. When Lieutenant Neale told Faulkner he could hit the lead British boat, the major ordered Neale to open fire. Just as the big 18- and 24-pounders belched fire, the lead British boats grounded on the shoal off Craney Island, still several hundred yards from shore. Neale, true to his word, hit Hanchett's lead boat with his second shot, killing one Frenchman and wounding eight British soldiers. The shot knocked down Hanchett, who was standing in the bow wrapped in a Union Jack, ready to lead his troops. He got back to his feet and began to wave his hat as a warning to the boats behind his, but another salvo from Neale's battery sent splinters flying, wounding Hanchett in the left thigh. The trailing boats continued to pile up on the shoal, creating confusion among the landing force. Boat officers screamed out commands to "Pull to port," "Pull to starboard," "Give way ahead," and "Back astern."

The shouted commands caused even more confusion among the British, who were now directly under the guns of the American defenders. Cannon fire struck one of the rocket boats and four launches. Lieutenant Westphal, pushing forward in one of the trailing boats, jumped out on the shoal and began to wade toward the beach in a vain attempt to convince the amphibious force to follow. Pechell rowed over from his column of boats and saw the beginnings of a rout. Perhaps hearing from Westphal that Beckwith already had withdrawn, he ordered a general retreat.[16]

As the British tried to back their boats off the shoal, Faulkner decided to snatch as many prisoners as he could. He ordered some of his riflemen to wade out and herd as many of the floundering enemy as they could to the shore. He also ordered Neale to form a salvage party of sailors to grab Hanchett's gig, which was empty and aground on the shoal.[17]

When the two parties set out, Faulkner ordered the gunners to change from grape and canister to round shot to avoid hitting their own men. The American riflemen charged into the water and quickly rounded up twenty-two prisoners. They also became embroiled in a controversial fight at the water's edge that would have tragic consequences for Cockburn's next target. The British claimed the riflemen brutally massacred a number of Frenchmen who were struggling to get out of a barge. Taylor, who eventually convened a board of inquiry into the charge, found the claim baseless.[18]

The American guns ceased firing around 9 a.m. Part of Pechell's force joined with Beckwith on the far bank of Hoffleur's Creek while the remainder stood offshore, out of artillery range, preparing for a second assault. As his men settled in to wait, Faulkner sent one of the 6-pounders to cover the footbridge leading to the island. General Taylor sent 120 volunteer reinforcements as well as Lt. Col. Armistead Mason's 5th Infantry Regiment. Mason took up a position from which he could attack Beckwith's force from the rear should it try once again to land on the island.[19]

At 3:30 p.m., as the tide came back in, the British once more rowed for the island. Once again the shoal stopped the attack. British accounts assert that the "boats pulled manfully to the contest but with the same unfortunate result. As on the first attempt, we again formed a solid mass instead of an extended line, and the enterprise was abandoned." The log of the *San Domingo* states the American battery opened fire and continued to fire until 6 p.m., when the attackers finally withdrew. There is no record of this second attack in any American account.[20]

The debacle on Craney Island took the British by surprise. Admiral Warren tried to play down the defeat in his report to the Admiralty, saying he "considered in consequence of the representation of the officer commanding the troops of the difficulty of their passing over [to Craney Island] from the land, that the persevering effort would cost more men than the number of us would permit."[21]

Warren mentioned neither Pechell, who was his nephew, nor the loss of his personal boat in his reports. Beckwith submitted no report other than his casualty list. The combined official British casualty report was three dead, sixteen wounded, and sixty-two missing, including the twenty-five Frenchmen who scampered off at the start of the attack. Not a single American defender was killed or wounded. A force of seven hundred men, most of them militia, flanked by a gunboat flotilla, had turned back an invasion force of more than four thousand men supported by twenty ships of war. The thoroughly humiliated Warren's self-serving description of Norfolk's impregnability was such that the British avoided the Elizabeth River for the remainder of the war.[22]

While the British wondered how everything could have gone so wrong, the Americans celebrated. In his report Faulkner singled out Neale and the men from the *Constellation*, saying, "A more determined set of men, if an opportunity existed, I never witnessed."[23] Taylor gave Faulkner the credit for the victory and promoted him to command of the defensive ring to the rear of Norfolk.

In the aftermath of the battle, interservice rivalries dimmed the victory as some of the officers began to bicker over who exactly did what in combat. Lieutenant Colonel Beatty, who was in overall command but apparently never moved to the scene of the fighting, praised Faulkner in his report and singled out several individuals for commendation, including Tarbell. The *Constellation* officer, however, was upset that Beatty had allowed sutlers on the island immediately after the battle, and reported that the militiamen were frequently intoxicated. On June 30 Taylor ordered Beatty to evict the sutlers. Beatty did so, telling Taylor that Tarbell's men were among those frequently drunk.

In early July one of Beatty's company commanders, Capt. Thomas Gregg, sent a letter to Taylor demanding Beatty's arrest for, among other things, "showing a disposition to strike the colors in the face of the enemy before they approached with musket shot." Gregg alleged that Major Waggoner had to physically prevent Beatty from ordering a retreat when the British landed. Beatty had not mentioned Gregg, who fought in the battle, in his report. Taylor ordered an inquiry that vindicated Beatty when Waggoner sent a letter completely disavowing Gregg's assertions. Beatty and Gregg continued to serve in the 4th Infantry until October, when the regiment was reconstituted with new officers and soldiers.[24]

Warren did not give his men time to brood over the fiasco at Craney Island, which Napier said "dampened us all." Instead, he turned his energy toward mounting an assault on Hampton, a small, isolated village across from Norfolk at the end of the long peninsula separating the James River from the York River. Warren justified his decision to the Admiralty by claiming the Americans had a "considerable corps" at Hampton that controlled communications to Richmond, which he believed necessary to interrupt. He also said he selected Hampton because it was a perfect place to get freshwater. Beckwith, however, justified the choice to his superiors by saying the Americans were gathering troops there and erecting batteries in the vicinity that would allow them to control Hampton Roads.[25]

The British troops had barely returned to their transports on June 24 when they began to disembark for the attack on Hampton. The ships' boats, cutters, and flats began loading Beckwith's 2,600-man land force around midnight. The first to shove off was Napier's advance guard consisting of his 102nd Foot, both companies of Independent Foreigners, three companies of ship's marines, and a company of Royal Marine Artillery with two 6-pounder field guns and Congreve rockets. Lt. Col. Richard Williams of the Royal Marines led the main body, consisting of two battalions of marines. Admiral Cockburn took command of the naval operations, and Captain Pechell went on board the *Mohawk* to supervise Beckwith's landing. Cockburn himself took personal command of the eight tenders that transferred the second wave of marines to the flats.[26]

Facing the British was a motley group of militia under the command of Maj. Stapleton Crutchfield. Most of the men came from the vicinity of James City and York, Virginia. Crutchfield had, on paper, seven companies of light infantry, one company of riflemen, a cavalry company, and an artillery detachment of four long 12-pounders and three 6-pounders. As impressive as that sounded, what should have been a regiment-sized force barely mustered a battalion's strength. Crutchfield had just 349 infantry, 25 cavalry, and 62 artillerymen.[27]

The militia took up positions at Little England, the ancestral home of the Barron family and former estate of Commodore James Barron, the disgraced commander of the U.S. frigate *Chesapeake*. At the time, the widow of Samuel Barron, James' older brother, lived at the estate, which was just south of the town on the Hampton River between Salters Creek and Sunset Creek. A small plank bridge across Salters Creek provided direct access to the property from the heart of town. The infantry dug a trench in front of their camp and built a high embankment in front of it. Crutchfield placed his guns in two places to project into the river, providing lines of fire to the narrow entrance of the river at Blackbeard's Point. He put the three light guns on a point near the mouth of Sunset Creek and the heavy guns on a point four hundred yards to the north.[28]

The first British troops waded ashore at a farm two miles west of town around 3:30 a.m. on June 25. Napier's advance force of nine hundred men quickly formed up and moved out. By 5 a.m. Beckwith had his entire force ashore and formed into columns, and had started inland. Cockburn took the *Highflyer* and other tenders together with thirty barges and two rocket boats and headed directly for Hampton to engage the militia from the river while Beckwith approached from their rear. One of Cockburn's launches, the barge from the *San Domingo*, carried an 8-inch howitzer manned by Royal Marine artillerymen with which Cockburn planned to take the American batteries in the flank as the boats sailed along the shoreline. The Americans had revealed the positions of their batteries on June 24 when two British officers, using a local pilot and a captured boat, entered the harbor and provoked them into firing.[29]

Cavalry captain John B. Cooper brought Crutchfield news of the British landing at 4:30 a.m. Cooper had his dragoons on patrol near Celeys Road when the first redcoats splashed ashore. He followed the British as they moved out, shadowing them for about an hour. At 5:30 he rode to Crutchfield's headquarters to report on Beckwith's activities. Crutchfield ordered Capt. Richard Servant to take his company of riflemen and a 6-pounder field gun to intercept and harass the land force while Crutchfield waited to see what the barges would do. He did not have long to wait.[30]

At almost the same time Crutchfield was giving Servant his orders the British barges began entering the Hampton River. The British officer in charge had his men row cautiously upriver, stood up to see if there were any defenders, and then signaled the trailing vessels to move forward. The American artillery commander, Capt. Brazure W. Pryor, let several British boats move into the river before he opened up with the 12-pounders, followed by the 6-pounders. The British replied with rockets, grape, and canister. The American fire drove the British boats back to Blackbeard's Point, where the tenders joined in the fight with 12- and 18-pounder carronade fire. The cannon duel lasted more than two hours. The rockets did little damage to the town or the American infantry, who were safe in their entrenchments.[31]

The first British troops to approach the American position were the three hundred Frenchmen of the Independent Foreigners. The unit was something of an experiment gone wrong for the British army. The British recruited the unit in Spain among French prisoners of war, with the promise they would not face their countrymen. The Frenchmen who enlisted did so more because they wanted to escape prison than because they enjoyed being soldiers. The two companies were notoriously ill disciplined and had mutinied while in Bermuda. The British, to give the Frenchmen some esprit de corps, dubbed the units Chasseurs Britanniques, or British light infantry. It did not help. New name or not, the Frenchmen remained hard to control.

As the Chasseurs advanced, they ran into Servant's riflemen. Cooper, commander of the few American cavalry troops, watched as the riflemen and the 6-pounder opened fire and ripped into the ranks of the Chasseurs, throwing the French into confusion. After several minutes the Chasseurs rallied and turned on their attackers. "They then gave the most incessant fire that I ever heard in my life," Cooper reported. "It was like the long roll of twenty drums at least and they pursued Captain Servant's men through the woods."[32] A party of Royal Marine artillerymen engaged the sergeant in charge of the 6-pounder, and after a short exchange of musket fire drove off the Americans and captured the gun.[33]

Cooper rode back to Crutchfield, who could see the barges lying off Blackbeard's Point. He realized the main attack would come against his rear and at 6 a.m. ordered his men out of the trench. His second in command, Maj. Gawin Corbin, formed the men into a column by platoons and led them into a cornfield that led to the intersection of Celeys Road and Yorktown Road at the rear of the American position. They were two hundred yards from a gate that led to Celeys Road when the British opened a heavy fusillade from the woods next to the cornfield. Crutchfield ordered his troops to "form a line, march to the enemy, fire, and charge with the bayonet."[34]

The Americans wheeled to the left to form the line and had advanced about fifty yards when they received a discharge of rockets, grape, and canister from the British artillery. The blast stunned the militiamen, who were having problems maneuvering in the muddy cornfield. As the intensity of the fire grew, so too did confusion among the untrained American soldiers. Crutchfield ordered his men to form a column and rush the gate, but the continued British fire was proving too much for the Americans. When the British opened fire with the captured 6-pounder, the militiamen broke and ran. Seven Americans were killed in the cornfield and twelve were wounded, including Corbin, who was shot in the leg and right arm.[35]

Crutchfield, with the help of the wounded Corbin and Lt. John Armistead, tried to rally the militia. Two companies responded and joined with Servant's riflemen to hold off the British; the rest of the militia disappeared in every direction. One of the last acts in the cornfield came from an artillery officer identified only as Lieutenant Jones in official reports. Seeing the overwhelming numbers of British heading up Celeys Road, he withdrew his 6-pounder behind a hedge. Finding his slow match extinguished and the militia in flight, he ran to a nearby house, grabbed a brand from the hearth, and hid in a hollow. When the British drew near the apparently abandoned fieldpiece and almost filled the lane, Jones jumped out and fired the gun with devastating effect. During the confusion that followed, Jones hitched the horses to the gun and pulled the piece to safety.[36]

The British pushed on toward the town and ran into Servant's riflemen, who had reformed, and the two companies of militia that managed to rally. The Americans stopped several times to fire volleys at the British, but never stood their ground long enough to allow the enemy to close. Lieutenant Colonel Williams, with Capt. William Powell, Beckwith's adjutant, led two companies of Royal Marines to take possession of the footbridge that led to Little England. Two more companies of marines advanced across a field opposite Williams. Captain Pryor and two other officers held their positions at the upper battery until the British advanced to within seventy yards. Pryor then spiked his guns and led his men on a charge through the British ranks to

Western Creek, which the Americans swam across while carrying their carbines, all without losing a man.[37]

The battle was over by 7:30. The British reported five dead, thirty-three wounded, and ten missing (presumed deserters). Crutchfield reported seven killed, twelve wounded, and eleven missing. As the militia fled from the field, the British force moved into Hampton. They spent the next two days pillaging the town.[38] Reports differ wildly on which troops caused the most damage. Mrs. Barron reported the British stripped her house of everything, right down to the bedsheets. The pastor of St. John's Episcopal Church said British seamen carried off his communion set—along with everything else of real or perceived value. Crutchfield and Cooper wrote detailed reports of wanton cruelty and the rape of the town's women. The conduct Cockburn unleashed and encouraged at Havre de Grace, Fredericktown, and Georgetown reached a bloody climax at Hampton. The worst offenders were the Chasseurs.[39]

A rumor spread among the Americans that Cockburn had promised each Frenchman a cash bounty if the Chasseurs captured Norfolk. Having failed to do so, the Frenchmen took out their frustrations on Hampton. Additionally, there was the story of the American riflemen murdering helpless Frenchmen at Crancy Island. Whatever the cause, the Chasseurs ran riot in Hampton, and local and national newspapers in America were filled with lurid tales of rape, pillaging, and theft.[40]

The Chasseurs "have inspired the Americans with horror at their names and have plundered, pillaged and killed some individuals and committed some ravishments in their accustomed manner," Warren wrote to Henry Dundas, Lord Melville, the First Lord of the Admiralty.[41] Beckwith told Warren the Chasseurs had dispersed in every direction to plunder, and brutally assaulted the aged and infirm townspeople who could not flee. Napier was much harsher in his assessment of the events in Hampton. Beckwith "ought to have hanged several villains," Napier wrote. "Every horror was committed with impunity, rape, murder, pillage; and not a man was punished!" Napier specifically recounted how one Chasseur had robbed a prisoner and then, to avoid detection and punishment, killed the man when he turned his back.[42]

Beckwith and Taylor engaged in a very public war of words over the atrocities. Beckwith attempted to deflect responsibility by claiming the Americans had "fired upon and shot" several British soldiers at Craney Island after their boats had either overturned or floundered. Taylor dismissed Beckwith's assertions. He convened a special tribunal to investigate Beckwith's claims and found them baseless. Taylor forwarded his findings to Beckwith, asking the British commander to conduct a similar probe into the actions of the British at Hampton. Beckwith refused. After receiving the British officer's response, Taylor wrote to Secretary of War Armstrong that he expected no change in the way the British treated civilians.[43]

British troops continued to believe Beckwith's allegations of American atrocities at Craney Island, while Americans viewed those allegations as a British attempt to avoid responsibility for the excesses of their own soldiers. Beckwith himself believed the Americans' charges—at least as they applied to the Chasseurs. He withdrew the unit from service and shipped the men to Halifax, where they continued to cause problems. From Canada the unit went to England, but the British eventually disbanded it and returned the men to France after Napoleon abdicated.[44]

The Battle of Hampton had no real importance tactically, but its strategic implications would haunt the British. The American public and government were furious over the sacking of Hampton. Newspapers compared the Chasseurs to the Hessians the British had employed in the Revolutionary War. Support for the war solidified among the people living along the Chesapeake, many of whom were antiwar at the start of hostilities. Politically, the United States turned an insignificant defeat into a significant victory.[45]

CHAPTER 8

Off the Beaten Path

*T*HE ONSET OF SUMMER brought no relief—not for the Royal Navy forces blockading the bay, the merchants and shipowners who watched in growing despair as their cargoes rotted in ships' holds or on idle wharves, or the inhabitants of the Chesapeake, who lived in constant fear of the arrival of marauding British forces.[1]

As June turned to July, the pace of operations slowed as the British simply ran out of targets. Although some ships managed to slip past the blockade, the Royal Navy had essentially shut down the Chesapeake. The focus of the British effort shifted to the larger rivers that fed the bay—the Chester on the Eastern Shore and the Patuxent, Anacostia, Severn, and Potomac on the Western Shore. There was an air of safety in many of the small port towns on those rivers. Sandbars and shallows made it difficult for the larger British vessels to reach them, while the Royal Navy crews in the ships' boats and barges would have to row a considerable distance to get there. Those towns, however, were not completely out of reach, as many inhabitants and merchants were about to discover.[2]

The blockade forced many merchants to look for new routes to get their cargoes out of the Chesapeake. There was no point in sending anything overland to Norfolk or Richmond, or even to Philadelphia. Norfolk remained all but closed to vessels. Richmond, safe on the upper reaches of the James River, could certainly accommodate cargoes, but vessels leaving there had nowhere to go because the James emptied into the Chesapeake at Hampton Roads. Philadelphia, on the Delaware River, was relatively safe from British attack, but Admiral Warren, when he took command of the British North American Squadron, had sent ships to the mouth of the Delaware specifically to close off Philadelphia.[3] British warships also ranged off Charleston, South Carolina, and Savannah, Georgia; and in any case, those ports were too far away from the Chesapeake to permit rapid overland shipment of the goods rotting in Maryland and Virginia warehouses. Instead, shipowners and privateers alike gravitated toward the small ports that dotted the inlets and bays of the North Carolina coast. One of the best of those was Ocracoke Inlet.

With a thirteen-foot depth at the bar, Ocracoke was the only port in the region that could accommodate oceangoing vessels that drew more than eight feet. An inland route through Pamlico Sound and the Dismal Swamp Canal, which had opened in 1812, permitted waterborne cargo traffic between the port and Norfolk. The approach to Ocracoke, however, was treacherous. Two deep, narrow channels north and south of Ocracoke Island gave entrance into Pamlico Sound, which lies behind a chain of islands off the North Carolina coast that includes Ocracoke and Portsmouth. Shoals and sandbars made the channels exceedingly difficult to navigate, and the slightest deviation from the very center could put a vessel aground. The southern channel led directly into the port of Ocracoke, but ships entering the inlet had to make a sharp right turn and the entrance was narrow. Two American ships near Portsmouth Island guarded the channel entrance.

The British learned about Ocracoke when two privateers sailing from the port achieved spectacular success. The brig *Anaconda*, under Capt. Nathaniel Shaler, first captured the British packet boat *Express*, which carried 20,000 pounds sterling, and then took in quick succession the brigs *Mary* and *Harriott*, which carried cargoes valued at $185,000.[4] The schooner *Atlas* scored an even bigger capture that reputedly brought in prize cargo worth more than $600,000.[5]

Those successes, and rumors that Ocracoke was home to a large fleet of commercial ships and privateers, made the British want to find out for themselves just what was happening on the North Carolina coast. Lt. T. C. Lewis sailed the tender *Highflyer* down to Ocracoke from the Chesapeake on May 19. At first pretending to be an American vessel, Lewis approached the town carefully and hoisted a pilot flag. When the local mariners refused to guide the *Highflyer* over the bar, Lewis tried force. He commandeered a small pilot boat that had approached the *Highflyer* and announced his intention to enter the harbor, where he had spotted a revenue cutter and at least one large schooner. Local militia onshore saw the loaded pilot vessel coming into the harbor and immediately stood to arms. Greatly outnumbered, Lewis returned to the *Highflyer* and lingered just out of cannon range for two days. He returned to the Chesapeake on May 23 and reported to Admiral Warren what he had found.

Warren sat on the information until after the failed attempt to take Norfolk. On July 6 he decided to act. He reported to the Admiralty, "I have sent Rear Admiral Cockburn with a detachment to attack the port of Ocracoke at Pamlico Sound, the emporium of the commerce and rendezvous of the privateers of North Carolina."[6]

Cockburn set out for Ocracoke with the troopships *Fox*, *Romulus*, and *Nemesis*; the brig *Conflict*; and the 74-gun ship of the line *Sceptre*, to which he had transferred his flag from the *Marlborough* (which was due for an overhaul in Bermuda). He also had the *Sceptre*'s tender, the *Cockchafer*, as well the

Highflyer, *Mariner*, and *Hornet*. Loaded on the troopships were 301 marines of the First Battalion, 258 of the Second, and 223 men from Lieutenant Colonel Napier's 102nd Infantry. Additionally, *Conflict* carried a 20-man Royal Marine rocket battery.[7]

Cockburn's squadron fought contrary winds all the way to Cape Hatteras, finally arriving after dark on July 11. The British anchored a mile east of Ocracoke Inlet but nearly five miles from the protected anchorage. The inhabitants of Ocracoke Island watched as the British fleet dropped anchor. The locals quickly spread the alarm. A group rowed over to Portsmouth Island to warn the U.S. collector of revenue, Thomas Singleton, as well as the masters of the ships in the harbor, which included the *Anaconda* and the *Atlas*. Singleton buried his books and other valuables and ordered the revenue cutter *Mercury* to head for New Bern, more than forty miles inland along the Neuse River. Several other vessels went with the *Mercury*.[8]

Inside the harbor, the *Anaconda*'s first mate, John Farnum, and fourteen crewmen prepared to both defend and scuttle their vessel. The seamen loaded the ships' guns with grape and canister and put their personal belongings into two of the *Anaconda*'s boats. The crew of the *Atlas* did the same.[9]

The British began embarking the invasion force in the early hours of July 12. Lt. George Westphal, who had led the infantry attack on Havre de Grace, led the first division of 13 ships' boats, which carried 253 marines; Royal Navy commander Robert Russell and 24 sailors manned 3 boats carrying Congreve rockets. Four of the cutters carried 12-pounder carronades. The second division of 9 boats, under Capt. Daniel Paterson of the *Fox*, carried another 116 marines and 80 men of Capt. Thomas Parke's company of Royal Marine Artillery and two 6-pounder field guns.[10]

The boats shoved off at 2 a.m. through heavy surf that apparently bothered Napier but not Cockburn, both of whom accompanied the lead boats. "In landing at Ocracoke we were nearly all drowned; the same in coming off. . . . Cockburn trusts to luck and makes no provision for failure," Napier wrote.[11] The British advanced in darkness, unsure of what defenses lay ahead. Once inside the bar, the assault force labored to remain in the deepest part of the channel. Seven of Westphal's boats fell behind and did not reach the point marking the entrance to the port until daybreak. Once at the entrance, the British spotted the *Anaconda* and the *Atlas* lying at anchor. The British opened the distance between each boat to prevent one shot from damaging multiple boats and slowly advanced on the town, the launches firing their carronades and rockets.[12]

On board both the *Anaconda* and the *Atlas*, the sailors manned the cannon and fired on the approaching British. Despite several minutes of heavy fire, the privateer seamen failed to slow the oncoming British boats and had to flee. Farnum attempted to scuttle the *Anaconda* by firing two shots from a 9-pounder carronade into her bottom while his crew cut her anchor lines and set her jibs to drive her aground. The thirty men still on the *Atlas* also abandoned ship in the face of the oncoming English force. The *Atlas'* crew jumped into waiting boats and headed for Portsmouth Island, but Westphal's men pursued them and captured two boats carrying fifteen Americans. The follow-up British force took possession of both privateer ships and plugged the holes in the *Anaconda*.[13]

Cockburn had formed a third division under Cdr. Charles Ross on the *Sceptre* that followed the first two divisions at a safe distance, with the *Conflict* in the lead. The tenders were also part of the division, carrying the remainder of Napier's 102nd Infantry and two companies of Royal Marines. The *Cockchafer* grounded twice trying to enter the harbor, so the soldiers and marines debarked on the shore of Ocracoke Island and began marching overland to the port town. Westphal and Paterson had already landed their divisions. A combined force of 1,300 British troops converged on Ocracoke, whose 500 or so inhabitants submitted meekly to the avalanche of red-coated invaders.[14]

What happened next remains the subject of considerable debate. Cockburn's troops, in what was now a familiar scene, demanded food from the town, although they had orders to pay a "fair and reasonable price." They also demanded the inhabitants turn over any military stores. Prior to entering the town, Cockburn and Napier had signed an order to both the army and the marine troops forbidding indiscriminate plunder of residents who surrendered without "rancorous or litigious" opposition. Whether the officers ever distributed the order is questionable. Cockburn made no mention of it in his report to the Admiralty, and Napier later claimed the admiral signed but never issued the order. Whatever the truth, an American eyewitness claimed the British once more ran amok.

Revenue Collector Singleton, a resident of Ocracoke, wrote a report for North Carolina governor William Hawkins detailing the attack: "There was the most wanton, cruel and savage like destruction of property I have ever witnessed; furniture of all kinds split and broke in pieces, beds ripped open and the feathers scattered in the wind—women and children robbed of their clothing and indeed many little children have been left without a second suit to their backs."[15] Singleton said he suffered firsthand from the British pillaging. "They broke open my office and destroyed every paper they could lay their hands on . . . robbed me of all the books in my library except the law books, and these with savage fury they tore to pieces."[16]

Cockburn, in his report to the Admiralty, made no mention of any poor behavior on the part of his soldiers or marines. He singled out Napier and the officers and men of the 102nd for their "truly cheerful, ready and able cooperation" with the Royal Marines, saying the soldiers and marines had "tended to establish a confidence and understanding between our respective services which cannot fail to have the happiest effect on such future conjunct operations as may be hereafter undertaken by these forces."[17]

The British admiral did admit his troops rounded up and confiscated local cattle, although he insisted they paid for them. Singleton confirmed—up to a point—that contention. The log of the *Sceptre* contains an entry showing the British paid $1,600 for 83 bullocks and 9 calves. Singleton, however, claimed Cockburn's men actually grabbed 200 head of cattle, 400 sheep, and 1,600 fowl—for which they paid the $1,600.[18]

The invaders spent two days stripping the town and surrounding countryside of everything they could eat or use. When they returned to their ships, Cockburn's men brought with them the *Anaconda* and *Atlas*. The admiral incorporated both into his flotilla, renaming the *Atlas* HMS *St. Lawrence*. He was especially happy with the *Anaconda*. The brig weighed 387 tons, had a copper bottom, and carried eighteen long 9-pounders as well as carronades. Cockburn called her a "perfect model of beauty" and put Lieutenant Westphal in command of her.[19]

The capture of the two privateers made up for what was otherwise a somewhat hollow victory for the British. Most of the ships in Ocracoke, including the revenue cutter *Mercury*, had escaped up to New Bern along with their cargoes. Although Cockburn's invasion spread fear along the North Carolina coast, the minute the Royal Navy flotilla weighed anchor the privateers returned, and Ocracoke remained a viable option for shipping goods out of the Chesapeake for another year.[20]

Warren remained in the lower bay throughout June and July. While Cockburn went after Ocracoke, the commander of the North American Squadron wrestled with a more immediate and pressing need: freshwater.

Warships in the Age of Sail required massive quantities of freshwater, used for everything from hygiene and cooking to keeping the ship clean to prevent saltwater corrosion; during combat warships required freshwater for their cannon. The frigate *Diadem*, for example, could carry 240 tons of freshwater; her crew alone consumed 3 tons a day.[21] In addition to the Royal Navy crew, Warren also had to provide water for more than one thousand marines and army troops. The need for freshwater was paramount, and Warren looked for it every place he could.

The orders from the Admiralty forbidding Warren from establishing a permanent base prevented the British from setting up a central watering station and severely hampered the British flotilla. By the end of June the frigate *Junon* was down to just seven days' supply of water, and the *Diadem* had exhausted her supply and had to borrow a ton a day from other ships. The overriding need for water led Warren to reinterpret his orders. He sent Beck-with ashore with three companies of marines to seize Old Point Comfort near Hampton. There, under the cover of the squadron's cannon, the marines dug three wells, which would provide enough water for Warren to supply the troopships and his ships of the line. The rest of his ships—the frigates and flo-tilla of schooners and brigs—he sent up the James River to replenish their own water and bring off cattle and other livestock for the fleet.[22]

The *Barrosa, Junon, Narcissus, Laurestinus, Atalante, Mohawk, Moselle,* and the newly arrived brig *Contest,* along with a sizable flotilla of barges, launches, and tenders, set out to obey Warren's order to acquire freshwater "at the risk of every consequence." James Sanders of the *Junon* led the expedition and anchored his ship off the Warwick River while the rest of the flotilla sailed up the James as much as five miles farther to find water and food.[23]

As they moved upstream, the British ran into small groups of militia and engaged in several short, sharp skirmishes. In one such skirmish near James-town, militiamen killed two British sailors, wounded several others, and took several prisoners. The British gave as well as they received, pillaging planta-tions on both banks of the James while also levying payments of provisions in exchange for leaving buildings or fields untouched.[24]

The sailors worked in parties of twenty to thirty men and presented what should have been perfect targets to the militia in the area. The militia, how-ever, was on its way elsewhere. The appearance of the Royal Navy on the James River so alarmed the locals that many fled to Richmond, some one hundred miles inland. The panic induced Governor James Barbour to order all avail-able militia to Richmond in the expectation of an attack on the city. The mili-tia responded, leaving the countryside defenseless for nearly a week until the panic subsided.[25]

The process of procuring freshwater was labor-intensive. The sailors set out in boats carrying large wooden casks called butts. The James and its tributaries are brackish because of the tidal influence of the Chesapeake, so the watering parties had either to row several miles upstream or to dig wells on land. Once they found drinkable water, the sailors filled the butts, which when full weighed nearly a half ton. The sailors then rowed back to their ships, loaded the full casks, picked up empty ones, and repeated the process. Despite the backbreaking work, the British moved quickly and efficiently. The *Junon,* for example, collected forty tons of water in just six days, enough to last her for more than a month.[26]

The watering parties remained on the James River for a week. On July 2 the flotilla rejoined the main squadron off Hampton Roads. They stayed for another nine days, replenishing food supplies, before Warren decided to scout the Potomac River, one of the Americans' last refuges in the Tidewater region. The admiral took with him the *Marlborough, Diadem, Diomede, Barrosa,*

Laurestinus, Mariner, Dotterel, Mohawk, Contest, and six tenders. The departure of these ships, coupled with Cockburn's expedition to Ocracoke, left only
the *Junon* and the *Atalante* at Hampton Roads while the *Plantagenet* and
the *Surveyor* anchored off Lynnhaven Roads. The depleted blockading force
offered a tempting target to Capt. Charles Gordon, who continued to look for
any opportunity to harass the enemy and had acquired a novel weapon with
which to do it.

When he assembled his small, ad hoc squadron of borrowed ships to guard
Baltimore, Gordon learned from Navy secretary Jones of the existence of a
new weapon—the torpedo. The invention of Robert Fulton, who also built the
first steamship, the torpedoes of 1813 were not torpedoes in the modern sense
at all, but rather antiship mines. The U.S. Navy had clandestinely begun developing torpedoes in 1810 after Fulton, in a pair of experiments, destroyed a
large warship by exploding a powder charge under her keel. In June 1810 he
pitched a plan to President Madison to defend American harbors and naval
stations with his torpedoes. The main selling point was the price. Fulton said
he could build his torpedoes for just $150 apiece.[27]

The Navy worked with Elijah Mix, an entrepreneur who wanted to turn
Fulton's weapon against the British. Mix undoubtedly found his inspiration
in an 1813 act of Congress granting a bounty of half the ship's value to anyone who sank an English warship by use of "torpedoes, submarine instru-
ments, or any other destructive means." Mix offered to pay Fulton one-third
of the prize money from any ships he sank if Fulton provided the torpedoes.
Unfortunately, Mix tinkered with Fulton's design and came up with a "simpler"
version in which he changed the fuse mechanism—and doomed his torpedo
to failure.[28]

A British naval officer described the configuration of Mix's first torpedo.
The explosive charge was equal to about 6 barrels of gunpowder, or approxi-
mately 540 pounds. Mix placed the charge in a container he suspended twelve
feet below a plank raft. Two lines, each three hundred feet long and with a float
at its end, extended from the raft. The device was launched from a boat, with
the floats spread six hundred feet apart. The operator allowed the torpedo to
drift with the current and snag on the enemy ship's anchor chain. The raft
and explosive charge were then supposed to swing around with the current
to make contact with the ship. The operator in the boat detonated the torpedo
by pulling a lanyard. Fulton's torpedo had two charges, ensuring that at least
one of them would detonate. He also put his charges deeper in the water and
angled them so they would explode beneath a ship. Mix decided to use just

one charge and did not angle the torpedo, the result being the device would explode against the side of an enemy vessel rather than beneath it.

Gordon and Mix attempted their first attack while Cockburn was on the Patapsco River near Baltimore. The device failed to explode and the British recovered the torpedo, although they were unsure just what it was. After working with the device, Lt. James Scott deduced that it was a mine. He duly noted his discovery in a report to Cockburn, adding that each vessel in the Royal Navy squadron routinely used a line attached to a mooring buoy specifically to foil "torpedo" attacks.[29]

For the next two months Gordon tracked the British up and down the bay with his makeshift squadron of borrowed vessels and gunboats. Although Gordon did his best to goad the Royal Navy into committing some of its tenders and other small ships to combat, neither Cockburn nor Warren took the bait. When Warren split his forces and left just the *Junon* and the *Plantagenet*, along with their tenders, to guard the lower bay, Gordon turned to Mix to try to break the blockade.

On July 15 Mix and Midn. James McGlaughon set out on a small cutter called the *Chesapeake Revenge*. Mix watched the blockading ships for three days, observing that the *Plantagenet* remained at anchor the entire time. He settled on the English ship of the line as his target. On the night of July 18 Mix attacked. He and McGlaughon rowed to within 120 feet of the *Plantagenet* and were just about ready to release the torpedo when a lookout on the British ship hailed them. The two Americans quickly recovered their torpedo and fled. The next night Mix tried again. He and McGlaughon were under the bowsprit of the *Plantagenet* when British sentinels again spotted him. The *Plantagenet* fired flares to illuminate the *Chesapeake Revenge* while sailors and Royal Marines gave chase in the ships' boats. Despite heavy fire from the *Plantagenet*'s main battery Mix and McGlaughon managed to elude their pursuers and disappeared into the darkness.[30]

The two failed attacks were more than enough to convince the captain of the *Plantagenet* that he needed to do more to thwart the Americans than simply rely on his lookouts. Mix was unable to find the ship on his next three attempts, in part because the *Plantagenet*'s captain began shifting the ship's position each night. On July 24, however, Mix's luck changed and he caught the *Plantagenet* lying at anchor. He deployed his torpedo at a range of three hundred feet, relying on the tide and current to bring the device to its mark. The water conditions were no ally, however, and as the tide swept the torpedo toward the British warship, the device exploded prematurely. Mix, in his report to Secretary Jones, described the detonation as comparable to an earthquake that propelled a "luminous pyramid of water fifty feet in circumference and then created a yawning chasm" into which he said the *Plantagenet* rolled and nearly capsized. He went on to describe what he believed to be the panic the device caused among the crew.[31]

Mix could not have been more wrong. Instead of nearly capsizing the ship of the line, his torpedo barely singed the paint on her hull, a result the British leaked to local American papers. The *Plantagenet*'s log played down the incident, saying only, "Torpedo exploded by the enemy near the ship but no mischief." A later entry shows that Mix was well off target with his attack: "A torpedo exploded inshore."[32]

The disparity between the reports so enraged Jones that he fired off an angry letter to Mix, telling him, "Your statement of the effect of the attack on the *Plantagenet* was so excessively exaggerated as to greatly diminish the weight of your representations." Jones also took the unusual step of refusing to allow the *National Intelligencer*, a Washington, D.C., newspaper, to publish Mix's report.[33]

Jones' anger did little to stem Mix's enthusiasm for—or promotion of—his weapon. A week after his attack on the *Plantagenet*, Mix had another chance to strike the British, this time in the narrows between Annapolis and Kent Island, and did nothing. Jones slammed Mix for failing even to attempt an attack. Mix, however, had already decided the Chesapeake was too shallow for his weapon and was heading north to Long Island Sound, where he believed the waters off New London offered much better operating conditions.[34]

After he had sufficient water for his squadron, Warren began his push up the Potomac River. He left the heavy, deep-draft ships of the line at the mouth of the river near Smith Point, Virginia, and loaded Beckwith and three companies of marines, a marine artillery company, and a rocket battery onto the *Barrosa*, *Laurestinus*, and *Mohawk* for the push upriver, detailing the *Contest*, the *Liberty*, and another tender to accompany them. He put this flying squadron under the command of Capt. William Shirreff of the *Barrosa*, giving him orders to find and destroy the 28-gun U.S. corvette *Adams*, which Warren believed was hiding in the vicinity of the Port Tobacco River.[35]

The orders represented something of a shift in Warren's strategic outlook, one the Admiralty's prohibition on "general engagements" undoubtedly forced on him. When he first arrived in the Chesapeake, Warren wanted to immediately push up the Potomac and threaten Washington, because doing so would "insult" America and "oblige" the Americans to withdraw troops from the Canadian front to protect the national capital. The Admiralty orders, coupled with his split forces, had led Warren to change his mind about pushing toward the federal district.[36]

Warren's main target, the *Adams*, had been in ordinary at the Washington Navy Yard when the war began, along with the 36-gun *New York*. The *Adams*, at least, was seaworthy. The *New York*, which had not left the yard in more than a decade, was almost completely rotten.[37] Capt. Charles Morris, who commanded the *Adams*, had no intention of challenging Warren's overwhelming strength. He kept his ship close to Washington. Two vessels of the Potomac squadron, the *Scorpion* and the *Asp*, were in the lower Potomac when Shirreff entered the river on July 14, and they offered tempting targets to the British.

On July 5 Morris had ordered the *Scorpion*, under the command of Lt. George Read, and the *Asp*, under Midn. James B. Sigourney, to reconnoiter the mouth of the Potomac for signs of the British squadron. When Warren's flotilla appeared off Mattawoman Point, the two American vessels put into the Yeocomico River on the Virginia side. After Shirreff pushed farther up the river with his advance squadron, Read slipped the *Scorpion* out of her mooring and sailed to Washington, arriving on the morning of July 15 to report the British movements to both Morris and Navy secretary Jones.[38]

The news that the British were less than a day's sail away threw the capital into confusion. Jones, Secretary of War John Armstrong, and Secretary of State James Monroe met with Morris at Fort Washington, which guarded the Potomac approach to the district. Jones wanted to reinforce the fort, but Armstrong refused, saying he did not believe the British planned to attack the city. Monroe, who had been a cavalry officer during the Revolutionary War, led a mounted force downriver to determine the exact location of the invaders. He sent word that the British were still well below the city and showed no indication of ascending the Potomac.[39] Jones was not so sure, and when Armstrong refused to strengthen Fort Washington, he authorized Morris to erect a water battery near the shore below the fort and man it with sailors and Marines from the *Adams*. Armstrong continued to believe all of the fuss was unnecessary because Washington, in his opinion, had little in the way of strategic significance to the British.[40]

Shirreff, unaware of the confusion in Washington, continued to slowly make his way up the Potomac. After rounding Smith Point he spotted the *Asp* and decided to take her. Sigourney knew that the *Asp* was not as well built as the *Scorpion* and could not outrun his British pursuers. Instead Sigourney sailed to the small port town of Kinsale on the Yeocomico and intentionally grounded the *Asp* on a shoal. His crew tied up antiboarding nets and prepared to meet the British, who had chased him up the river in three ships' boats. Sigourney and his crew of twenty-two men, using the three cannon on the *Asp*, forced the British to retreat. After a short time the British boats returned with two more boats and pressed home the assault.[41]

The American crew resisted fiercely. Midn. Henry McClintock, the second lieutenant of the *Asp*, reported that his crew, armed with the ship's two carronades and long 9-pounder mounted on a pivot amidships, "continued doing the same as before but having so few men we were unable to repel the enemy." The British, McClintock said, "boarded us [and] they refused giving any quarters. There was upwards of fifty men on our decks which compelled us to leave the vessel, as the enemy had possessed it."[42]

Sigourney went down early in the attack, shot through the body. When the British swarmed across the deck, they found him slumped against the gunwales with the *Asp*'s flag flying above him. A Royal Marine smashed in Sigourney's skull with his musket butt, killing him. McClintock and nine men of the crew escaped overboard. Ten Americans died and three were wounded in the battle; the British reported two dead and six wounded.[43] The British attempted to burn the *Asp*, but the approach of a sizable force of militia forced them to retreat before they could completely destroy the schooner. McClintock and the nine men he had escaped with returned to the *Asp* and put out the flames with the help of the militia. When Read returned with the *Scorpion*, he towed the *Asp* to Washington for repairs.[44]

The day after the battle with the *Asp*, the *Barrosa* and the *Laurestinus* rejoined the *Mohawk* and the *Contest* and moved up the Potomac. The *Barrosa*, with Beckwith on board, and the *Mohawk* led the advance. Beckwith conducted several raids onshore but each time ran into considerable resistance. At Rossier Creek on July 15, a British raiding party under Lt. George Hext of the *Barrosa* ran into several companies of Virginia militia under Lt. Col. Richard Parker. The militia drove off the British, killing Hext and wounding five marines.[45]

The British incursion on the Potomac lasted a week. Shirreff rejoined Warren's main force on July 22 and transferred Beckwith's troops back to the *San Domingo*. Riding at anchor with Warren's force was Cockburn's squadron, which had returned from Ocracoke on July 19. Beckwith, in a July 20 letter to his superiors in London, expressed an opinion similar to Warren's about the expedition. "I do not venture to say anything with respect to the expediency of having made the Chesapeake the scene of our first operations, as I have no information respecting North America in a military point of view, nor have I fallen in with anyone who is capable of giving me any," he wrote. "I can only hope . . . the general alarm spread through the country has proven of essential service to Sir George Prevost [British commander of Canada]."[46] In fact, all the incursion did was to cause panic in Washington and eat up the supplies Warren had spent the first part of July collecting for his fleet. It failed to divert a single soldier from the Canadian front.

CHAPTER 9

The Long, Hot Summer

*T*HE ASSAULT UP THE POTOMAC pointed out to Admiral Warren the logistical Achilles heel of his campaign. Forbidden by the Admiralty to establish a permanent supply base on American soil, all Warren could do was strip various areas of what he needed, then move on to a new location and repeat the process. While in the Potomac, the British took possession of St. George and St. Clements Island, a fertile farming community and source of freshwater, and stripped the island bare. It still was not enough to feed and provide water for the entire squadron. On July 26 Rear Admiral Cockburn led the entire naval brigade and both battalions of Royal Marines ashore at Smith Point at the mouth of the Potomac on the Virginia side of the river. The first division, consisting of the 102nd Infantry and the First Battalion of Royal Marines, landed at Cornfield Point near the mouth of the Potomac on the Maryland side of the river. The Second Battalion and the Royal Marine artillery landed farther south. Cockburn, with the naval brigade, followed the Royal Marines ashore, and the British formed a cordon completely around Smith Point. They gathered 120 cattle, 100 sheep, and uncounted hogs, geese, and chickens, drove them all to the landing areas, and dispatched them to the ships that night.[1]

The spiteful behavior of the raiders particularly distressed the inhabitants. Even though Cockburn, Colonel Beckwith, and Lieutenant Colonel Napier were with the landing force, small raiding parties ran wild, seizing tableware, combs, scissors, kitchen utensils, and linens while smashing furniture and anything else of value they could not carry. When the owners appealed to Cockburn for compensation, the admiral brushed them off.[2]

The British foray up the Potomac came as a shock to the Americans. But even though it put the redcoats within miles of the national capital, Secretary of War John Armstrong remained unconvinced that Warren planned a push toward Washington. Capt. Charles Morris and Secretary of the Navy William Jones, however, believed otherwise and began planning for the defense of the capital. Morris wrote to Jones on July 18 detailing his ideas. He recommended building several batteries in areas that could rake the river as it snaked past

Alexandria, sinking a hulk opposite Alexandria to block the channel, and using the *Adams* as the main ship in an ad hoc flotilla. "I take for granted that should the enemy really intend proceeding as high as this place that their first object, is the destruction of the navy yard and its dependencies—the second object in point of military importance is the destruction of the foundry above Georgetown and the third, which in a moral point of view is equal to the others would be the removal of the seat of government which though of no real injury in itself would depress the public mind in this country, and naturally affect our reputation in Europe," Morris wrote.[3] The Navy captain expected Warren to attack with overwhelming strength, against which "our force here could make no effective resistance."

Jones agreed with Morris, up to a point. He ordered Morris to convince Armstrong of the need to adopt the defense plan but refused to sink any hulks or order new fortifications until the intentions of the British became clear. The departure of Warren's forces from the area near Washington convinced both Armstrong and Jones that the British had no plans to attack the city.[4]

In fact, Warren had no plans to attack *any* major city along or near the Chesapeake. He not only considered Norfolk and Washington beyond the reach of his frigates, he also dismissed Baltimore and Annapolis as targets. He explained to Lord Melville that shoal waters and seven thousand troops protected Baltimore, and five thousand soldiers were "around" Annapolis with more expected, although at the time Annapolis was essentially undefended. By declining to attack, Warren and Beckwith believed they were following the Admiralty's orders to harass the Americans without risking their ships or a major land engagement that could cost them heavy casualties. Warren was also keenly aware of the need to supply his force and to find, if not a permanent base, at least an area he could control as a central point at which to gather food and water for his fleet.[5] The squadron now consisted of five ships of the line; six frigates; four sloops; and more than a dozen brigs, schooners, and captured auxiliaries, all of which required massive amounts of food and water. Warren decided to move this force to Kent Island, across the bay from Annapolis and just twenty miles south of Baltimore. From the island Warren could send his barges and boats up the region's many creeks and rivers to gather provisions while he kept the Baltimore Squadron—Gordon's force of contracted ships and gunboats—bottled up in the upper bay.

Almost as important to Warren as supplies was the chance to get his sailors and Royal Marines off their ships. As July turned to August, the heat and humidity of the Maryland summer came as a shock to many of the British. A late July heat wave pushed temperatures above 90° Fahrenheit, and the humidity made the heat even more oppressive. The troops, confined to their transports, suffered horribly from heat exhaustion and thirst. Kent Island offered the best place for Warren to accomplish all of his self-appointed tasks before he left for Halifax for the winter.[6]

The Royal Navy squadron set sail for Kent Island on July 28. Gales and contrary winds turned what should have been an easy thirty-six-hour sail into a weeklong slog up the bay. Shirreff's advance flotilla reached Kent Island on August 4, and the rest of Warren's squadron straggled in over the next three days. When Beckwith arrived with the troop transports on August 7, he ordered all of the Royal Marines, including those on the various ships in the squadron, to disembark. He marched the force nearly twelve miles through 90° heat until it reached the two-hundred-acre farm of Jonathan Harrison, where the sea-weary foot soldiers pitched camp.[7]

Beckwith took over Harrison's farmhouse as his headquarters while his Royal Marines spread out over the well-cultivated fields and found fresh food in abundance. The sailors immediately sank wells, which they lined with old casks, and replenished their supply of freshwater. Lt. James Scott of the *Mohawk* later recalled that the immense quantities of beef, lamb, geese, turkeys, and other poultry, along with the mounds of fresh fruit and vegetables the men picked daily, provided a rare treat for both the seamen and the troops. Scott thought the main camp resembled an English gentleman's park, with the regularly spaced tents made of evergreen boughs forming a pretty vista. Not all the British had it so easy. The Royal Marine artillerymen and boat crews pitched their camp on the bank of the Chester River, near a marsh that bred swarms of mosquitoes that nightly tormented the British.[8]

The British force near the center of the Chesapeake, just four miles from the state capital at Annapolis, was a source of curiosity and consternation among the inhabitants. Maryland residents on both sides of the bay stared in wonder at the ships of the line with their two decks of guns protruding ominously in the direction of Annapolis. There were frigates, sleek and powerful, their captains and crews prowling the decks, keeping an eye on American actions in the Severn River and the port of Annapolis; and there was a veritable forest of auxiliaries spread out and posted to prevent attack. Curiosity was so strong that on August 8 the steamboat *Chesapeake*, the first of its kind on the bay, brought a capacity crowd to the mouth of the Patapsco River to gawk at the Royal Navy vessels.[9]

Maryland governor Levin Winder was far less curious about the looks of the British squadron than he was about its intentions. Almost the minute Warren's squadron dropped anchor in the Severn River near Annapolis, Winder dashed off yet another letter to Secretary of War Armstrong and Secretary of the Navy Jones pleading for men to replace those the War Department had stripped from the city's two forts and sent to Canada. This time Jones acted, ordering Capt. Charles Morris and the entire crew of the *Adams* to head to Annapolis.

Morris arrived on the morning of August 13 and set about examining the forts that guarded the city and the entrance to the Severn River. Fort Madison, on the north bank of the river, was a masonry structure built to house 169 men and 13 guns. Morris found only 12 cannon that were mounted on decayed carriages sitting atop an incomplete platform. Across the river, Fort Severn, which could accommodate 104 men and 8 guns, had only 7 cannon in place, 2 without carriages. Neither fort had any spare parts or any grape or canister to use against ships' boats. Fort Madison and Fort Severn together contained only 118 round shot.[10] The city's two earthworks—Fort Nonsense, which protected the heights near Fort Madison, and Fort Horn, which guarded the entrance to Spa Creek south of Fort Severn—were in equally poor condition, inadequately manned and armed.

Morris quickly set his men to work, putting Marine Corps captain Samuel Miller in charge of the work at Fort Severn while he personally supervised the work at Fort Madison. He sent a request for 770 round shot and 550 grape and canister rounds to the War Department. A week later he received word from the War Department that he should search for what he needed in Baltimore. By then the panic of Warren's arrival was passing. A full regiment of militia was in Annapolis as well as Morris' crew, and it was clear the British had no intention of attacking. Morris and his crew left the city when the British departed from Kent Island.[11]

The British treated the inhabitants of Kent Island far better than they treated residents of other areas in which they operated, probably because Warren and Beckwith were present and firmly in control of the occupation force. The British ordered militiamen to surrender their weapons or face deportation and plundered only the homes of absentee owners. More than forty slaves living on the island sought refuge with the fleet, but in comparison with other places the British had visited along the lower bay, it was a small price for the islanders to pay.[12]

Warren tried to take advantage of the better relationship to convince the locals of the folly of supporting Madison's war. His officers actively campaigned for Federalist candidates in the upcoming elections for both the U.S. House and the Maryland House of Delegates. The British officers repeatedly told the islanders they wanted peace with America and they "hoped that the American administration would be changed by the election of Federalists to office." Failure to secure a peace, they warned, could result in the destruction of Baltimore and the complete desolation of both sides of the bay.[13] To counter Warren's propaganda, the *Easton Star* reported a conversation Oswald Tilghman said had taken place between his grandfather, farm owner Jonathan

Harrison, and an aide to Beckwith, a Captain Powell of the Royal Marines. The conversation revealed the true feelings of the invaders when, after Harrison said that he as a Federalist had no ill will toward the British, Powell retorted that the British would whip the Democrats for being enemies of his country and drub the Federalists for being enemies of their own nation.[14]

Warren did not give his weary sailors and marines a long respite. Even before landing on Kent Island he had cast his eyes on the town of St. Michaels. Nestled on an L-shaped peninsula on an arm of the Chesapeake called the Eastern Bay, St. Michaels lies on the west bank of the Miles River. In 1813 the town had a population of a few hundred people living in about sixty houses clustered near a square adjacent to a well-sheltered small harbor that split into five creeks. The primary business of St. Michaels was shipbuilding. Yards in the small town turned out many of the famed privateers that captains and owners prized. As many as six ships were reported on the stocks in August, and Warren was determined to prevent those vessels from plundering British shipping.[15]

The locals were aware of the town's importance. Brig. Gen. Perry Benson, a former captain in the Continental Army, commanded the 12th Brigade of Maryland militia from his headquarters in Easton. The town was also the headquarters of the 4th Infantry Regiment of the militia along with a large volunteer company of artillery under Lt. Col. William Smith. In St. Michaels, Lt. Col. Hugh Auld and his Saint Michaels Patriotic Blues, the 26th Infantry Regiment of the state militia, defended the town. The Blues were among the better-equipped and -uniformed regiments on the Eastern Shore.

British activity in the spring had alerted Auld to the possibility of attack. He ordered his men to erect a small breastwork to protect the entrance to the harbor and mounted a 9-pounder and three 6-pounder field guns on it. Capt. William Dodson commanded the garrison of thirty men. When his sister presented a handmade flag from the ladies of St. Michael's to Dodson's command, the soldiers hoisted the banner over their little earthwork and vowed to defend it to the last man.[16]

Auld had his troops erect a second small battery at Impy Dawson's shipyard to guard the entrance to the town. Auld placed two brass 6-pounders in the new battery and assigned thirty infantrymen under Lt. John Graham as a garrison. When Benson learned of the British landing on Kent Island, he suspected Warren planned to strike St. Michaels. On August 7 he ordered his brigade artillery under Capt. Samuel Thomas to take a position just north of the town to prevent a possible flank attack. Benson also deployed pickets along the Eastern Bay to give warning of a British approach and called up several hundred more militia to defend the town. According to an artilleryman in Graham's detachment, the town's defenders blocked the entrance to the inner harbor with a boom of chained-together logs.[17]

Warren ordered Cdr. Henry Baker of the brig *Conflict* to lead the expedition to St. Michaels, with Lieutenant Polkinghorne of the *San Domingo* in command of the 219 sailors and marines detailed for the attack. Polkinghorne set out on the night of August 8 with ten barges to transport his troops.[18] The British spent two days slowly making their way up the Miles River, marking channels and setting out buoys as they went. Just after midnight on August 10, Baker sent Polkinghorne toward St. Michaels while he anchored the brig two miles north of the town at a point where the river abruptly narrows.[19]

Polkinghorne's force rowed silently past St. Michaels, searching for armed vessels lying at anchor. Finding none, Polkinghorne crossed to the opposite bank and silently ran northward until just before daybreak, when he reached a beach two hundred yards south of Dodson's gun battery and began disembarking his troops. The British lieutenant likely had a local pilot helping him on his approach. The channel up the Miles River is very circuitous, and the rapidity and accuracy with which Polkinghorne was able to maneuver in the dark deepened the locals' suspicion that a collaborator was helping the British.[20]

As the British troops waded ashore and began forming a column, a sentinel who heard the officers' commands shouted the alarm and fired his musket. The sudden materialization of an attacking force at close quarters panicked most of Dodson's men, who quickly forgot their vow to defend their position to the last man, threw down their muskets, and ran toward town. Three men remained at their posts: Dodson, Pvt. Frank Gossage, and Pvt. John Stevens, "a mulatto man . . . [who] served faithfully in the battery."[21] The three men wheeled around the 9-pounder they had charged the night before with grape and canister and added a 27-pound bundle of langrage (a bag containing metal scraps), "which filled it to the muzzle." When they fired the gun, the massive charge caused a recoil so strong the barrel of the gun flew off the carriage and landed in a ditch. British officer J. C. Adams said the blast contained "damned spike nails" that wounded two men.[22] Dodson, Gossage, and Stevens then fled through a cornfield. Dodson, before he ran, grabbed the banner the ladies of St. Michaels made for the battery and took it with him.[23]

When the Royal Marines entered the earthwork, they spiked the two remaining cannon and gave three cheers that could be heard in town. They also destroyed whatever stores they could find. They continued to mill around the breastwork, making themselves perfect targets for Lieutenant Graham and his battery of field guns, which began firing on the battery site. Polkinghorne "deemed the object of the enterprise fulfilled" and ordered his troops to reembark on the barges, and they moved out under the cover of carronade fire.[24] The British pushed off for the inner harbor but never entered it. Whether they encountered the log boom or simply retreated under fire is unknown. Whatever the reason, Polkinghorne's men withdrew to their boats and began firing cannon on the town. Graham returned their fire, and Lt. Clement Vickars joined in with two more field guns. The two American batteries fired fifteen rounds, damaging at least one boat. The British caused little damage to the town, and the Americans suffered no casualties in the encounter.[25]

The British attack on St. Michaels was more ruse than raid. Had Warren wanted to pillage and destroy the town, he would have sent a much larger force. Instead, the admiral's goal was apparently to pin down as much militia as he could while he consolidated his hold on Kent Island. Cockburn, in his journal, characterized the effort as "annoying the enemy," and the British accomplished that objective.[26] The attack threw the area into turmoil and caused a considerable amount of expense as the Talbot County militia brigade spent the entire month of August in the field under arms. Whether that was any comfort to the 250 Royal Navy sailors and Royal Marines who spent 48 hours—including a rainy night—in open boats but captured no prizes is unknown.

On August 10 an American officer appeared before the British camp at Kent Island under a flag of truce. Gustavus Wright was a captain in the 6th Brigade Artillery, which was attached to the local regiment of militia, the 38th Infantry of Queen Anne's County. Once in the British camp he met with Capt. Frederick Robertson, a Royal Artillery officer who was on Beckwith's staff. Wright's mission was simple: he challenged the British to come out and fight and offered to face Robertson in single combat. The astute artilleryman declined the offer of single combat but made a return visit to Wright's camp under a flag of truce, using the trip as an opportunity to scout the land leading to Queenstown, where Wright and the militia were based. Robertson observed that a large marsh dominated the shore across from Kent Island, with a narrow causeway running through it. Thick woods adjoined the marsh and lined the road leading to Queenstown, a village of ten or twelve houses that lay six miles inland from the British camp on an inlet that created a natural harbor.[27]

Robertson's report on the topography undoubtedly reinforced his superiors' intent to surprise and capture the entire American force, which Warren believed was "several corps." He left the planning up to Beckwith, who decided on a two-pronged assault. Moving at night, the colonel would take the entire Second Battalion of Royal Marines along with Lieutenant Colonel Napier's 102nd Infantry Regiment directly overland to Queenstown. Simultaneously, the First Battalion of Royal Marines would deploy by boat, enter Queenstown harbor, and attack the Americans from behind. Rear Admiral Cockburn took charge of the waterborne attack but delegated operational control to Capt. James Paterson and Capt. John Maude, who had taken part in the attack on Ocracoke. In all, Beckwith planned to hit the Americans with nearly 2,600 soldiers, sailors, and marines.[28]

Facing the British was a militia regiment of just 244 effectives under the command of Maj. William H. Nicholson. The American force also had one hundred cavalry under the command of Maj. Thomas Emory, plus Gustavus Wright's artillery company of thirty-five men and two 6-pound field guns. Nicholson divided his regiment into six companies, and Emory split his men into three troops. The Americans billeted the infantry and artillery in and around the town while Emory's horse soldiers camped about a mile away because there was no room for them in town.[29]

The British began preparing to move out on August 12. Nicholson, on hearing the bustle on Kent Island, sent two of his infantry companies to a location near the edge of the swamp to monitor Beckwith's actions. Capt. Charles Hobbs and Capt. John Taylor took up a position across from Kent Narrows with sixty-two infantry along with four cavalry to act as couriers. Nicholson gave his advance force explicit instructions "to by no means invite an attack . . . [and] they were not to occupy the same position any two nights successively." Nicholson then arrayed the rest of his meager forces at Queenstown to meet an attack by either land or water, although he admitted, "Against an attack from two or three points, I felt the insufficiency of my force."[30]

Nicholson went to sleep around midnight, only to have an aide awaken him two hours later with a message from Hobbs that Beckwith's men were beginning to embark. The First Battalion of Royal Marines, by the light of a full moon, began moving out several hours before the remainder the British force started to cross at Kent Narrows. Capt. Charles Ross of the *Sceptre* supervised the embarkation of Beckwith's marines and Napier's soldiers, moving 1,200 men across the narrows in just an hour. Captain Robertson led the column along the mosquito-infested causeway. As they marched toward Queenstown, Hobbs and Taylor sent word to Nicholson of the enormous force on its way. Nicholson awakened his officers and ordered a picket force of eighteen men under Capt. James Massey to take up a position two miles west of town at a previously prepared place the locals called Slippery Hill. Taking cover along the sunken road the British had to follow to reach Queenstown, they waited for Beckwith's force.[31]

Nicholson deployed his troops across the same road about a half mile outside town. He set one flank on Queenstown Creek and the other on the Wye River. Wright's artillery deployed with the main force, while Nicholson put Emory's cavalry in some woods along the Chester River where they could harass Beckwith's right flank as the British approached. The Americans took up their positions at 3:15 a.m. As they deployed into a line of battle a second message arrived from Hobbs and Taylor reporting that Beckwith had crossed Kent Narrows and was approaching Queenstown with an overwhelming force, and resistance was impossible. The captains had had to abandon their position but were confident they could escape.[32]

Nicholson now feared for Massey and the pickets stationed at Slippery Hill. "I immediately mounted my horse and pressed forward toward my picket," Nicholson reported. "When I had advanced within a half-mile of their post the firing commenced between them and the enemy and the volleys of musketry left me without a hope that an individual of them was alive."[33]

Nicholson, however, was wrong. Massey was very much alive, as were his men. The pickets had opened fire on the advance element of the British force when it moved within thirty yards of their position. The volley unnerved Capt. William Dymock, the senior marine officer from the *Sceptre* and commander of the advance guard. At the first shot, Dymock threw himself to the ground "in a disgracefully incapable state" and ordered his men to return fire, despite orders from Beckwith and Napier to the contrary. Beckwith and Napier galloped to the sound of gunfire and, finding the advance force in disarray, ordered Robertson to relieve Dymock and take command of the unit. Two days later Dymock would report to his ship's surgeon complaining of suffering from "temporary paroxysms of mental derangement rendering him incompetent to perform any of the important duties active service requires."[34]

Beckwith and Napier attempted to restore order to the column of British troops, but the damage was already done. The Royal Marines began firing wildly at shadows and at each other. Two marines died and another was wounded before the two senior officers could restore order.[35]

By the time the British resumed their advance. Massey and his men had taken up a new position in a cornfield closer to the town. Sheltering behind a fence, the Americans again opened fire on the Royal Marines as they approached and once more caused panic among them. Beckwith and Napier again rode to the front, exposing themselves to the effective fire of Massey's picket—fire that made the British believe they were up against more than just eighteen militiamen. Beckwith's horse was shot out from under him, but when Robertson begged Napier to dismount, the lieutenant colonel refused, "saying the state of troops would not allow of care for himself."[36]

Massey and his men fell back once more, retreating to the main American line around 4 a.m. only four hundred yards ahead of the enemy. At that point the couriers from Emory arrived with word of Cockburn's seaborne force. The new British force of forty-five barges arrayed itself in a line across the harbor and fired a signal that Beckwith's land force answered. It was now after daybreak, and Nicholson could plainly see Beckwith's troops massed just 150 yards to his front. He also had a British force assembling to his rear. "In this situation I concluded that nothing but a silent retreat could effect my escape," Nicholson reported. He ordered his men to withdraw. They fell back under British rocket, round, and grape fire but maintained their order and did not lose a man.[37] Major Emory, in a letter to the *Easton Star*, said a delay of just five minutes would have resulted in the loss of the entire command.[38]

Nicholson retreated about a mile and a half down the road to Centerville, a small village eight miles from Queenstown. He pulled his regiment all the way back to Centerville after a messenger arrived with news the British had landed a second waterborne force at the north entrance of Queenstown harbor. As Nicholson's men pitched camp, Hobbs and Taylor and their sixty-four infantrymen rejoined the main command. The two captains had bypassed the direct road to Queenstown to escape from Beckwith, crossed the Wye River in canoes, and marched through the woods.[39]

The British force marched into Queenstown only to find it empty. Beckwith spared the homes, collected whatever materiel the Americans had abandoned, then turned back toward Kent Island. Cockburn was far less genial. The admiral vented his frustration at not catching the militia by pillaging the homes of those who had sheltered an American fighter. He was particularly brutal to the owner of the farm Nicholson had used as his headquarters. His men drove off all the cattle and poultry, confiscated the luxurious silverware and china that belonged to the owner, smashed the furniture and cut up mattresses, and even vandalized family portraits.[40]

The march against Queenstown accomplished very little for the British, who reported two men dead, several wounded, and eleven deserters. It was essentially the last major offensive Warren undertook on the bay. As the oppressive heat and humidity of August wore on, disease and desertion turned a force of some 2,600 effectives into one of slightly more than 2,000, of whom 25 to 35 percent were incapacitated by "fever and ague." Captain Robertson, in a rather glum assessment of the British situation, wrote, "The prospects of Sir J. Warren, at whose disposal Beckwith and the troops were placed, were now exhausted and he had done nothing."[41]

The British left Kent Island on August 22 somewhat disheartened. The one senior officer still itching for a fight was Napier, who wanted to restore the self-esteem of his soldiers and "clear them of the Queenstown business." After an abortive attempt to trap a force of militia on Bayside, a peninsula that jutted into the bay from the Eastern Shore, Napier demanded approval of a plan to march his regiment to St. Michaels and attack the defenders with bayonets only. Beckwith turned him down. Napier then suggested attacking the town with the 102nd, two companies of marines, and a battery of marine artillery. Beckwith turned down that plan, too. Exasperated, Napier called for an all-out attack on St. Michaels using the entire British force. Beckwith again said no. Instead, Beckwith deployed the ground forces and Cockburn's naval brigade in an attempt to round up all of the militia in and around St. Michaels. He sent Napier with the 102nd and two companies of marines to attack a reported force of five hundred militiamen camped north of St. Michaels.[42]

When he arrived at the spot where the militiamen were supposed to be, Napier found only "a miserable picket" of about fifty Americans, who promptly fled at the sight of the redcoats. Napier's men gave chase and rounded up fifteen prisoners, but it was scant consolation to an officer looking to vindicate himself and his soldiers. Napier, his soldiers, and Cockburn and the Royal Marines continued chasing shadows and rumors throughout the night but found nothing. At daybreak they pressed Beckwith to allow a direct assault on St. Michaels, but again he refused, instead ordering both officers to return to the barges. "We re-embarked," Napier wrote, "having landed for no purpose, done nothing and retired to our ships, with the Yankee videttes quietly following us—to see us off!"[43]

CHAPTER 10

Bay Blues

*T*HE BRITISH CAMPAIGN in the Chesapeake failed to accomplish its main goal of relieving pressure on the Canadian frontier. In fact, it failed to divert a single American soldier from heading north, including Regular Army and volunteer units from Maryland and Virginia. It also failed to prevent the United States from consolidating its hold over the vast swath of territory acquired from France, an area Britain wanted to see remain in Native American hands as a bulwark against American expansion. The Admiralty laid those failures, and one more, squarely on the shoulders of Adm. Sir John Borlase Warren.

The force of soldiers, sailors, and marines that once marched with pride on towns from Elkton to Norfolk was now merely a group of worn-out men. Weeks of confinement on board ship had taken a massive toll on morale and discipline. Throughout the long, hot summer months on the Chesapeake, the Admiralty received a litany of requests for transfers as junior officers invented reasons for a move away from Maryland. Sickness was rampant because mosquitoes transmitted numerous diseases, including the dreaded yellow fever. When Capt. George Paterson of the *Fox* contracted the fever, there were no doctors available to treat him because so many other men throughout the squadron were sick. Paterson died a week later.[1]

Morale was also extremely low. Every day, sailors and marines, either singly or in small groups, looked for ways to desert. One group of five tried to steal the ship's barge off the *Conflict*, but an astute guard caught them. Warren summarily ordered the five men hanged and made the entire squadron watch the executions.[2]

When news of what was happening in the Chesapeake reached London, the Admiralty took the step of rebuking its North American Station commander. In a stern letter the commissioners of the Admiralty dressed Warren down not only for the harshness of the punishments but for failing to keep accurate records of the proceedings he used in handing down the executions. At the same time, John W. Croker, the secretary of the Admiralty, never a supporter of Warren, wrote to the admiral relieving him of command. Neither letter would reach Warren until January 1814.[3]

Unaware of developments in England, Warren left the Chesapeake on September 6 with most of the fleet and all of the troops. Sir George Prevost, the British commander in chief in Canada, welcomed the arrival of the two battalions of Royal Marines and Napier's 102nd Infantry Regiment as much-needed reinforcements. For the soldiers and marines, the transition from the bay, where the temperature hit 96° on the day they left, to the cold hills of Nova Scotia, where temperatures at night dipped to 36°, was jarring. "In the morning it is a concert to hear 1600 men's teeth chattering and it screws up my wounded cheek wonderfully," Napier said. Napier's men, at least, had only a brief sojourn in Canada before they left for Bermuda; the marines and Beckwith moved to Montreal to augment the city's garrison.[4]

Rear Admiral Cockburn also left the Chesapeake on September 6, sailing for Bermuda with his flagship, the ship of the line *Sceptre*, as well as a small group of frigates, brigs, and tenders, with orders to take overall command of the British blockade from the Delaware Capes to Savannah, Georgia. The Admiralty also put Cockburn in charge of the Bermuda station.[5]

The departure of Warren and Cockburn left Capt. Robert Barrie of the *Dragon* in charge of a greatly reduced blockade. Although he now had command of his own flotilla, Barrie was unhappy about having to remain in the Chesapeake. He confided to his mother, "This blockading affair is a sad disappointment to me who expected a cruise off New York," where Commodore John Rodgers, a Marylander, commanded a small U.S. Navy squadron that included the 44-gun frigate *President*. Despite his disappointment on missing out on potential ship-to-ship combat, Barrie had hopes of capturing prizes: "If the Americans venture to run any of their French traders during the winter I hope to catch a few of them. . . . Nathan [a derogatory British term for Americans, along with "Jonathan"] has not had any trade whatever during the summer. I hope he will dash a little now the bad weather is coming in."[6]

Poor weather and slow-moving news made the early autumn dull for Barrie. His flotilla was tiny compared with the force that had once bottled up the bay. Barrie had his flagship, the 74-gun ship of the line *Dragon*; two frigates, the *Armide* and the *Lacedaemonian*; the brigs *Acteon* and *Mohawk*; and the tenders *Cockchafer*, *Snapdragon*, *Hampton*, and *Liberty*; but few if any American vessels tested the blockade. Winds on the Chesapeake are notoriously fickle in the late summer and early fall, and no captain wanted his ship to get caught in the afternoon calms that often plague the bay. Instead, Barrie kept his men busy looking for "coasters," small schooners or sloops that carried produce or cargo in the shallow areas of the bay. The British also engaged American militia in a cat-and-mouse conflict over water. The Americans had grown increasingly adroit at ambushing British watering parties, and the two sides clashed in a series of skirmishes.

On September 21, militia under Lt. Col. Kendall Addison attacked a force of eighty-five sailors and Royal Marines under Lt. Richard Maw who were trying to cut out a schooner they had spotted in Cherrystone Inlet on the Virginia Eastern Shore. Maw's force managed to board the schooner and two other boats, but Addison's men, numbering about two hundred with a pair of 12-pounder field guns, lined both sides of the shore and drove off the British. The raiders set fire to the boats, but the militiamen quickly doused the flames. The British suffered one dead and two wounded while the Americans had no casualties.[7]

Winter commenced early that year, with fierce storms lashing the Chesapeake in early October. Barrie pulled his force back to the shelter of Lynnhaven Bay but could not escape the harsh weather. The *Liberty* foundered and sank, and the *Hampton* suffered so much damage in one storm that the British simply broke her up. The *Mohawk* also suffered extensive damage, but Barrie could not afford to send her to Bermuda for repairs until he received a replacement ship.[8]

The bad weather continued throughout October. It rarely hampered the blockade, although an early October snowstorm supplied cover for fifteen schooners to run the British gauntlet. Capt. Samuel Jackson gave chase with the *Lacedaemonian*, but the schooners disappeared into the storm. Those ships were the exception, however. Barrie claimed seventy-two prizes from the day he took over the blockade to the end of year as the blockade continued to choke American commerce.[9]

The British also continued to terrorize the local population. On October 30 Barrie anchored the *Dragon* off St. George Island on the Maryland side of the Potomac River to search for water. A landing party dug twenty shallow wells that yielded plentiful clean water, and the entire squadron soon moved to the island. The few inhabitants of the island fled, and the British pillaged their homes and then burned houses, barns, and crops—everything they could find. As American militia moved into the area to harass the watering operation, the British grew nastier, destroying fences and cutting down most of the trees to use as lumber or kindling on board the ship.[10]

The British had problems other than the near-continuous sniping of American militiamen. Morale remained low in the reduced squadron, and five men took the opportunity to take "French leave," running off into the brush. Barrie's marines and sailors spent five days scouring the island for them, and although the search party found and stole numerous hogs and chickens, they had to resort to setting the marsh grasses on fire and literally scorching the island before the deserters gave up.[11]

On November 5 Barrie dispatched Lt. George Pedlar and thirty-five men in five armed barges to capture three ships anchored in St. Inigoes Creek located off the bay in St. Mary's County, Maryland. Pedlar and his men, guided by a British sympathizer, quickly found and seized the ships. American militia who were lying in wait engaged the small party with musket and cannon fire. The British boarding party returned fire and managed to bring off one of the boats, the 350-ton, copper-bottomed schooner *Quintessence*, and set fire to the other two. Barrie took the captured vessel into British service as a tender.[12]

Late on the night of November 21, one of the more unusual ships to leave Baltimore slipped past Barrie's entire squadron, which was patrolling off Cape Charles at the mouth of the Chesapeake. The *Ultor* was a three-masted xebec, a type of ship common in the Mediterranean but almost unheard of in American waters. Rigged with lateen sails, the *Ultor* cut an unlikely figure among the brigs and schooners that plied the Chesapeake. Her rig, however, made her nimble in light winds and easy to maneuver. The British were already familiar with the *Ultor*. In October the xebec, under the command of Capt. John Cook, had tried to run the blockade. The *Lacedaemonian* gave chase, but the square-rigged British warship could not match the speedy *Ultor* in the prevailing winds, and the American ship easily avoided capture. Several weeks later Cook tried again, with Barrie fuming as the *Ultor* easily sailed past the *Dragon* bound for Cape Henry and the Atlantic. Something, however, caused Cook to turn back at the last moment, and the last thing Barrie saw that day was the xebec again sailing past his ship.

On November 21 the *Ultor*, now under the command of Sailing Master James Matthews, once more dared the blockade as she sought to break out into the Atlantic. First the *Lacedaemonian* and then the *Cockchafer* chased the xebec to no avail. As Barrie looked on from the *Dragon*, the *Ultor* outran both British warships, rounded Cape Charles, and disappeared. She would go on to have an exceptionally active though not very profitable career.[13]

The Admiralty might have been more sympathetic toward Warren had they known just how badly the British blockade was hurting the American economy. James Madison certainly knew how effective Warren's blockade had been. Exports, which totaled $75 million in 1812, dropped to $45 million in 1813. Customs duties on imports, which provided the federal government with its chief source of income, went from $96 million in 1812 to slightly more than $13 million in 1813.[14]

The lack of income forced Madison to get approval from Congress to secure loans just to keep the government afloat. Congress approved borrowing $27 million, but even that was not enough. The cost of the war hit $24 million in 1813 as U.S. forces fought from Canada to Alabama.[15] In a somewhat gloomy assessment for 1814, the Treasury Department expected the cost of the conflict to increase to more than $32 million, with all expenses for the federal government topping $45 million. Without more income the government would go broke by October 1814, and expenses mounted daily.[16] Each time Madison's government called up and federalized state militia, the War Department had to pay to feed, clothe, arm, and equip the troops while they were in federal service. Present-day Department of Commerce estimates put the costs of the militia alone at 2.7 percent of the nation's gross domestic product.[17]

The Indian uprisings in the South came as a particularly nasty shock to Madison. The Creeks, who lived in western Georgia, Alabama, and Mississippi, had lived peacefully with the European Americans for several generations. In 1812, with British backing, Tecumseh convinced a band of Creeks to rise up against American encroachment. The uprising turned into a civil war when other bands of Creeks refused to take part. The governors of Georgia and Tennessee allied with the "loyal" Creeks and called out their militias. Because the Army had no troops to send, the state troops operated under a federal mandate and were put on the War Department payroll, adding to the costs of the war.[18]

The economic situation Madison faced was similar to that of Governor Winder of Maryland and, to a lesser extent, Governor Barbour of Virginia. Winder also had to take the extraordinary step of getting legislative approval to take out loans so he could pay for and try to equip the militia. Those expenses would eventually be passed on to the federal government, but that was small consolation to Winder as 1813 turned into 1814. Maryland and Virginia needed their militias, and not just to repel the British.

As Warren and Cockburn operated on the Chesapeake, fears of a slave uprising grew. Capt. Charles Napier, cousin of the colonel of the 102nd Regiment, boasted that he could assemble a slave army of more than 100,000 that could seize control of the entire Chesapeake region.[19] Robert Barrie, commanding the blockade in Cockburn's absence, came to believe the region's slaves offered a valuable source of manpower and intelligence. "There is no doubt but that the blacks of Virginia and Maryland would cheerfully take up arms and join us against the Americans," he wrote to Warren.[20] Although the British had strict orders not to foment a revolt, rumors and whispers mounted with every British raid. Both Winder and Barbour had their militia out not only to fight the British but also to keep a careful watch on the restive population in chains.

The constant loss of slaves seeking freedom was already a drain on the local economy. Crops needed to be planted and harvested. The shipping industry used slave labor to move cargo to wharves. The fishing industry depended heavily on slaves, as did shipbuilding, at least for its raw materials. Landowners who provided the lumber for building ships often used slave labor to harvest the wood.[21] Like the country as a whole, the Chesapeake region teetered on economic collapse as the British choked American trade.

Politically, the country continued to tear at itself. Federalists and Democrats remained locked in a bitter debate over the war. Connecticut, which at the end of 1813 was the only New England state under blockade, continued to refuse to send troops to Canada or anywhere else. Merchants fumed when the British extended the blockade to include all of New England, but the brunt of the blame fell on Madison. New Englanders castigated the president for his inability to safeguard the American coast and for the costs the states incurred in erecting batteries, calling out militia, and commissioning warships to protect their shores. The British blockade also spawned a call among New Englanders to strike their own deal with Great Britain in which New England would essentially declare regional neutrality while the rest of the country continued the war. By the end of 1814 this unorthodox idea had morphed into a call for secession, although that idea never gained widespread support.[22]

Diplomatically, time was not on America's side. Napoleon was in retreat everywhere, and it was just a matter of time before the British-led allied forces defeated and dethroned the French emperor.[23] Madison was eager to end the war before Britain could bring the full weight of its military to bear on the United States. When Alexander I of Russia offered to mediate, Madison jumped at the chance, sending Albert Gallatin to St. Petersburg as part of a peace delegation. Gallatin arrived in July 1813 and for the next six months cooled his heels as the Russians tried to convince the English to join in the peace talks. The Russian czar had never been happy about the American war. He wanted nothing to distract Britain from the war in France.

What Alexander did not take into account was Britain's desire for revenge against the United States. British newspapers railed against Madison and slaveholders in particular, likening the American declaration of war to a stab in the back. The British viewed their war against Napoleon as a war against a global tyranny, and if any country should support a war of freedom, Britain believed it was the new United States. The American declaration of war, as the British saw it, showed support for Napoleon. By the onset of spring 1814, Britain smelled blood—Napoleon's and Madison's. As victory over Napoleon became a foregone conclusion, England turned its focus on America. Although Britain had to keep the bulk of its forces in France to maintain order and prevent insurrection, four brigades of Wellington's army were made available for duty in North America. The peace talks went nowhere, and in April 1814, just days after Napoleon abdicated, Gallatin wrote to Madison, "To use their own language they mean to inflict on America a chastisement that will teach her that war is not to be declared against Great Britain with impunity."[24]

Vice Adm. Sir Alexander Forrester
Inglis Cochrane, the leader of
Britain's 1814 campaign in the
Chesapeake. Cochrane earned the
enmity of many in Maryland and
Virginia with his early version
of total war. NATIONAL PORTRAIT
GALLERY, LONDON

After sacking Warren in November 1813, the Admiralty turned to Vice Adm. Sir Alexander Forrester Inglis Cochrane, an officer with a known hatred of America. The sixth son of an impoverished minor Scottish noble, Cochrane entered the Royal Navy in 1776 at the age of fifteen as a midshipman and steadily advanced through the ranks thanks to the sponsorship of Adm. Sir George Rodney. He served in North America during the Revolutionary War and gained his first reason to despise Americans when his older brother, Charles, died in combat at Yorktown.[25]

As the war came to a close in 1783, Cochrane was serving on a ship stationed in New York. He met many loyalists who were hurriedly packing their belongings to flee the city along with the British forces. Cochrane had American relatives who had remained loyal to the king during the Revolution, and they were among the many preparing to leave New York. He also met his future wife, Maria Shaw, while on duty in New York. Shaw was from a prominent loyalist family who would lose their fortune when they left New York and "patriots" confiscated their property. It was the same for Cochrane's family and many other loyalist families. Bands of "patriots" roamed New York searching for loyalists, whom they robbed, beat, and abused.[26]

By 1794 Cochrane was a full captain in command of the frigate *Thetis*, operating out of Halifax. He found his in-laws and his own relatives living in relative poverty after the United States reneged on its Treaty of Paris obligations to compensate loyalists for their lost property. That enraged Cochrane and deepened his hatred of America. Also deepening his hatred was an incident that occurred in the summer of 1794 after the *Thetis* was caught in a storm while operating off Norfolk. When he brought the ship into port for repairs, he came in contact with numerous slaves and slaveholders and witnessed firsthand the brutal nature of slavery and the burning desire of the slaves to be free.[27] These experiences led Cochrane to despise Americans, whom he called a "perfidious enemy. . . . They are a whining, canting race much like the spaniel and require the same treatment—must be drubbed into good manners."[28]

Cochrane's expertise in amphibious operations was even more dangerous to America than his hatred. In 1800 he had trained two hundred officers to command an immense amphibious force of seventy flat-bottomed boats and dozens of barges. On March 1, 1801, he personally led a division of this force ashore at Aboukir Bay in Egypt in the face of stiff resistance from 30,000 French infantry and artillery. He landed his entire force of 16,000 over the next 3 days along with artillery, baggage, and supplies from a fleet of 70 warships plus transports lying 7 miles offshore.[29]

Cochrane became commander of the Leeward Islands Station in the Caribbean in 1805, and played a central role in the British victory over a French squadron at the Battle of Santo Domingo on February 6, 1806. Cochrane, acting under the command of Adm. Sir John Thomas Duckworth, helped smash the French battle line, driving the enemy's flagship, the *Imperial*, and another ship of the line, the *Diomede*, aground. Cochrane deployed his marines and sailors in ships' boats to seize the two vessels before the French could set them on fire. His men beat off the French, but neither ship was seaworthy and the British completed the destruction of both. He was awarded a knighthood for his role in the battle and was promoted to vice admiral in 1809 after he led the force that captured the French island of Martinique. By 1812 he was governor of Guadeloupe, although he returned to London late in 1813. On December 27, 1813, the Admiralty's orders officially put Cochrane in command of a reorganized North America Station that now ran from Halifax to Bermuda.[30]

While in England, Cochrane apparently read a paper British foreign secretary Robert Stewart Lord Castlereagh wrote on the coming campaign in North America. Castlereagh envisioned recruiting a land and sea force of 15,000 men in Canada that would take control of the Great Lakes. He also advocated the annexation of U.S. territory south of the lakes to create a buffer zone that would protect Canada; the capture of New Orleans and "freeing" of all the land America had acquired in the Louisiana Purchase; arming and equipping all of the Indian tribes west of the Appalachian Mountains and turning them into a force capable of blunting any further American expansion; and undertaking a campaign to sever New England from the rest of the country and allow it to become an independent nation.[31]

Although somewhat fanciful, the Castlereagh paper had a direct influence on Cochrane's plans because the capture of New Orleans was one of his main goals as well. Cochrane, however, added to the foreign secretary's plan, requesting arms and uniforms for freed slaves he planned to enlist into a corps of Colonial Marines. Current British policy mandated the Royal Navy to resettle to Trinidad any slaves who fled their masters. Now they were to become soldiers for the Crown in return for their freedom.[32]

At first, Cochrane planned to recruit slaves only from Virginia, North and South Carolina, and Georgia as punishment for those states' continuing support for Madison and the war. The British government expanded on Cochrane's idea, telling the admiral he should recruit and free slaves from any U.S. state. Slaves who preferred resettlement to service were to receive transport, with "northern slaves" going to Nova Scotia and "southern slaves" traveling to Trinidad. The government's orders, however, failed to define the difference between a northern slave and a southern one.[33]

Cochrane arrived in Bermuda on March 6 and quickly set about formulating his plan to make Jonathan regret declaring war on England. He wrote Lord Melville on March 10 that he believed "all the country southwest of the Chesapeake might be restored to the dominion of Great Britain, if under the command of enterprising generals."[34] Two weeks later his schemes included kidnapping political leaders close to the Madison administration. On March 25 he envisioned an attack on the Portsmouth Navy Yard in New Hampshire that would occur in conjunction with an invasion from the north under Sir George Prevost, all with the goal of severing New England from the rest of the country. As for the Chesapeake, the admiral believed disaffected blacks could be recruited to fight the Americans on the doorstep of their own capital.[35]

Throughout his time in command Cochrane remained committed to the freeing and recruiting of slaves to aid England's war effort. On March 28 he ordered Cockburn, who had spent the winter in Bermuda, to return to the Chesapeake and set up a fortified base on Tangier Island, where he was to begin accepting black recruits for the Colonial Marines. He also ordered Cockburn to map the mouth of the Patuxent River in southern Maryland and search for a suitable place to land a large force of soldiers. On April 1 Cochrane extended the British blockade to cover both New England and New Orleans.[36]

Cochrane conducted all of his scheming without knowing the size of the force he would have to work with. He convinced himself he would receive at least 15,000 of Wellington's "Invincibles," as the Peninsular War force was known. On some days he expected up to 20,000 men.[37] Above all, he continued to expect and plan for massive slave defections to the British. "The great point to be attained," he wrote to Cockburn on July 1, "is the cordial support of the black population. With them properly armed and backed with 10,000 British troops, Mr. Madison will be hurled from his throne."[38]

Meanwhile, events in Europe and England were developing without Cochrane's knowledge. Lord Castlereagh wanted to send a total of 25,000 soldiers to North America; he got just 10,000. Wellington, who was never a supporter of the war with America, refused to release any of his light infantry for duty in Canada and said he needed the bulk of his forces to maintain order in France. On April 11 Lord Bathurst, the secretary of state for war and colonies, ordered 7,000 men to Canada. On May 18 Bathurst requested the Admiralty to transport three regiments from France to Bermuda for operations in the Chesapeake. Two days later Bathurst named Maj. Gen. Robert Ross to command the troops bound for the bay. All told, 2,814 men from the 4th, 44th, and 85th Regiments of Foot boarded transports in Bordeaux. Led by the 74-gun ship of the line HMS *Royal Oak*, the convoy of fourteen warships and three transports set off for Bermuda and, from there, to America.[39]

Ross was a popular choice as a land commander. The forty-seven-year-old Irishman had forged a reputation as both a stern disciplinarian and a soldier's soldier. At the Battle of Coruna in Spain, he personally led his 20th Foot in action, losing fewer men than any other regiment despite being in the thick of the battle. At Pamplona, two horses were shot out from under him and he was wounded twice, yet he remained on the field. He was the type of leader the hard-bitten men from Wellington's army appreciated.[40]

Bathurst's orders to Ross, transmitted through Cochrane, were strikingly similar to those under which Warren and Beckwith had operated in 1813. Ross would command the land forces, but Cochrane was to pick the targets. Bathurst told the Peninsular War veteran "to effect a diversion on the coast of the United States of America in favor of the army to be employed in the defense of Upper Canada." He warned Ross, "This force will not permit you to engage in extended operations at a distance from the coast," although Ross could use his own discretion to "decline engaging in any operations which he feels may either fail or expose his troops to losses disproportionate to any potential advantages."[41]

Finally, Bathurst told Ross, "You will not encourage any disposition which may be manifested by the Negroes to rise upon their masters. The humanity which ever influences His Royal Highness . . . [forbids] the atrocities inseparable from commotions of such a description." Ross, in keeping with Cochrane's plans, could enlist any slaves who desired British protection and who wished to serve, but he had to provide transportation to Trinidad for any who simply wished to be free and not to serve.[42]

Ross did not arrive in Bermuda until late June. By then Cochrane had already moved forward with his plan to arm runaway slaves and use them against their former masters. On April 2, 1814, he issued a proclamation directly to the slaves, promising "That All Those who May be Disposed to Emigrate from the United States Will, with Their Families, be Received on Board of His Majesty's Ships Or Vessels of War . . . when They Will Have Their Choice of Either Entering Into His Majesty's Sea Or Land Forces, Or Being Sent as Free Settlers to the British Possessions in North America Or the West Indies."[43]

The proclamation sent a clear signal that Cochrane intended to wreck the economy of the southern states by encouraging slaves to run away. It also came close to violating Bathurst's order not to foment a slave rebellion. Although Cochrane never called on slaves to rise up against their masters, his Colonial Marines raised the specter of a slave revolt among southern whites. American papers vilified Cochrane and his proclamation, and Governor Winder warned Maryland militia commanders, "Should we be attacked there will be great danger of the blacks rising, and to prevent this, patrols are very necessary, to keep them in awe."[44]

When he learned of the proclamation on May 20, President Madison fired off a note to Secretary of War Armstrong asking for advice. Although Madison, a slaveholder, did not address his own concerns about a slave uprising, he did write of his concerns for the capital—his first such admission since the scare of 1813. "I am just possessed of the intelligence last from Great Britain and France and the proclamation of Cochrane addressed to the blacks," Madison wrote. "They admonish to be prepared for the worst the enemy may be able to effect against us. The date concurs with the measure proclaiming to indicate inveterate ferocity against the Southern states and which may be expected to show itself against every object within the vindictive enterprise. Among these the seat of government cannot fail to be a favorable one."[45]

CHAPTER 11

Sloops, Frigates, and Galleys

NONE OF THE PLANNING, scheming, or dreaming in London or Bermuda did much to help Capt. Robert Barrie. The commander of the greatly diminished Chesapeake blockade squadron had to count on the fickle bay winter weather as much as his own ships to prevent American merchantmen and privateers from reaching the Atlantic. There were two ships Barrie could not allow to leave, the two ships the British coveted the most as prizes: the *Constellation* and the sloop of war *Adams.*

The *Constellation,* commanded by Capt. Charles Gordon, remained bottled up on the Elizabeth River near Norfolk. Barrie had no recent information on the location of the 28-gun warship *Adams,* under the command of Capt. Charles Morris. On a hunch, he deployed his meager force of blockaders close to the Potomac River, where he believed the *Adams* was lurking, in case the American warship tried to break out.

Breaking out was exactly what Morris intended. One of the many officers whose careers took off under Commodore Edward Preble during the First Barbary War in 1803–4, Morris was born on July 26, 1784, in Woodstock, Connecticut. He entered the Navy as an acting midshipman in 1799 and received his warrant the following year. He served alongside Stephen Decatur, Charles Stewart, Richard Somers, Isaac Hull, James Lawrence, and Thomas Macdonough in the Mediterranean, and was part of Decatur's daring raid to burn the captured frigate *Philadelphia* in Tripoli's harbor.

At the outbreak of the war Morris was first lieutenant on the *Constitution* under Hull. He was wounded in the abdomen during the victorious fight with the *Guerriere* and was promoted to full captain, a promotion that raised the hackles of his brother officers. Many, most notably James Lawrence and Jacob Jones, were senior to him and resented Morris jumping above them in rank. Morris, to his credit, made no attempt to influence the Senate, which had to approve the promotion. On October 5, 1812, Secretary of the Navy Jones put Morris in command of the *Adams,* which was then undergoing a complete refit at the Washington Navy Yard. A month later the Senate approved his promotion to captain—along with those of Lawrence and Jones, keeping Morris junior to both on the seniority list.[1]

After his promotion Morris received his orders to proceed to Washington to take command of the *Adams* and oversee her overhaul. While directing the work, Morris joined with Stewart in testifying before the Naval Committee of the Senate, arguing for the expansion of the Navy. It was likely an easier task than the overhaul of the *Adams* proved to be. Then a 32-gun frigate, the *Adams* required nearly a complete rebuild after lying in ordinary since 1807. Workers at the Washington Navy Yard completed the refit in May 1813, but the British blockade kept the *Adams* from getting to sea. Instead, Morris and his crew reported to Annapolis and manned the two forts guarding the city. Morris also put together a plan to defend Washington, a plan Armstrong ignored.

Two short cruises on the Potomac convinced Morris and a board of other officers that the frigate was still not ready for sea. Although always a fast vessel, the *Adams* had design flaws that hampered her success as a warship. She was too sharp on the bottom and drew too much water when loaded. Josiah Fox had suggested converting the *Adams* into a flush-deck sloop of war as early as 1807, but work on completely converting the frigate did not begin in earnest until August 1813.[2] Workers cut the ship in half and lengthened her fifteen feet by adding a section amidships. The *Adams* relaunched on November 18, 1813, as a 28-gun sloop of war armed with "short 18-pounders" and a crew of officers and men whom Morris described as "all young."[3]

Despite the renovation, the officers and crew—including Morris—were not particularly happy with how the *Adams* sailed. "I regret that the ship gives but little satisfaction either to myself or officers," Morris wrote to Jones. "They are so little satisfied with her that they would willingly change to any other vessel that can get to sea, but will not apply for a removal while I remain in her. They do not consider her a safe cruising vessel."[4]

The problems with the *Adams* were many. Her rudder shook so violently at any speed faster than a crawl that Morris believed it might actually rip away from the ship. A bigger problem was the shape of the bow, which did not channel water properly around the ship. Instead it pooled water that formed eddies right behind the rudder. Whether it was an old problem or a new one caused by lengthening the ship, Morris did not say.[5]

In spite of his ship's shortcomings, Morris brought the *Adams* down to the mouth of the Potomac at the beginning of January 1814, "ready to take advantage of any favorable opportunity." He admitted, however, that his "situation was not very agreeable, being always exposed to an attack by superior force, with all the rivers closed above us by ice."[6]

Each day the *Adams* spent waiting for favorable winds increased the tension on board. The crew and officers alike expected to see Royal Navy blockaders sail into sight while their own ship was helpless. Finally, on January 18 at

5 p.m., Morris guided the *Adams* out of the Potomac and into the Chesapeake. A strong northwest wind pushed her at nearly twelve knots, and darkness and snow squalls hid her from view. Although he was out of the Potomac, Morris was hardly out of danger. "All the lights [aids to navigation] in the bay had been discontinued, and the two persons who acted as pilots were imperfectly qualified for the duty," Morris reported. "The rate of sailing was so rapid that correct soundings were not obtained, and it was only fortunate chance that we were not carried upon the shoals."[7]

The *Adams* continued on her course until a light onshore was mistaken for a channel light and she scraped over a large shoal, grounding her keel twice "with considerable force." Morris quickly changed course and found deeper water. His two pilots "differed widely as to our place in the bay and it became necessary to depend entirely on my own judgment, which happened to prove correct." Although some of the crew worried the ship might have been holed passing over the shoal, Morris decided to continue, with even those worried about possible damage agreeing. "Everybody was willing to encounter these risks for the chance of escaping the species of imprisonment to which we had been so long subjected."[8]

Just past midnight the *Adams* passed Lynnhaven Bay, where Barrie was anchored with his 74-gun flagship, the *Dragon*. The British never even saw Morris' vessel pass. "When daylight broke upon us," Morris said, "neither the enemy nor land was in sight."[9] For the Americans it was the first sea victory in the Chesapeake in more than a year, and Morris had not fired a shot.

Capt. Charles Gordon did not have Morris' luck. Gordon arrived in Norfolk in September to take command of the frigate *Constellation*, expecting to get her to sea as soon as he spotted a hole in the British blockade. It would be the culmination of his dream to finally take the war to the British. Revenge was also likely a motivation for Gordon. His close friend Capt. James Lawrence had been killed in June 1813 while commanding the frigate *Chesapeake* in a losing battle with the British warship *Shannon*. Gordon no doubt had dreams of avenging Lawrence, although he never put those thoughts on paper.[10]

Gordon found his new command anything but ready for sea. The crew was scattered. Some remained on temporary duty on the gunboats that helped repel the attack on Craney Island. Others were detailed to the defenses of Norfolk or were working in the Gosport Navy Yard. On October 12 he reported to Navy secretary Jones, "I found the Ship without order or arrangement in any degree owing to her crew being so long absent and indeed had become almost strangers to the ship, to their stations and to every thing like system and regularity. For in the Gun Boat service they cannot be kept in that state of discipline necessary for a man of war."[11]

The crew was only part of the problem. "The ship will require re-fitting from her keelson up and her crew reorganized and trained as though she were just from the ordinary," Gordon wrote to Jones. "She will require a quantity of running rigging; one set of top sails and courses to replace those that have been bent and have become mildewed and rotten; two bower cables; one mizzen top mast to replace a white pine one she has now."[12] Finally, the *Constellation* had no powder. The skeleton crew left on the frigate had allowed several feet of water to accumulate in the hold that destroyed all the stores, including the ship's one ton of gunpowder.

Gordon laid much of the blame for the poor condition of the *Constellation* on Capt. Joseph Tarbell, who commanded the ship during the summer after Charles Stewart went to Boston and before Gordon could arrive from Baltimore. Tarbell appeared to be indifferent about the *Constellation*, knowing he was not destined to take her to sea. "There being no inventory taken and no receipt from Capt. Tarbell to Capt. Stewart when the change took place, I find it difficult to ascertain precisely what is deficient or where the deficiencies are," Gordon reported.

Jones took the extraordinary step of writing to Stewart, asking him about the state of the *Constellation* when he left for Boston. Stewart replied to Jones' inquiry with incredulity. "It is truly mortifying to me that there should have arisen any necessity for calling on me at this period to show the state and condition of that ship at the time I surrendered her to the charge of Captain Tarbell; particularly as her books of indent and expenditure were left on board, made up to the day of my leaving her; by reference to them it will be seen what had been received on board, as stores, and what was expended."[13]

Both Stewart and Jones wanted to know the location of the ship's furniture. Gordon reported on his arrival that the *Constellation* had been stripped of everything. Of even greater concern, however, was the wet, useless gunpowder. Jones ordered Capt. John Cassin, commander of the navy yard, to investigate, but nothing apparently came of the probe. Tarbell attempted to shift responsibility for the ship to Sailing Master Benjamin Bryan, saying Bryan had been in charge of the frigate while the rest of the crew was fighting in the gunboats. Bryan responded to the charge of negligence by detailing his actions and exact whereabouts—and those of the ranking officers on the *Constellation*—from February through October 1813. He reported that he never found more than twelve or fifteen inches of water in the bilges (a normal condition for a wooden ship), an amount that could not have damaged the powder. "I do not merit the stigma attempted to be cast on me," he wrote to Jones. "It will appear from the foregoing statement that I was not at any one time longer in charge of the ship than 48 hours."[14]

The entire affair exasperated Jones, and he was particularly unhappy with what he saw as buck-passing among his senior officers. On October 28 he wrote to Gordon, telling him to find out exactly who was responsible for the mess on the frigate:

> The disorganization, waste, and negligence, on board the *Constellation*, subsequent to your command, are, I believe, without a parallel in the service; sails rotting on the yards, seven feet water in her hold, 2000 lbs. of powder utterly destroyed, and great part of the furniture, etc. dilapidated or lost; and the responsibility attempted to be shifted from the commander to a warrant officer, who is said to have been left with the entire command, under the pretext of the commander and lieutenants being engaged in flotilla expeditions, and on Craney Island. This may account to you for the necessity of my enquiry, in order to investigate and trace the negligence to its proper source.[15]

Work on the *Constellation* progressed throughout the fall. Captain Cassin made the frigate the yard's priority, and Gordon reported the ship ready for service in early December. A quirk in the command structure prevented Gordon from leaving, however, when he lost his crew to Tarbell. Because he equaled Gordon and Cassin in rank, Tarbell believed he could essentially do what he wanted. Tarbell commanded the Navy gunboats at Norfolk and decided to use them to strike at British watering parties operating in the York River. He launched his expedition on December 1 and immediately drew the attention of most of Barrie's squadron. The British commander left only the frigate *Lacedaemonian* to watch Norfolk while he pursued Tarbell with his brigs and frigates. It was a perfect opportunity for the *Constellation* to slip out of Norfolk and possibly to attack and capture an enemy frigate.

The departure of the gunboats left only the *Constellation* to guard the city, however, and Gordon was unwilling to leave Norfolk defenseless. He also raised the possibility that the British might sail around the gunboat flotilla and cut it off from Norfolk. "The strange and distant conduct of Capt. Tarbell to me on this occasion, and the great risk of having all his disposable force," led Gordon to ask Jones to clarify the command situation. It was not that he desired command of all the naval forces in Norfolk, he wrote. All he wanted was to ensure coordination, so should another opportunity to run the blockade arise, he would not miss it because of the actions of one of his fellow captains. On December 28 Gordon sailed the *Constellation* to Point Lookout, near the mouth of the Elizabeth River. He was ready, he wrote Jones, to slip past the blockade. From his anchorage he could see that Barrie had left one frigate to guard the river while others were "looking out off the capes or up the bay." All he needed was good weather; but that was in short supply. The usual conditions were "thick blustering and variable," Gordon reported. Good weather lasted only a day before it changed to marginal, and without the right winds the *Constellation* could go nowhere.[16]

Gordon remained at anchor near Craney Island for more than a week, always looking for a way past the blockade, but contrary winds and squalls kept the frigate tied to her moorings. Once he did get into the Atlantic, Gordon's orders were to attack merchant ships. "The commerce of the enemy is the most vulnerable interest we can assail," Jones had written to him, "and your main efforts should be directed to its destruction."[17] Gordon tried to set sail on January 3 but had to turn back when the wind suddenly veered. He tried again ten days later, and five days after that. He made his final attempt on February 11, but once again the weather worked against him. "So baffling was the wind and so extremely thick with squalls and calms from the south," he reported to Jones, that "we were kept in this state of anxiety and uncertainty until the morning, when it broke away with the wind at west and exposed us to the full view of the Enemy—one frigate in Lynnhaven Bay, and a ship of the line, a frigate and a large brig off Back River. As I could not then proceed without being pursued by the whole of their force, I remained in the [Hampton] roads."[18]

Almost as bad as the weather was the bickering that continued between Tarbell and Gordon. Throughout January and February, Tarbell wore out couriers with letters to the Navy Department, all of them complaining about Gordon. On February 15 Tarbell whined to Jones, "I beg I may not be considered attempting anything to the prejudice of a brother officer, but really Capt. Gordon's demands on the flotilla has been so great, and so severe, that I have been compelled to refuse him." Gordon's repeated attempts to slip past the blockade had kept the gunboats and schooners of the flotilla constantly at work, Tarbell complained, preventing him from conducting his campaign against the British.[19] Gordon retorted that as the senior officer, it was his right to suborn the flotilla to his needs.[20]

Jones finally had enough of both men. It was bad enough that the *Constellation* remained in Norfolk. He did not need two of his senior officers engaging in a war of words as well, especially when it took up the secretary's time. As British reinforcements began to arrive, strengthening the blockade, it was readily apparent that Gordon would not get to sea. On April 15 Jones ended the command debate. "In the present state and probable continuance of the Blockade, the prospect of your getting to sea is not only hopeless but it would be temerity to make the attempt," he wrote to Gordon. "Therefore your attention will be exclusively directed to the efficient employment of the whole of the Naval force on the Norfolk station, for which purpose you are invested with the entire command of that force, and Captain Tarbell will report himself to you accordingly."[21] The command question was settled, but the *Constellation* would remain stuck for the rest of the year.

The success the British enjoyed raiding up and down the Chesapeake throughout 1813 convinced both Secretary of War Armstrong and Secretary of the Navy Jones of the need for some type of defensive force on the bay, one that could cover the principal cities of the upper Chesapeake, including Baltimore and Annapolis, as well as Washington. Thanks to the lobbying efforts of Morris, Stewart, and other officers, Congress, when it approved the $16 million loan to continue funding the war, approved using a portion of the funds to build several new warships. Six of those vessels were to be sloops of war, with two of them built in Baltimore and one at the Washington Navy Yard. Work on the new vessels began in the fall, but the blockade hampered the construction because contractors could not ship materials to the shipwrights.[22]

Although the sloops would be effective warships, there was still a need for inshore defense boats that could match the British barges and cutters and challenge the raiding parties. Charles Gordon's leased flotilla of privateers were returned to their owners in September 1813, leaving just one U.S. Navy gunboat to defend the city. On the Potomac, the U.S. block sloop *Scorpion* and schooner *Asp* were the only vessels left of that flotilla after the British incursion up the river. What both Jones and Armstrong needed was a cost-effective, hard-hitting way to fight the British.

Joshua Barney, arguably the most accomplished naval officer not in the U.S. Navy, gave the secretaries exactly what they wanted in July 1813 when he submitted a plan to defend the Chesapeake using a novel type of warship. Barney was already something of a legend. Born in Baltimore on July 6, 1759, to a well-to-do family, he was one of fourteen children. He professed his desire to go to sea when he was ten years old, although his parents kept him on land for two more years. He made his first transatlantic voyage at age sixteen and became a captain by default on his next voyage when the captain of the merchant ship on which Barney was sailing died at sea. Barney saved the ship from sinking in a storm and, after many months of wrangling, sold the cargo and returned to Philadelphia to find the colonies in revolt against England.

Barney immediately offered his services to the Continental Navy and was appointed the master's mate of the *Hornet*, one of the ships in Commodore Esek Hopkins' flotilla that attacked New Providence in the Bahamas. He soon became the lieutenant in command of the *Wasp* and later of the *Andrea Doria*. He also served as a successful privateer. He was captured three times and exchanged twice. The third time the British cast him into the infamous Old Mill Prison outside Plymouth, England. He escaped by bribing a guard,

Commodore Joshua Barney, commander of the Chesapeake Flotilla that fought the Royal Navy throughout the summer of 1814. Portrait by Rembrandt Peale. MARYLAND HISTORICAL SOCIETY, BALTIMORE

dressing in a homemade British officer's uniform, and then stealing a fishing boat. He was caught before he could flee from English soil but escaped again, once more using his fake uniform to boldly evade patrols looking for him. He managed to reach Holland, where he secured passage back to the United States. On his return he took command of the *Hyder Ally*, a Philadelphia privateer, and captured the British warship *General Monk*.

Barney had a reputation for honorably treating his prisoners. In 1782, after capturing the *General Monk*, Barney used his own money to arrange for the treatment of the wounded British captain. Although he treated his prisoners well and harbored no hatred toward the British, Barney did develop a lifelong desire to punish them for his cruel treatment at their hands.

Barney was also known for his fearlessness and resourcefulness. During the battle with the *General Monk*, Barney stood on the binnacle that housed the ship's compass so he could better direct his sailors. The perch made him a perfect target for English sharpshooters, who peppered his uniform and hat with musket balls. He only abandoned his exposed position when a cannonball hit the binnacle and tumbled him to the deck. Later, he proudly recalled that his example had inspired a young sailor who had been frozen with fear. Barney had noticed the young man just before he was knocked off the binnacle. When he stood up, he saw the young man working his gun.[23]

After the Revolution, Barney became a successful merchant captain and shipowner who made frequent voyages to France. He became enamored of the Republican ideals of revolutionary France and in 1795 accepted an offer to serve in the French navy. He spent seven years, off and on, commanding frigates and commissioning privateers, two of which were wildly successful. He turned down a commission in the nascent U.S. Navy in 1797 when the United States and France entered into an undeclared naval war, believing he was not high enough on the seniority list.

Barney remained in French service until 1802, when, with the ascent of Napoleon and the demise of the French Republic, he returned permanently to Baltimore. At the outbreak of the war with England Barney commanded the Baltimore-built privateer *Rossie*. He set out on July 12, 1812, on a ninety-day cruise. When it ended, Barney had captured or destroyed 20 British ships totaling 3,698 tons worth an estimated $1.5 million and had taken 217 prisoners. It was among the most successful runs of any American privateer during the war. By the summer of 1813 he was back in Baltimore and, like many in Maryland, watching in horror as Cockburn's waterborne marauders operated with impunity.[24]

In July 1813 Barney wrote to Jones detailing a plan to defend the Chesapeake with a "flying squadron" of sail-and-row galleys. These boats, Barney wrote, would be "so constructed, as to draw a small draft of water, to carry oars, light sails, and one heavy long gun, these vessels may be built in a short time, (say 3 weeks). . . . Add to this squadron three or four, light fast-sailing vessels, prepared as fireships, which could with ease, (under cover of the Barges) be run onboard any of the enemies ships, if they should attempt to anchor, or remain in our narrow rivers, or harbors."[25]

Barney's idea dovetailed with a plan Senator Samuel Smith of Maryland had rammed through Congress in June that ordered the federal government to provide adequate defenses for harbors and ports. Smith's plan called for the use of galleys in two classes, one 70 feet long, the other 50 feet.[26] Jones was against the idea. "The number of men required in proportion to the efficient force of a barge is excessively great," he explained to Smith, "and it will be recollected that a vast number of our seamen are still employed in licensed merchantmen abroad and in our public and private armed vessels." Jones also saw problems supplying the boats, finding the money to build them, and in the chain of command.[27] Moreover, Jones believed Smith secretly wanted the federal government to absorb the costs the city of Baltimore had incurred when it purchased several barges for local defense during Warren's spring campaign.

The Maryland senator, however, had the political clout to push his idea, and Jones acquiesced, with one caveat. He made sure command of any battle group of galleys would be outside the normal Navy establishment. When Barney's memo arrived, Jones jumped at the chance to offer Barney the job. Naming Barney was also something of a shot across Smith's bow because Barney and Smith were political rivals and barely on speaking terms. If Smith expected to exert influence over the flotilla, he would find in Barney an implacable foe.[28]

Jones tendered Barney the command of the "United States Flotilla on the upper part of the Chesapeake" on August 20. Barney quickly accepted even though the flotilla would not be as he had envisioned it. Whereas Barney's plan called for 100-foot galleys with crews of fifty sailors and officers and twenty-five "soldiers," Jones had shipyards in Baltimore, Washington, and St. Michaels building 75-foot and 50-foot vessels, each with a different size crew and no differentiation between sailors and soldiers. The armament was also different. Barney called for just one cannon in each galley while Jones had two guns on each boat. Under Jones' plan, each galley was to carry a single 24-pounder long cannon in the bow and a 42-pounder carronade in the stern. Jones later changed the armament to an 18-pounder cannon and 32-pounder carronades because the Navy had a surplus of those weapons.[29]

If Barney had any misgivings about the vessels' design, he never expressed them. After accepting his appointment as an acting master commandant in the "U.S. Flotilla Service," Barney began recruiting men. He estimated that at a minimum he needed 750 sailors to man the 11 galleys, the cutters *Scorpion* and *Asp*, and the two U.S. Navy gunboats that made up his flotilla. It was possible, though, that he would need more. Shipyards continued to build galleys that could add to his flotilla, and Barney also wanted to buy several of the galleys the city of Baltimore had built for local defense. The city government of Baltimore actually offered all of its vessels and their captains to Barney, knowing those boats could eventually play a large role in thwarting any British attack on the city. He picked up his first recruit from Baltimore as well when Lt. Solomon Rutter resigned from a local defense unit and joined the flotilla. Barney even bought Rutter's ship, the 45-foot *Vigilant*, which was reputed to be exceptionally fast.[30]

Those additions aside, Barney found recruiting men extremely difficult. He had to compete for men and officers with the militia, the Army, the Navy, and privateers. The Army was then recruiting men for the 36th Infantry Regiment and offering cash bounties to recruits. Barney asked for permission to do likewise, but Jones turned him down. In December, Barney went to Annapolis, found 138 men willing to leave the 36th Infantry, and asked Jones for permission to enlist them into the flotilla. The Navy secretary agreed, but the company commander, Capt. Joseph Merrick, refused to discharge any of his soldiers for service in the flotilla. Barney complained to Jones, who wrote to Secretary of War Armstrong, who ordered Merrick to release the men. Twenty-six soldiers joined the flotilla, and the Army never forgot it.[31]

Barney used every means he could find to recruit men. He attempted to absorb the Baltimore detachment of 104 men of the "Corps of Sea Fencibles," an ad hoc force under the tenuous command of the Army that was solely for defense of harbors and ports. When that plan failed, he turned to Maryland state senator Solomon Frazier, a veteran of the Revolution and a popular Eastern Shore lawmaker. Barney made Frazier a lieutenant in the flotilla and tasked him with recruiting men from his home district in the St. Michaels area. He also played on Marylanders' patriotism and badgered local militiamen and shipowners. It all paid off, somewhat. By year's end he had two hundred men—not enough to man all of his warships, but it was a start.[32] He would continue to recruit into the new year, when an old enemy returned to the Chesapeake smelling blood.

Old Tricks

R EAR ADM. GEORGE COCKBURN returned to Chesapeake Bay on February 23, 1814, following a six-week voyage from Bermuda that took him first to the blockade off New London, Connecticut. The New England weather was frigid, and Cockburn suffered a mild case of frostbite. While off Long Island he decided to change flagships because the *Sceptre* had undergone a full refit in Bermuda that made her so top-heavy Cockburn feared she would capsize in heavy seas. He transferred his flag to the 74-gun *Albion* and made his way south. He stopped at Cape May at the mouth of the Delaware Bay to check on the blockaders there before finally arriving in the Chesapeake.[1]

The admiral spent a month rearranging the Chesapeake blockade before receiving orders from Vice Admiral Cochrane to locate a suitable place to establish a fortified base. Cockburn chose Tangier Island, centrally located between the Virginia shores of the bay and close to the mouth of the Potomac. The island offered deep-water anchorage and a protected land area where he could execute Cochrane's order to gather and recruit slaves for either service or resettlement. Although it provided a change of pace, the occupation of the island and the construction of a fort, which Cockburn named Fort Albion, did little to relieve the monotony of maintaining the blockade. Robert Barrie, who had spent the winter in charge of the blockade, lamented to his half-sister Eliza Clayton, "I am tired of blockading and long to be sent to the Eastward to cruise.... [H]ere we are very cold and ... very dissatisfied at doing nothing."[2]

The monotony of the blockade was in stark contrast to the frenzied activity in Bermuda. Cochrane, still dreaming up schemes of a massive invasion of the American South, first had to quell a question of command. His predecessor, Admiral Warren, refused to believe the Admiralty had relieved him. Even after he saw Cochrane's orders and received Lord Melville's letter of the previous November relieving him of command, Warren remained at Bermuda issuing orders before he finally accepted that he was no longer in charge.[3]

Cochrane, with the command issue settled, wrote to Cockburn in April with orders that undoubtedly made Cockburn extremely happy. "You are at perfect liberty as soon as you can muster a sufficient force to act with the utmost Hostility against the shores of the United States," Cochrane wrote. "This is now the more necessary to draw off their attention from Canada, where I am told they are sending their entire military force. Their sea port towns laid in ashes and country wasted will be some sort of retaliation for their savage conduct in Canada. . . . [I]t is therefore but just, that retaliation shall be made near to the seat of their government, from whence those orders emanated."[4]

The pace of British operations picked up at the start of April 1814, when Cockburn began sending out parties in search of runaway slaves and supplies. Food was becoming a major problem as the number of African refugees increased at Fort Albion. At one point the entire squadron was down to barely a one-week supply of bread and beef. The arrival of a supply ship from Bermuda helped avert dissolution of the blockade and allowed Cockburn to resume his campaign against the inhabitants of both shores of the Chesapeake.[5] He ordered Barrie to take the 74-gun *Dragon*; the 7-gun schooner *St. Lawrence* (the former American privateer *Atlas*); and three tenders, the *Catch-Up-a-Little*, *Erie*, and *Utility*, up the Potomac to replenish the squadron's water supply while seeking out both American militia and runaway slaves. Cockburn was already finding the refugee slaves a problem because they consumed supplies, tied up troops to provide protection, and demanded transport to Halifax—not Bermuda—in keeping with Cochrane's proclamation. Cockburn's doubts about Cochrane's grand scheme to recruit an army of freed slaves grew.[6]

As the operational tempo began increasing, and more and more refugee blacks arrived on Tangier Island, Cockburn wrote to Cochrane:

> If you attach importance to forming a Corps of these blacks to act against their former masters, I think my dear sir your proclamation should not so distinctly hold out to them the option of being sent as free settlers to British Settlements, which they will most certainly all prefer to the danger and fatigue of joining us in arms; in the temptations I now hold out to them I shall therefore only mention generally our willingness and readiness to receive and protect them, and to put arms in their hands if they choose to use them in conjunction with us.[7]

By mid-May Cockburn had gathered 242 refugees, 151 of whom he sent to Bermuda. He kept 38 men who had enlisted in the Colonial Marines and made Royal Marine sergeant major William Hammond their drill instructor. By the end of the campaign, the Colonial Marines numbered 250 men. Under Hammond's training the escaped slaves evolved into one of Cockburn's most reliable units, although Cockburn had been quite skeptical when Hammond began training the first 38 recruits. "They are naturally neither very valorous nor very active," Cockburn wrote to Cochrane on April 29.[8] In another letter

Cockburn added that they "pretend to be very bold and very ready to join us in any expedition against their old masters," but he doubted their usefulness in combat.[9]

The Colonial Marines soon dispelled those doubts. In mid-May the force, now numbering eighty men, saw its first action. Their steadfastness and eagerness soon had Cockburn boasting that "they have induced me to alter the bad opinion I had of their whole Race and I now really believe these, we are training, will neither show want of zeal or courage when employed by us in attacking their old masters."[10]

The Colonial Marines provided a measure of loyalty Cockburn's British sailors and Royal Marines did not, because the black soldiers did not desert. The only disappointment the British had in the former slaves was their unwillingness to serve in army units in the West Indies. They were willing to fight in the local unit because it afforded them revenge against their former masters, while service in the West Indies appeared to them as exchanging one master for another.[11]

The desperation of the slaves to escape bondage was heart-rending. On May 2, two women gave birth while making their escape in canoes. Another woman who tried to escape with an infant handed the baby boy to British sailors while she went back to retrieve a possession she had left behind. The woman never returned, and the baby grew up on Royal Navy vessels. The *Albion*'s cook, who was black, cared for the boy while the flagship's captain, James Ross, looked after his welfare. The boy remained a ward of the Royal Navy until he died in an accident when he was eighteen.[12]

Cockburn picked up in April 1814 where he had left off in November 1813, once again terrorizing the inhabitants of the Chesapeake. He was well aware that the Admiralty had relieved Admiral Warren in part for his perceived soft touch with the detested Yankees. Cockburn was not about to make that mistake. His boat crews fanned out across the lower Chesapeake burning storehouses, seizing grain and livestock, and carrying off tobacco, which was sold for prize money.[13] On April 20, 1814, a party of seamen and Royal Marines chased a fleet of forty fishing boats trying to slip into the Potomac. Most of the vessels made it to safety, but the British managed to capture and burn seven of them. Five of the destroyed boats came from the little fishing port of Onancock, and their loss devastated the town.[14]

Ten days later, Capt. George Edward Watts of the brig *Jaseur* spotted a large American privateer hiding in the East River near St. Michaels. He ordered Lt. Henry West to cut out the ship with twenty-four sailors and marines. On the night of May 2, West and six men boarded the schooner and overpowered her captain and the seven men standing watch. The British fastened the hatches, trapping twenty more Americans below deck, then quietly slipped the schooner from her moorings and took her out, much to the elation of Captain

Watts. The schooner was the 228-ton *Grecian*, a veteran privateer owned by a friend of Joshua Barney. Watts said the schooner was "one of the fleetest and most beautiful schooners in America, coppered and copper-fastened, pierced for 20 guns." In addition to the twenty prisoners the *Grecian* was carrying a cargo of munitions and arms, which Watt confiscated.[15] The Royal Navy took the ship into service, also under the name *Grecian*.

The British activity on Tangier Island did not go unnoticed. The supply and recruiting parties quickly earned the attention of militias along the Virginia coast. The Americans harassed Cockburn's units as they searched for food and water—and in doing so played right into Cockburn's hands. The rear admiral used his watering and foraging parties to lure American militia into the open. If the local citizen-soldiers refused to show themselves, Cockburn developed an information network that could point them out. A boat from one of the warships would land a group of sailors and marines, who would seek out a friendly black man to act as a local guide and "facilitator." This man, aside from pointing out where to find provisions, would run from plantation to plantation spreading word of the British offer of freedom and leading any slaves willing to run to the British. The facilitators also acted as an informal intelligence network providing Cockburn and his officers with details on where the militia had their camps, their strength, and their movements.

It was through this loose intelligence network that Cockburn learned the 2nd Virginia Militia Regiment constituted the main resistance to his current operations. The American commander, Lt. Col. Thomas Bayley, had established four camps from which to operate and monitor the British, not knowing that each time his soldiers tried to ambush a recruiting or foraging party they gave the British more information on their location. By May 27 Lt. James Scott of the *Albion* believed he could pinpoint one camp located on Pungoteague Creek, some fifteen miles south of Tangier Island. The militiamen operating from that camp had already gained Cockburn's attention when they attempted to destroy the buoys the British placed to mark the shallows around Tangier Island. On May 28 Cockburn ordered Captain Ross to take 11 boats with 250 sailors and Royal Marines to teach the militia a lesson. Ross had problems finding the camp in the dark, and the noise his boats made alerted a second American detachment at Onancock Creek. When Ross finally found his bearings, he landed his men about a mile upstream from the Pungoteague camp.

The British expected to find a "six-gun battery" but instead found a lone 4-pounder field gun, which opened fire on the British as soon as they came into view. At the same time, thirty militia from the Onancock camp hustled to where the British had landed and opened fire with their muskets. The British replied with cannon and rocket fire from three of their boats and chased the militia from the field. Leading the pursuit were thirty Colonial Marines experiencing combat for the first time. As the unit approached the fieldpiece, the

American crew fired a devastating blast of canister that killed one Colonial Marine and wounded another. The British pillaged several farmhouses as they chased the militia, but after two hours, threatened by a growing number of militia reinforcements, they returned to their boats.[16]

The little skirmish was somewhat costly to Ross' force, which reported three dead and eleven wounded; the Americans reported just one man wounded. The British destroyed two barrack houses in addition to pillaging the local farms.[17] The Colonial Marines, in particular, showed great discipline, order, and bravery. The slain Colonial Marine was Michael Harding, who was at the forefront of the British charge and, according to newspaper accounts, was found on the field in full uniform with four dollars in his pocket.[18]

On May 30 Cockburn decided to undertake another "gallant little affair." He readied three boats from the *Albion* under Lieutenant Scott and was ready to send them in search of a militia camp when a seemingly minor incident occurred that set the pattern for military operations on the Chesapeake for the next three months. An informant told Cockburn that an American flotilla had left Baltimore with plans to join forces with warships from Washington and Norfolk, with the intent of capturing any small British vessels they encountered.

Cockburn at first discounted the information. He had heard stories about Joshua Barney and his "flying squadron" but had been unable to substantiate them. Something about the latest report, however, made Cockburn wonder if there was some truth to the news. He canceled the raid on the militia camp and sent the three boats of *Albion* sailors and marines and a group of Colonial Marines to reinforce Barrie, who was operating at the mouth of the Potomac. He ordered Barrie to take his task force and locate and either capture or destroy the American flotilla. Cockburn was about to find out not only that the report of Barney leaving Baltimore was true, but that the American flotilla was hunting for the British.[19]

Joshua Barney held a unique position. As a captain in the U.S. Flotilla Service he received the same pay and held the same authority as a captain in the U.S. Navy, but he and his command were outside the normal Navy chain of command. Barney reported directly to Secretary of the Navy Jones, and his command was separate from, but equal to, the Navy squadrons in Norfolk and Baltimore.[20] The flotilla was an amalgam of vessels. The flagship was the block sloop *Scorpion*, which, along with Barney's second-largest ship, the schooner *Asp*, had once been part of the Potomac Flotilla. The *Asp* needed overhaul and had yet to join Barney's force. Barney had two U.S. Navy gunboats, *No. 137* and *No. 138*, which he stripped of armament and used primarily as supply vessels. The flotilla also included the *Vigilant*, a 45-foot "barge" built in Baltimore. Barney acquired a small pilot boat that he named *Lookout Boat* for use as a messenger boat and twelve galleys, or "barges," built in Baltimore and St. Michaels.

Barney spent all winter recruiting for and fitting out his flotilla, with varying levels of success. Shipwrights turned out two types of barges—a 75-foot-long galley Barney dubbed a "first-rate" and the 50-foot-long "second-rates." Arming the barges, however, was more difficult than expected because shortages plagued Barney. "I have been severely disappointed in the delivery of the guns (light 18-pounders)," he wrote to Secretary Jones on April 4, 1813.[21] As for the heavier ordnance, Barney quickly realized that 24-pounder long guns and 42-pounder carronades were too heavy for his barges. He received a shipment of 18-pounder long guns and 32-pounder carronades, but those proved too heavy for the second-rate barges, and Barney eventually swapped the 18-pounders for 12-pounders.[22]

The commander of the Chesapeake Flotilla actually had more boats than he could man. With shipyards in Baltimore, Washington, and St. Michaels on the Eastern Shore churning out barges, Barney had twenty-six vessels in Baltimore by spring. He was able to man barely half of them. Competition for manpower remained intense. The Army and Navy were both recruiting in Baltimore. The Navy was building two new sloops of war, the *Ontario* and the *Erie*, and had plans to begin construction of a 44-gun frigate, the *Java*. The Army was looking to augment its strength by recruiting "Sea Fencibles," a home defense force for ports. The Army had recruited two companies in Baltimore who were to serve under Maj. George Armistead, commander at Fort McHenry. John Gill, commander of one of the two companies, approached Barney with the idea of transferring his 104-man unit to the flotilla. Barney liked the idea but told Gill to forward his request directly to Jones. The transfer died when Barney's political rival, Samuel Smith, exerted pressure on both Jones and Secretary of War Armstrong to keep the Fencibles out of the flotilla.[23]

Barney's efforts to recruit on the Eastern Shore also ran into political problems of a different sort. Local elections were due in October, and politicians from both parties were loath to see potential voters leave. Lt. Solomon Frazier, Barney's first lieutenant, was in charge of superintending the construction of barges and recruiting in the St. Michaels area, and he told Barney about the problems with enlisting men. Barney somewhat wryly told Frazier to "promise all Democrats" they would be home in time to vote that October.[24]

Not even the Navy Department, it seemed, could solve the recruiting problem, even when it ordered its own personnel to the flotilla. Jones told Capt. Robert Spence, superintendent of the sloop of war *Ontario*, to transfer all of his enlisted men to Barney. The *Ontario*, Jones said, was not going anywhere because of the blockade, and Barney had the greater need for sailors.

Spence sent 85 of his 105 sailors. Of those, 68 reported for duty so drunk that Barney put them in irons; the other 17 men were on the sick list.[25]

As Barney prepared to put to sea, his flotilla remained undermanned. In April he somewhat derisively wrote Jones, "If I had the Sea Fencibles, which are doing worse than nothing at the fort [McHenry], I could man five more barges."[26] On April 17 he set out on his first shakedown cruise with ten barges, each short at least ten men, on a course for Annapolis. He quickly learned the deficiencies of his galleys. The 50-foot barges did "not answer well, shipped [took on] much water and are dangerous in anything of a sea." Construction was faulty on at least three of the barges, which lost their rudders during the short transit down the bay, Barney added.[27]

On April 28 Barney received some good news. The Senate confirmed his special status as a captain in the U.S. Flotilla Service and conferred the rank of lieutenant on his two subcommanders, Frazier and Solomon Rutter. Because he commanded his own flotilla, Barney assumed the title of commodore.

Barney set out on a second cruise from Baltimore on April 29, and within days reported that his smaller galleys continued to suffer from construction and design defects. "I had to take everything out of the barges of the second class, even their shot (except fifteen rounds) and put it into the large boats," he wrote Jones. "In going down, and whilst laying off Point Lookout at anchor, I was very near losing them, as they took in great quantities of Water; to remedy which, I have concluded to have Wash-boards put round them about eight Inches high, which will keep out the water and of course make them more safe, I am Obliged to do this as the men are very unwilling to remain in them in their present state."[28]

The flotilla encountered fierce gales as it proceeded down the bay, and Barney put in for shelter at Drum Point at the mouth of the Patuxent River. He sent out scouts to investigate reports that the British were active on the Potomac. The scouts returned with word that the British were evacuating slaves. On May 3 Barney sent the *Vigilant* and the *Lookout Boat* to scout the Potomac. On learning the river was clear of British warships, he moved his entire flotilla there and anchored in the Potomac from May 8 to May 9. Once again the second-rate barges wallowed in heavy weather, even at anchor. Barney told Jones that had it not been for the weather, he would have "gone into Tangier Sound for a day or two," even with the faulty second-rate barges.[29]

Logistics were another of Barney's concerns. Gunboat *No. 137*, his supply vessel, was a disaster. The gunboat was a dreadfully poor sailor and, worse, could barely carry the provisions Barney needed. He reported to Jones,

> On examining the Bread put onboard the gunboat I found a great quantity has been wet by leaks in her deck, which Obliges me to take every thing out and to have her caulked, before she can serve again; indeed sir, she and *No. 138* are both such

miserable tools I do not know what to do with them, they cannot carry any thing more than their own armament, as 3500
lb. bread bags filled her, the salt provision on deck where their
men were obliged to sleep, and they sail so bad, that I am afraid
to trust them out of my sight ahead or astern.[30]

The flotilla returned to Baltimore on May 11, and Barney begged Jones
for permission to hire a schooner to act as a supply and hospital boat. Jones
denied the request, telling the commodore to make do with what he had and
suggesting he use the *Asp* as his supply ship. The *Asp*, however, was still at the
Washington Navy Yard undergoing refit and would never join the flotilla.[31]
The shakedown cruises *did* embolden Barney and cement his belief in the ability of his flotilla to elude the British. He slipped past the ship of the line *Dragon*
unseen off Kent Island on his first cruise, and on the second he boldly entered
and anchored in the Potomac, sailing unseen past multiple Royal Navy patrols.

Now back in Baltimore, Barney began planning for his next voyage, one
in which he was determined to bring his enemy to action. On May 29 he set
out with a force of eighteen ships. Among them were his flagship, the *Scorpion*, armed with one long 24-pounder cannon, one 18-pounder, and two
12-pounder carronades; the *Vigilant*, armed with a long 18-pounder cannon; the *Lookout Boat*, armed with an 18-pounder carronade; three first-rate
barges each armed with a long 24-pounder cannon and one 42-pounder carronade; four first-rate barges each armed with a long 18-pounder cannon and
a 32-pounder carronade; two second-rate barges each armed with one long
18-pounder cannon and a 24-pounder carronade; and four second-rate barges
each armed with one long 12-pounder cannon and one 24-pounder carronade; as well as gunboat *No. 138*, armed with a long 18-pound cannon and two
12-pound carronades, and gunboat *No. 137*, which was unarmed and carried
the flotilla's supplies. The flotilla arrived off the mouth of the Patuxent River
just as the British were preparing for their next operation.

Capt. George Watts of the frigate *Jaseur* must have been surprised when he
looked north off the quarterdeck of the brig on the morning of June 1, 1814,
and saw a forest of masts moving toward him. The *Jaseur* was anchored off
Kedges Strait, near Smith Island on the Eastern Shore. The force moving
toward her was the Chesapeake Flotilla.

Barney had reached the Patuxent River after a two-day transit from Baltimore. He set out at 3 a.m. on June 1 with the intention of attacking and
capturing one of the smaller British warships operating near the Royal Navy
anchorage on Tangier Island. A convoy of seven merchant ships intent on running the blockade sailed with the flotilla.

Operating alone, the *Jaseur* offered a tempting target. At 5 a.m., however, Barney's lookouts spotted the 7-gun schooner *St. Lawrence*. The schooner was operating near the mouth of the Potomac in support of the ships' boats and barges Admiral Cockburn had sent to reinforce Capt. Robert Barrie. Barney turned his sights from the *Jaseur* to the *St. Lawrence* and the boats he could see operating near the schooner.

Barrie had orders from Cockburn to "do any mischief on either side of the Potomac which you may find within your power" and had the authority to extend his operations as far upriver as Point Lookout or as far west as he pleased. He was "at full liberty to act as circumstance may point out to you as being most advisable for the service."[32] Barrie had set off at 8 p.m. on May 31 with three barges of sailors and marines from the *Albion* under Lt. George Urmston and four barges from the *Dragon* under Lt. George Pedlar. The British rowed through the night and at daybreak arrived off St. Jerome Creek, which flows into the Chesapeake just north of the Potomac. Barrie signaled the *St. Lawrence* to move into a covering position. Lt. David Boyd, commanding the former American privateer, moved toward the mouth of the creek with the tenders *Catch-Up-a-Little* and *Erie* trailing behind. Barrie ordered his boat crews to begin scouting the area, and around 9 a.m. on June 1 the British spotted the flotilla, although they still had no idea what it was.[33]

The Chesapeake Flotilla advanced toward the British arrayed in three divisions, each flying a broad red, white, or blue pennant. Barney commanded the red division, leaving his son, Maj. William Barney, in charge of the *Scorpion*. Lieutenant Frazier commanded the white division, and Lieutenant Rutter the blue. Using "sails and oars," as Barney put it, the Americans steered toward Barrie, smelling blood.[34]

Barney's aggressive approach put Barrie at an immediate disadvantage. Barrie believed that he was under attack from twenty-five vessels, not knowing that seven of the American vessels were unarmed merchant ships. He realized his force of seven barges was no match for the Americans bearing down on him and ordered a hasty retreat toward the *St. Lawrence*. He also played his trump card, signaling the *Dragon* to come to his assistance. The 74-gun ship of the line weighed anchor, but contrary winds at first prevented her from joining the brewing fight.[35]

The Chesapeake Flotilla bore down on the *St. Lawrence* on a wind from the north. Barney's force arrived off St. Jerome Creek at 1 p.m., and then the weather that had so favored the Americans shifted. The winds became light and variable before swinging around to the south, bringing with them one of the summer storms that mark that season on the Chesapeake. The wind shift allowed the *Dragon* to raise sail and head to Point Lookout, directly toward the flotilla, a move that caught Barney off guard. He ordered the flotilla, which was sailing south, to head north into the Patuxent ahead of the British behemoth because the Royal Navy force now had the Potomac blocked. The flotillamen, with the British in pursuit, rowed mightily for Cedar Point, which marks the southern mouth of the Patuxent River. The British attempted to slow the Americans by firing rockets at the flotilla's barges. The rockets had a longer range than the carronades several of the ships' boats carried but were much less accurate. The noise and smoke they made, however, alarmed the American sailors.[36]

The American boats reversed course and moved into the shelter of the Patuxent, all except gunboat *No. 137*, which labored against the wind and the heavy sea. The gunboat was crucial to Barney because she carried most of the flotilla's provisions, and as the British pursuers closed on her Barney ordered the *Scorpion* and gunboat *No. 138* to cover *No. 137* while the rest of the flotilla again turned about. Barney "sent men onboard *137* to row and tow her in, the tide and wind being against us." While the extra hands attempted to row *No. 137* away from Barrie, Barney reported, the *Scorpion* and *No. 138* "opened a fire on the large schooner [the *St. Lawrence*], who was leading in with a number of barges." The *St. Lawrence* bore off under the combined weight of the flotilla's guns, giving the American mariners the opportunity they needed to row *No. 137* to safety.[37]

After he saw Barney's force safely enter the Patuxent, Barrie tried to lure the flotilla back into open water by attacking the seven merchant ships that had followed Barney down the bay. "I endeavored to tempt him to separate his forces by directing Lt. Pedlar with the *Dragon*'s barge and cutter, to cut off a schooner under Cove Point."[38] Barney, however, refused to permit Barrie to goad him into combat, instead allowing the British to capture and burn one of the merchant boats.

Barney had eluded the British for a third time, although he failed in his objective to attack the Royal Navy anchorage. The British use of rocket barges caught him somewhat by surprise, even though Cockburn had used them throughout his 1813 campaign. Barney wrote to Jones, "I find they can be thrown further than we can our shot; and conclude from this essay, this will be their mode of warfare against the flotilla."[39]

The Chesapeake Flotilla anchored three miles up the Patuxent River while the *Dragon* and the *St. Lawrence* anchored at the mouth of the river along with most of the barges. Barrie sent several of the ships' cutters back to Cockburn for reinforcements. Barney expected the move, writing to Jones, "Some attempt may probably be made to attack us. . . . In a day or two I expect the enemy will make their arrangements." He asked Jones to send any troops in the area to help prevent a land attack on his anchorage.

After sealing off the mouth of the river, Barrie asked Cockburn to send the brig *Jaseur* and at least one frigate, which would allow him to "venture up the river, as our boats would be able to tow the frigate should it be necessary."

The additional force would tip the balance back in the Royal Navy's favor in any direct encounter with the Americans.[40]

Both sides began moving reinforcements to the area. Cockburn ordered Capt. Alexander Kerr to bring up the *Loire* from Lynnhaven Bay "with any other ships of war" anchored there,[41] while Maj. Alexander Stuart marched to St. Leonard Town in St. Mary's County, Maryland, with a three-hundred-man battalion of the 36th U.S. Infantry Regiment. Once they arrived, the troops would guard against the overland attack Barney expected. However, they would be of no use against the tactics Barrie and Cockburn decided to employ against the flotilla and the people living along the Patuxent River.

CHAPTER 13

Up a Creek

COMMODORE JOSHUA BARNEY probably felt safe on June 2 as his Chesapeake Flotilla lay at anchor three miles up the Patuxent River. In his report to Jones, Barney bemoaned his lack of a furnace to heat cannonballs for red-hot shot and again asked for permission to abandon the two Navy gunboats and hire a small sloop or schooner to act as a supply vessel. Despite his perceived handicaps, Barney confidently assured the Navy secretary, "I shall observe [the British] motions and act accordingly."[1]

In his response Jones expressed his approval of Barney's actions, commiserating with the commodore that he was unable to reach the Potomac and the safety of the Washington Navy Yard but expressing confidence in Barney's ability to evade the Royal Navy. The secretary even included plans for the future of the flotilla, telling the commodore, "When you return to Baltimore you may have a brick furnace constructed on board the *Asp* or either of the other vessels or in a good stout launch which might be kept for that special purpose." Jones gave Barney permission to hire a supply ship, albeit at a low price, and added that he could mount a new expedition against Cockburn "should an opportunity occur when the calm season commences, and you deem the object practicable."[2]

While Jones gloated in Washington, Capt. Robert Barrie was working on a plan to force Barney to leave his protected anchorage. "I fear it will be impossible to follow the flotilla up the river in the *Dragon*," he wrote to Cockburn. He needed more barges because "had we been anything like a match for the enemy, I am certain we should have given a good account of him."[3] Until those reinforcements arrived, Barrie decided to borrow a page from Cockburn's playbook. First, he attempted to woo the local population with offers of hard specie for provisions. On June 2 Barrie sent Lt. George Urmston to buy livestock at the plantation of Nicholas Sewall near Cedar Point. Urmston sailed under a flag of truce, but his small force met with a group of American militia officers who refused to allow the British to conduct business. One of the officers, Capt. James Jarboe, was particularly vocal in his condemnation of the British. He urged his fellow officers to seize Urmston and hang him. The British lieutenant,

132

who had only a couple of sailors with him, remained just offshore and out of reach. When the colonel in charge of the officers rebuked Jarboe, the captain continued to scowl and mutter nastily at Urmston, something the British officer did not forget to mention when he reported back to Barrie.

After that incident Barrie copied another of Cockburn's tactics. If the local Americans would not cooperate, he would take what he needed and destroy everything else. He sent Urmston back to Sewall's plantation that night, and this time the British came in force. The sailors and Royal Marines took all the livestock and burned the farm buildings. They also freed six slaves, one of whom offered to lead the British to the home of Captain Jarboe. Barrie and Urmston quickly accepted.

On June 4 a force of twenty Royal Marines, twenty Colonial Marines, and a handful of sailors under Urmston followed the former slave straight to Jarboe's home. As Urmston pounded on the front door, Jarboe sent a messenger running to Maj. Alexander Stuart, who had arrived at St. Leonard Town with three hundred men of the 36th U.S. Infantry. Urmston correctly deduced the reason for Jarboe's delaying tactics and kicked in the front door. He chased Jarboe into a bedroom and cornered the American at sword point. Despite the pleas of his wife of three days, Urmston led away Jarboe and his slave overseer, Josiah Smith. Barrie later released Smith, but Jarboe, "due to the peculiar circumstances" that prompted the raid on his home, went to England as a prisoner of war.[4]

Barrie's attempt to lure Barney into a fight by attacking the inhabitants failed; the commodore refused to take the bait. Instead, he watched as British reinforcements arrived off the mouth of the Patuxent on June 6. One of the new arrivals was the 38-gun frigate *Loire* under Capt. Thomas Brown. The Royal Navy had cut the captured French frigate down into a razee with a fully flush upper deck. The *Loire* could easily operate in the deep channel of the Patuxent. The schooner *St. Lawrence* and the brig *Jaseur* also moved into the river, all covered by the ship of the line *Dragon*.

Barney knew it was time to move upriver to a more defensible position. On the night of June 6 he brought the flotilla into St. Leonard Creek, where he anchored his barges in a line from bank to bank and waited for the British to react. The creek was too shallow for the larger British warships to pursue him, and he believed the position would allow him to engage any enemy barges on nearly equal terms.[5]

Barrie was surprised on the morning of June 7 to find that Barney had entered St. Leonard Creek. He ordered his barges and ships' boats to conduct soundings of the Patuxent and set out buoys, and he stationed the *Loire*, *St. Lawrence*, *Jaseur*, and the tender *Catch-Up-a-Little* at the mouth of the creek to block Barney's exit. Barrie also had help on the way. Cockburn, eager to corner Barney, promised Barrie, "You may depend on my sending everything to you as it arrives as the destruction of these fellows would be a point of great importance."[6] He stripped the *Albion* of every Royal Marine and sailor he could spare and sent six boats of reinforcements to Barrie.

Barney's decision to enter St. Leonard Creek was shrewd. Barrie described the position as "in few places more than a Musket shot wide, and in many not above two cables length. Its banks are covered with trees and the land is generally high." Bluffs lining the creek offered excellent fields of fire if land troops arrived to help Barney.[7] Barrie also found "it impossible to attack the Enemy in our Boats" because of the way Barney had positioned the flotilla.[8]

Barrie's first move was to send in a screening force of boats to sound the creek and "to annoy [Barney] from our boats and provoke him to chase them within gunshot of the frigate" *Loire*, which was waiting at the mouth of the creek.[9] For two days the British probed the Americans' defenses, but each time they retreated before a concentrated hail of shot. When Barney attempted to pursue the British, they adeptly used sails and oars to skirt back to the safety of the guns of the *Loire*.

The cat-and-mouse game continued for two days as each side looked for an opportunity to strike either a decisive or at least a crippling blow. Barrie gained an early advantage when he again deployed his rocket barges, a weapon Barney feared almost as much as the *Dragon*. On June 8 Barrie sent his rocket barges in ahead of his cannon-armed boats. A barrage of rockets screamed toward the American line, nearly all of them missing the mark. One rocket, however, sped toward barge *No. 4* and struck, killing one man and landing in the magazine, where it exploded and started a fire. The blaze spread rapidly, igniting a barrel of powder and another of musket cartridges. Both blew up, hurling sailors into the water and forcing the barge commander to order the rest of his crew to abandon ship.

Barney ordered another officer to board the barge to fight the fire before it destroyed the vessel. His son, Maj. William Barney, volunteered. He leapt on board the barge with several sailors and promptly began dousing the flames. The younger Barney was an accomplished mariner as well as a major in the 5th Maryland Cavalry, a Baltimore County militia unit. Although there were some who complained about the commodore appointing his son to command the *Scorpion*, the flotilla's flagship, the younger Barney put those doubts to rest as he fought the fire on barge *No. 4*. The major and his men frantically poured buckets of water and rocked the barge from side to side while flames lapped at the magazine. They succeeded in extinguishing the flames, and the commodore ordered the crew back onto the barge and sent her back into action.[10]

While his son was fighting the fire, the commodore was fighting the British. He ordered the flotilla to move forward and began blasting away at Barrie's force. Once more the British retreated to the safety of the guns of the *St. Lawrence*. Barney, satisfied with blunting the British attack, returned to his anchorage having suffered no damage other than to barge *No. 4* plus one man killed and three men wounded. Several of Barrie's boats had been hit, and the British suffered losses of three dead and two wounded.[11]

Barrie hauled off and spent the rest of June 9 realigning his forces, which included ships his own men had captured as well as some that Cockburn had sent to him. Among the vessels his raiding parties captured on June 7 was a small schooner. The British burned the cargo of lumber the schooner carried and took the little vessel into their service, arming her with a pair of 32-pounder carronades. Barrie also received the *Erie*, the tender to the *Dragon*. The *Erie* was a small, gaff-rigged topsail schooner armed with an 18-pounder carronade. He now had fifteen barges, the two small schooners, the *Jaseur*, the *St. Lawrence*, the *Loire*, and the *Dragon* to face Barney's force of a block sloop, two Navy gunboats (one unarmed), and thirteen barges. Thanks to a concerted effort, Barney's mariners had managed to repair the barge damaged on June 9 and put her back into action.[12]

Barrie kept his men at quarters throughout the night as June 9 turned into June 10, expecting either an American night attack or a dawn raid. Sometime after daybreak his lookouts spotted wagons moving onto the peninsula that jutted out into the Patuxent at the mouth of St. Leonard Creek and boats carrying men across the waterway. Barrie sent in several of his own boats to chase them, but without success. The wagons signaled reinforcements for Barney: Major Stuart and his battalion of Regulars as well as several companies of Maryland militia had arrived. The land forces gave Barney the cover he needed to execute his own attack plan. He set up a battery on a bluff on the eastern side of the creek and stationed infantry on the western side to defend against a British land attack. He anchored the flotilla in a single line across the creek in between the camps. Barney knew Barrie would again attempt to lure him out; this time the commodore planned to oblige.

Barney used the night of June 9–10 to prepare his flotilla for the coming action. He stripped the sails from his barges to make them easier to move by oar, hoping to use speed to surprise Barrie. He left the *Scorpion* and the two Navy gunboats in his anchorage because they were too clumsy for close-in fighting, while putting his own flag on the *Lookout Boat* and reorganizing his three divisions. The commodore took command of the red division at the center of the line, Rutter took the white division, and Frazier had the blue division. Major Barney served as his father's aide-de-camp on board the commodore's gig. All told, the flotilla numbered 450 men advancing against a force of close to 800.[13]

At 8 a.m., to the accompaniment of the *Dragon*'s band, Barrie began preparing his force of barges and small schooners. The martial music echoed across the still waters of St. Leonard Creek, alerting Barney that something was afoot in the British anchorage. It took Barrie the entire morning and part of the afternoon to assemble his assault force of twenty-one barges and ships' boats, a rocket barge, the *Erie*, the captured lumber schooner, and the *St. Lawrence*. The British shoved off at 2 p.m. with flags flying and the barges towing the two small schooners. The force anchored well out of cannon range around 4 p.m. and the Congreve rocket barge prepared to open fire. As the sailors rowed the barge into position, however, they saw what they least expected: the entire Chesapeake Flotilla was heading straight toward them.[14]

The minute Barney heard the music he ordered his boats to move down the creek. The waterway had several twists that hid his vessels from view as the flotillamen rowed toward the British. Almost the minute he was able to see Barrie's boats, Barney ordered the flotilla to open fire. Although outnumbered, the Americans had the advantage because their single line of warships was able to cover the entire creek. The British were deployed in three lines, giving Barney a tactical numerical advantage as he advanced toward the first line of boats. Barney's flotilla opened fire, using their 18- and 24-pounder long guns to outrange the carronades on Barrie's vessels. The two sides traded fire for several minutes as Barrie held his position while Barney continued to push toward him.

On board barge *No. 1*, Sailing Master Claudius Besse found himself at the center of a firestorm. Every British gun appeared to be aimed directly at his 50-foot boat. His oarsmen strained to keep the boat directed at the British line. In the bow, his gunners went through the constant evolutions of loading, firing, sponging, and reloading the long 18-pounder gun. Each time it fired, the recoil pushed the barge backward in the water, putting more strain on the oarsmen. The gunners sent round after round thundering at the British boats in front of them and received round after round in return. The British fire pounded Besse's barge, holing it below the waterline and causing it to begin to founder and sink. The strain of the fight took a toll not only on the crew but on Besse too, who "appeared so much deranged" that Barney relieved him of command.[15]

The closer the two sides came, the hotter the action became. The longer-ranged American guns began to smash into the British boats, driving the front line back on the second. The British responded with grape, canister, and rockets. Smoke filled St. Leonard Creek and, thanks to a westerly breeze, drifted toward the British boats. Barney's gunners began scoring hits at a range of about a half mile. A round shot smashed through one of the boats of the *Loire*, killing two Royal Marines and two sailors. Another shot sank a boat from the *Jaseur*, killing two seamen and wounding two. All told, the rocket barge bore the brunt of the American onslaught as grape and canister swept over the vessel, knocking her out of action.

The British force, once arrayed in three neat lines, was quickly becoming a jumbled mess. To Barney's eye, the British, "struck with sudden confusion, began to give way." The accuracy of that observation is debatable. Barrie all along had planned to use his barges and boats to lure Barney's flotilla into open water where the *Loire* and *Jaseur* could engage them. The volume of American fire certainly caused disorder, although Barrie made no mention of it in his report.

With the British barges pulling back, Barney pressed home his assault. The British boats became tangled up with the lumber schooner and the *Erie*, allowing the American flotilla to pound both. Barney's men raked the schooner, sending shots smashing through her stern. The *Erie* also took several shots, but Barney fixed his eyes on the *St. Lawrence*. The big schooner offered a tempting target, and Barney ordered his red division to engage her. The British could not maneuver well in the shallow water, and within minutes of being engaged the crew had put the *St. Lawrence* on a sandbar. The flotilla surged forward and opened a fierce barrage on the stranded vessel that dismounted her guns, pierced her port quarter at the waterline, fractured her foremast, tore up her deck and rigging, and temporarily drove the crew from the vessel. It also gave Barrie the chance to spring his trap.

On the *Loire* and the *Jaseur*, gun captains pulled lanyards, activating the flintlock firing mechanisms on the long 18s on the frigate and the 32-pounder carronades on the brig. Both ships disappeared behind a wall of smoke as they sent a hail of round shot toward the flotilla. At first most of the shots missed, and Barney, even as he closed on the British, continued to use the geography of the creek to his advantage. He positioned the flotilla in a cove where it could engage the *St. Lawrence* from behind a thirty-foot point near the mouth of the creek that shielded his barges from the heavy British ships. Barrie responded by sending officers aloft where they could see the mastheads of the American barges and direct fire. The gunners on the *Loire* and *Jaseur* quickly found the range and sent shot careening over the point and into the flotilla.

Barney again reacted quickly. He ordered his men to step the masts—drop them to the decks—to make his barges "disappear." The next threat, however, was one Barney could not fight. Barrie sent Capt. Thomas Carter and a party of Royal and Colonial Marines ashore and ordered them to scale the bluffs that shielded the flotilla. As the fire from the frigate and the brig reached a crescendo, Barney began to feel the strain and ordered his men to begin rowing back up the creek. Barrie saw what he said was "great disorder" among the American boats and ordered his boats to give chase, but after exchanging a few shots the British gave up their pursuit.

The British squadron fired more than seven hundred rounds at the American flotilla, yet caused, according to Barney, scant damage. Besse's barge was sunk, and the *Vigilant* took two shots through her hull. A 24-pounder gun on another barge burst during the height of the battle, but beyond that, Barney reported no damage and no casualties. In his report to Jones, the commodore claimed the British

> suffered much, the large schooner was nearly destroyed, hav-
> ing several shot through her at the water's edge, her deck torn
> up, gun dismounted, and main-mast nearly cut off about half
> way up, and rendered unserviceable; she was otherwise much
> cut up. The Commodore's boat was cut in two, a shot went
> through the rocket boat, one of the small schooners carrying
> two 32-pounders had a shot which raked her from aft, forward;
> the boats generally suffered, but I have not ascertained what
> loss they sustained in men.[16]

Barrie, in his report to Cockburn, reported only minimal casualties. He said the *St. Lawrence*, "notwithstanding the exposed position," took only four hits because "the enemy's guns were so ill-directed." He at first reported just three men killed and two wounded, although later he amended that to six dead and twelve wounded.[17]

The flotilla retreated to its anchorage near St. Leonard Town, where Barney found Maj. Alexander Stuart and his battalion of Regulars waiting. He directed Stuart to take up positions along the east bank of the creek while local militia occupied a position on the western side. His carpenters began working on barge *No. 1* and quickly restored her to action. He replaced the burst cannon with one from gunboat *No. 138* and also repaired the *Vigilant*.

His inability to smash the flotilla chagrined Barrie, but there was little the Royal Navy captain could do. Barney, now safe in his anchorage with infantry securing his flanks, was all but unassailable. As much as he wanted to grapple again with the American commodore, the battle on June 10, later dubbed the First Battle of St. Leonard, taught Barrie a healthy respect for both the Americans and their commander. Barney told Jones that after the battle the British "have remained in-active this way," and it was true. Barrie had no intention of attacking Barney head on. Instead, he began to look for an indirect way to strike at his foe.

American newspapers proclaimed the action a "resounding victory," and news of it quickly spread, reaching Norfolk within a few days. The news stirred arguably the most frustrated officer in the U.S. Navy to look for some way to help Barney.

Capt. Charles Gordon was still desperate for a chance to fight the British. When he had received command of the 36-gun frigate *Constellation*, he thought his moment was at hand. The British blockade, however, stymied his efforts to get the frigate to sea. Instead, he found himself bottled up in Norfolk, chafing to get at the British. When the news of the battle at St. Leonard Creek reached him on June 12, he saw an opportunity. "Finding that the Baltimore

Flotilla is certainly blockaded in the Patuxent, I have determined on attempting a diversion . . . to raise his blockade if possible," he wrote to Jones. Gordon envisioned an attack on the few ships Cockburn still had around Tangier Island, although he said he could not evict the British from their base because he was "not sufficiently strong to attempt a landing there."[18]

Gordon planned to use a small force of schooners, tenders, and ships' boats for his attack. The *Constellation*, the most powerful American warship in the Chesapeake theater, was not part of his plan because she had no crew. The enlistment period of most of his sailors had expired and the men had scattered. Gordon had sent those who remained to man the flotilla of gunboats and barges that made up the bulk of the sea force guarding Norfolk. Those men fell under Tarbell's command, and although Gordon had seniority and commanded all naval forces, his ongoing feud with Tarbell limited his ability to augment his planned attack.

Even more galling to Gordon was the fact that Cockburn had stripped the blockading force off Norfolk to a bare minimum. If Gordon could batter the ships around Tangier Island, he believed, then Cockburn would have no choice but to pull all the ships away from Norfolk to protect his base. Should that happen, Gordon believed he could slip out of Norfolk with the *Constellation*, provided he could recruit enough sailors to man the ship.[19]

Gordon set out on June 14 with 3 schooners, a tender, and 150 men loaded in ships' boats. He found the frigate *Acasta* waiting off Craney Island while the ship of the line *Albion* hovered nearby. Gordon knew the *Albion* had only a skeleton crew but was not sure what other vessels Capt. Thomas Kerr of the *Acasta* had around him. Gordon decided to lay up his flotilla off Craney Island and observe the British. He waited for more than a week, seeking an opportunity to use his boats and schooners to launch an attack. On June 20, however, the frigate *Narcissus* arrived and the window for attack closed. "Finding ultimately that the two frigates kept their position with their tenders close under their Guns every night, and the men in my Launches requiring rest, having slept [on] the boats and messed upon the beach for a week or 10 days," he wrote to Jones, "I returned to the squadron, regretting very much that the inactivity of my force together with its importance to the defense of this place deprives me the satisfaction of assisting Barney in any way at present."[20]

Gordon did not immediately give up on his plan for helping Barney by launching an attack from Norfolk, but by the end of June there was little he could do. He had twenty gunboats and barges but could man only ten because crews had reached the limit of their enlistments. He had already stripped the *Constellation* of her sailors and Marines to man the boats, but even that measure was wanting. He told Jones he simply could not compete for recruits with the Army, which offered a bounty to any man who enlisted, or to privateers, which offered the lure of prize money. "We are now discharging men so fast from the crew of the *Constellation*, as well as from the flotilla that I shall be reduced to the necessity of laying up several of the gun boats in a few days or at least to send them up to the yard so soon as the enemy may make any threatening movement, as I am only keeping them at present for appearances," Gordon wrote to Jones. Gordon implored Jones to allow him to set up recruiting stations elsewhere in Virginia as well as in North Carolina, South Carolina, and Georgia. He wanted to pay a ten-dollar bounty to entice recruits, but Jones refused. As Gordon's sailors drifted away, so too did his chance to get the *Constellation* to sea. Although he never stopped believing that he could run the blockade—"No exertions shall be wanting on our part," he told Jones—Gordon had to accept the fact that there was little he could do to help Barney.[21]

CHAPTER 14

Fire on the Patuxent

APT. SAMUEL MILLER marched out of the Marine Barracks at Eighth and I Streets in Washington, D.C., on June 12 bound for St. Leonard Town, the small port where the Chesapeake Flotilla lay at anchor. Miller was new to his rank but not new to the Marine Corps. Born on October 12, 1775, in Massachusetts, Miller had been appointed a second lieutenant in the Corps in 1809 at the somewhat advanced age of thirty-two. He reported for duty at the Marine Barracks in Washington, the first permanent post in the Marine Corps, and was appointed adjutant to the Commandant, Lt. Col. Franklin Wharton. He would hold that post, off and on, for nearly a decade. He was promoted to first lieutenant after just nine months in the Corps.[1]

Marine officers assigned to the Washington Barracks often found themselves detailed to service for the federal government in addition to their duties for the Corps. Company-grade officers served as couriers for diplomatic correspondence and carried bullion, and sometimes even took secret messages to and from senior government officials. Miller spent two years, from 1810 to the beginning of 1812, alternating between his duties as the Commandant's adjutant and as a diplomatic courier, including nine months in 1811 carrying secret dispatches to France. When the war broke out in June 1812 he was among the senior lieutenants in Washington.[2]

Miller spent the opening months of the war helping Wharton find enough Marines to serve on board ships, defend Navy yards, and man harbor fortifications. It was not easy. Although Congress authorized the enlargement of both the Regular Army and Navy early in January and again in June 1812, it failed to augment the Marine Corps, leaving Wharton the task of fulfilling ever increasing requests for Marines without having the authority to recruit beyond the Corps' legislated strength of just 483 enlisted men. It took Congress two years to increase the authorized strength to 2,652, although the Corps never really approached that number.[3]

On June 10—the same day Barney was battling Barrie—Jones sent Wharton orders to ready "such aid the Marine Corps at headquarters is capable of affording to march to the scene of action." Jones ordered Wharton to put

Miller in command of the company, which was to have "as many officers as necessary and as many Marines as can possibly be spared from duty at this post with all the field pieces that are mounted, together with every company necessary for the detachment to act efficiently as artillery or infantry."

To Miller, Jones sent explicit orders that his Marines were to "act under the immediate orders of this [Navy] department." He was to report directly to Commodore Barney "on the best means of protecting the flotilla and annoying the enemy." The last order would serve to exacerbate the rift between Barney and the Army.[4]

In those same orders Jones promoted Miller to captain, giving him command of the six lieutenants Wharton had managed to scrape up to help lead the Marine company. Finding Marines, however, was even more difficult than finding officers. The Marines in Washington occupied a somewhat unique position in the Corps—part ceremonial, part sentry, and part sea Marine. According to the official Marine Corps history, "The detachment performing military duty at Headquarters was particularly well-drilled and thoroughly acquainted with the various military ceremonies. It was paraded regularly and ceremoniously mounted guard daily."[5] All that time spent parading left little time for combat drill, and drill was crucial. The Marines acted as both artillery and infantry on land and sea, and their ability to switch seamlessly between the two duties set the Marines apart from their more specialized Army and Navy counterparts. Wharton and Miller assembled 125 enlisted men, 40 of whom were new recruits. Miller was so hard-pressed for men that he tapped into the Marine Corps Band, taking seven musicians to serve as infantrymen.[6] For artillery, Miller had two 12-pounder cannon mounted on carriages. On June 12 he set out for Barney's headquarters.[7]

Other reinforcements were also moving to aid the flotilla. Col. Henry Carberry, commander of the 36th U.S. Infantry, received orders to march his entire six-hundred-man 2nd Battalion to St. Leonard Town. Carberry's force was to replace Stuart's battalion of the same regiment because Stuart had orders to return to his position in St. Mary's County. Jones convinced Secretary of War Armstrong to release Maj. George Keyser and his 38th U.S. Infantry battalion of raw recruits from the defenses of Baltimore and send them to Barney's anchorage as well.

Finally there was the local militia. The Calvert County Regiment, officially the 31st Maryland militia, had mobilized, but Barney had a dim view of militia, and the Calvert County men did little to change that view. "Like most other troops of that class, they were to be seen everywhere but just where they were wanted," Barney said. "Whenever the enemy appeared, they disappeared and their commander was never able to bring them into action. . . . [T]hey rendered no assistance whatever to the flotilla, nor did they even attempt to defend their own houses and plantations from pillage and conflagration."[8]

Carberry's battalion was the first of the reinforcements to arrive at St. Leonard Town, marching into camp on June 14. The colonel chafed at finding himself under Barney's command and almost immediately began sniping at him. Carberry had neither forgotten nor forgiven Barney's attempt to entice recruits from the 36th Infantry into flotilla service, and he publicly condemned Barney for entering the creek and bottling up the flotilla. On June 16, without informing Barney, Carberry abruptly withdrew from his camp and moved his men several miles to the rear into the surrounding countryside, claiming they were "much fatigued and worried."[9]

The commodore, for his part, had little good to say about Carberry. "His conduct does not please me in more ways than one," Barney wrote to Jones. "He finds much fault publicly to the Inhabitants about my coming into this creek, he seems to have no disposition to give me real assistance."[10] Carberry's soldiers, Barney reported, were no better. "The fact is, there is no order or discipline in that corps. The Col. disaffected, the other officers without experience and in two parties, the men under no control, ranging through the country, committing depredations, on the persons and property of the Inhabitants, leaving their camp when they please."[11] He also pilloried Carberry for moving his men, reminding the Army officer that his own flotilla crews had remained at quarters every night while performing active duty every day.

In addition to releasing the two Regular Army battalions, Secretary of War Armstrong also offered the service of Col. Decius Wadsworth, Army Commissary General of Ordnance. Jones embraced Wadsworth's proposal to drive the British from the mouth of St. Leonard Creek "with a few pieces of cannon." Wadsworth volunteered to set up a battery of two 18-pounder field guns. Armstrong agreed, augmenting that force with three 4-pounder field guns and a detachment of gunners from the Army Corps of Artillery in Washington under the command of Lt. Thomas Harrison.[12]

Capt. Robert Barrie, angry and frustrated at his inability to defeat Barney, had decided to once more draw Barney into open water by attacking the local population. "I conceived by destroying some of the tobacco stores, the inhabitants would be induced to urge Commodore Barney to put out and defend their property," Barrie wrote to Cockburn.[13]

He began his campaign on June 11, sending Capt. Samuel Carter and 104 Royal Marines plus 30 Colonial Marines to raid tobacco plantations 4 miles up the creek. The British landed at the farm of James Pattison and moved inland. They carried off all the tobacco in Pattison's storehouses and then torched the entire plantation. Next Carter's force burned the plantation of John S. Skinner, the purser of Barney's flotilla. On June 12 Carter and his men went ashore across the Patuxent in St. Mary's County to purchase livestock, which a local farmer refused to sell them. A force of three hundred militiamen was in the area as well, something Barrie duly noted.[14]

Barrie decided to make an example of that plantation, and on June 13 he ordered Carter with 140 Royal Marines and 30 Colonial Marines to teach the owner a lesson. The plantation's overseer, John Platter, son of the sixth governor of Maryland, had castigated the British the previous day for their ruthless destruction of Pattison's and Skinner's plantations. Now the British were back, and this time there was no refusing their demand for livestock. The local militia "did not think it prudent to face this force but allowed the tobacco store and three houses which were most excellent military posts, to be burnt without opposition."[15]

The success of the raids spurred Barrie to intensify and spread his campaign of terror. He received a boost on June 12 when the 32-gun frigate *Narcissus* under Capt. John Richard Lumley arrived. Two days later Barrie accompanied his entire landing force up the Patuxent River to the town of Benedict, twelve miles north of St. Leonard Creek. The British found the town deserted. They quietly took possession of the place and found 360 hogsheads of tobacco awaiting shipment. Barrie left a small party to guard the tobacco, which the British loaded onto a captured schooner and their own boats. A company of militia had been stationed at the town, Barrie reported, but they "fled at our approach, leaving muskets, knapsacks and part of their camp equipage behind them." Barrie added, "They also left a six pounder which was spiked."[16]

The British spent June 15 in Benedict before moving out the following day. A raiding party of sixty Royal Marines crossed the river into Calvert County and descended on the plantation of Benjamin Mackall, a local militia officer. The marines burned the house, which had stood on the shore of the Patuxent at Hallowing Point since 1635, and then pushed farther upriver to the tobacco port of Lower Marlboro, where Barrie expected to find more tobacco and other valuables. For good measure, he wrote to Cockburn, "as Marlborough is near the Seat of Government, I thought an attack on the town would be a sad annoyance to the enemy and oblige the regulars and militia to try their strength with us."[17]

Barrie and his troops arrived in Lower Marlboro around 6 p.m. The inhabitants and militia fled on seeing the approaching British force, giving Barrie uncontested control of the town. Barrie let his men run wild, and they plundered with abandon. "They opened all the feather beds they could find, broke the doors and windows out and so tore the houses to pieces inside as to render them of very little value," reported an inhabitant.[18] Small detachments of British marines pushed into the countryside where they "stole with impunity from a widow lady, thirteen slaves and done considerable damage by the destruction of furniture, etc., at other places."[19]

British troops spread outward from Lower Marlboro, pillaging plantations and burning storehouses. "Tobacco, slaves, farm stock of all kinds and
household furniture, became the objects of their daily enterprises, and possession of them in large quantities was the reward of their honorable achievements," one account derisively described Barrie's raids. "What they could not
conveniently carry away, they destroyed by burning."[20]

The British left Lower Marlboro on June 17 and continued to burn their
way along the river. They destroyed two large tobacco warehouses at Magruder's Landing, a mile below and opposite the Prince George's County side of the
river from Lower Marlboro, as well as Coles Landing in St. Mary's County.
Only once did any of the raiders report seeing defenders, and even then the few
shots directed at the British failed to do anything except bring on a retaliatory
attack. Other than those few shots, the British enjoyed an uncontested trip
back to Benedict, where Barrie found the *Jaseur* waiting to escort the entire
force back to the area around St. Leonard Creek.[21] Upon arriving at his original station, Barrie received orders from Cockburn to take the *Dragon* north to
Halifax, Nova Scotia, for a long-overdue overhaul. He turned command of the
blockade over to Capt. Thomas Brown of the *Loire*, who continued to bottle up
the flotilla with his ship and the *Narcissus*.[22]

The British raids caused panic up and down the Patuxent. Residents on both
sides of the river fled, taking with them everything they could carry. Groups
appeared in St. Leonard Town asking Barney to do something about the British
depredations, but there was little the commodore could do. Each day, Barney
looked for the opportunity to strike the British. On June 16, while Barrie was
burning farms, Barney took a handful of barges downstream and ambushed
a British barge foraging for freshwater. Waiting until the last moment to open
fire, Barney's barges completely surprised the British. "She then discovered
us but our round shot was very near destroying her," Barney reported. "I saw
two oars cut off and was told, two men fell overboard, or jumped over. Several
bodies of dead men have floated onshore in the creek and river."[23]

Barney received more reinforcements that same day when Miller and his
company of Marines arrived, greatly fatigued from a tougher-than-expected
march. After leaving Washington on June 12, the company first marched
toward Queen Anne Town on the Patuxent River in Prince George's County,
but a massive rainstorm turned the roads into a quagmire. After stopping
overnight, the Marines spent the next day wading through water as roads
flooded along their route, covering fifteen miles before they finally halted at
a mill in Anne Arundel County, north of Barney's position. On June 14 the
Marines set out again, using double horse teams to pull their cannon and

wagons. Miller's force slogged for two days through twenty miles of ankle- and sometimes knee-deep mud, finally reaching St. Leonard on the afternoon of June 16. Miller allowed his men to rest while he reported to Barney.[24]

Afterward Miller examined the ground and decided to place his company and three 12-pounder field guns on a high hill to the east of the flotilla anchorage, and had his men erect a breastwork there for the cannon. First Lt. Benjamin Richardson said the arrival of the Marines and Miller's choice of position pleased Barney, who commented on the "very appropriate" placement of their three artillery pieces as well as the demeanor of the Marines, which was in stark contrast to that of Carberry's Regular Army contingent.[25]

The Marines remained in their position for a few days until Miller learned the British were sending in one or two boats to raid local farms at the mouth of the creek. He decided to attempt to ambush one of the raiding parties and selected eighty men and five officers to punish the British. Miller led his party on an overnight march to a point just east of the entrance to St. Leonard Creek. There the Marines waited, watching as the British ships in the Patuxent maintained the blockade. After several hours Miller saw at least one enemy landing party come ashore, but the British never ventured from their landing site. Miller waited most of the day before moving his men back to camp under the cover of darkness.[26]

The Marines' arrival, welcome as it was to the commodore, exacerbated an already difficult logistical situation for Barney. His purser, John Skinner, had to buy supplies from as far away as Baltimore and find a way to transport them to the anchorage. On June 20 Barney wrote to Jones, "I have been obliged to take the wagons of the Marine Corps to send for provisions to South River [thirty miles north of St. Leonard Town] where it seems Mr. Skinner has received some from Baltimore. I am under the necessity of furnishing the Marines with rations; we are much at a loss for some person to purchase articles and procure supplies, the wagons want money advanced to them, and horses to ride express, I am not provided with money for that purpose."[27]

Jones, however, had worries other than how to feed the flotilla. In the days following the June 10 battle the Navy secretary had been enthusiastic about the role the barges could play in the Chesapeake. On June 13 he wrote to Barney, "As no force that he can bring against you in Boats can endanger the flotilla, so long as the Banks of the Creek are protected by our Military, the position appears to me as favorable as any in which we may expect to attack him. I shall be mistaken if ultimately he is not made to suffer extremely for his temerity."[28] Within a week, however, Jones was concerned about the future of Barney's "flying squadron." Barrie's total control of the Patuxent and his ability to strike at will convinced Jones that Barney's position was precarious. "Should they continue the blockade of the flotilla, without any further attempt with their present force," he wrote Barney, "it will be with a design to await the arrival of an additional force from the coast, with which they may attack some other point, while you are locked up."

Jones' solution was mobility, of a sort. "I am satisfied that the whole of the barges may be transported [overland] from the head of St. Leonard's Creek to the [Chesapeake] Bay with great facility. I believe the distance is not more than four miles, and I am told the road is tolerably good and free from any serious impediment," he wrote to the commodore. Jones actually believed the sailors could strip the barges of all equipment and bolt wheels to the bottom of each vessel. "One of the large barges stripped of every moveable article will not weigh more than six tons—about the weight of a cable for a 44[-gun frigate]," he told Barney. "Two pair of dray wheels with a stout bolster and a chock to fit the bottom and raise it clear of the wheels would carry a Barge. There are plenty of oxen I am told, and in different places you have manual force to assist."[29]

The idea stunned Barney, who expected and continued to plan for a breakout from his anchorage. He never envisioned moving his entire squadron overland to escape from the Royal Navy, and he immediately saw numerous flaws in the idea. "There is nothing to prevent the enemy's ships from laying near the shore, so that we should not be able to launch, arm, and get away our barges after they are transported, for if we place artillery to cover us from the shipping, we cannot defend the blockade," the commodore wrote to Jones. "I am well convinced that in four hours after we begin to prepare for transportation, the enemy will be informed of our intentions, by the people of this district, who are all disaffected."[30] Despite his misgivings, Barney began trying to procure wheels, blocks, and animals. He had Maj. William Barney price the equipment necessary for hauling the barges from St. Leonard Creek to the Chesapeake.

Jones continued to badger the commodore about moving the flotilla, although he seemed to back off the immediacy of the idea. On June 18 he wrote Barney, "The plan of transporting the barges overland to the Bay, was not suggested without a view to the possible difficulties you have stated, but my local knowledge was not sufficiently distinct to determine the nature and degree of the obstacles. It is for you to determine the practicability of rearming and equipping the Barges on the Bay side in the face of the enemy. If his heavy ships can approach the beach within a point blank shot, I should deem it impracticable."[31]

As the days ticked by, Jones became more and more convinced that each passing hour sealed the fate of the flotilla, even hinting to Barney that scuttling the barges was preferable to the flotilla either remaining blockaded or, worse, being captured or destroyed by the British. "The enemy appears to attach great importance to the blockade of the flotilla, and their agent has been heard to say, that if you had double your force, the blockade would not be raised," he wrote Barney. "Should the enemy increase his force in the Bay, it may be necessary ultimately to secure your flotilla if practicable, and transfer your men to the barges at Baltimore and this place, and endeavor to raise the blockade outside."[32]

Barney refused to contemplate abandoning or destroying his barges. Using information he gleaned from six deserters from the *Narcissus*, he told Jones he believed he could in fact run the now-diminished blockade. He informed the Navy secretary that any attempt to haul the flotilla overland would mean the loss of four of his vessels—the two Navy gunboats, the *Lookout Boat*, and his flagship, the *Scorpion*.[33] The commodore also reported problems in assembling the necessary equipment, tools, and draft animals to move the barges. On June 20, finally convinced that the plan would not work, Jones gave Barney a drastic order: "These considerations have induced the determination to destroy effectually the whole of the flotilla under your command, after stripping them of every moveable article, which you will transport as soon and as conveniently as possible to Baltimore for the equipment of other barges."[34]

Barney protested as strongly as he could. "I acknowledge the justness of the reasoning, and the precaution in your orders, but I feel a depression of Spirits on the occasion, indescribable," the commodore wrote. "I must be cautious in mentioning to my officers and men the final result, they are in high spirits and anxious to meet the enemy, who we look on as defeated and beaten, I shall break the matter to them as we progress." Barney had one final argument to change Jones' mind. The British, he told Jones, were off on one of their raids with the *St. Lawrence*, *Erie*, *Jaseur*, and most of their ships' boats. That left just two frigates—the *Narcissus* and the *Loire*—near the mouth of the creek. If he could establish land batteries that could engage the frigates, the commodore believed he could break out.[35] Secretary of War Armstrong had sent just the man for the job—Col. Decius Wadsworth. If anyone could set up land batteries that could drive off the British, it was the Army commissary general of ordnance. The argument worked. On June 20 Jones sent a short note to Barney: "You will suspend the execution of my order."[36]

Barney immediately set to work restoring the cannon, masts, rudders, and other equipment on the barges while he waited for Wadsworth to arrive. The company of Washington Artillery, with three 12-pounder guns, had already marched into camp, but Wadsworth, with his heavier 18-pounder cannon and trains, was taking much longer. As Barney waited, the actions of the company of U.S. Marines continued to impress him.

From the moment he arrived, Miller consulted with Barney on his movements, campsite, and supply situation, even though he was under no obligation to do so. The Marine captain's willingness to confer and coordinate with Barney was a stark contrast to Carberry, who treated Barney as an antagonist. Miller was in something of an odd position. His orders, direct from Jones, said he was to report solely to the Navy Department, meaning the secretary.

As such, his command was completely independent of Barney, Carberry, and even Wadsworth. His somewhat ambiguous position pointed out the unusual position of the Marine Corps. At sea, the Marines fell under the command of the Navy. On land, however, it was unclear just where the Marines fit in. The Army wanted jurisdiction over the Marine Corps in land operations, but the Army was under the War Department while the Marines were part of the Navy Department, both cabinet-level departments. The question of which department the Marines reported to continued to be an issue and would cause problems later in the campaign.[37]

CHAPTER 15

The Battle of St. Leonard Creek

Col. Decius Wadsworth arrived at the anchorage of the Chesapeake Flotilla with orders to take command of all ground forces. He spent most of the day on June 24 scouting the ground near the mouth of St. Leonard Creek for the best position on which to place his guns and build a shot furnace. That night Wadsworth, Captain Miller, and Commodore Barney met to discuss strategy. All three agreed there was no possibility of making an attack on June 25. Wadsworth and Miller needed time to set up gun emplacements, and Barney wanted at least a day to ready his barges. The three commanders agreed to launch a breakout attempt on June 26. The meeting over, Wadsworth began to acquaint himself with the troops he would command. His opinion of the largest contingent of soldiers, the 2nd Battalion of the 36th U.S. Infantry, apparently was not much higher than Barney's opinion of its commander, Col. Henry Carberry.

Wadsworth and Carberry met on June 24 after the conference. The meeting between the two Army colonels was icy at best. Wadsworth barely acknowledged Carberry's presence when the battalion officers presented themselves at Wadsworth's headquarters. He peremptorily dismissed Carberry, giving him orders to return to his camp at the head of St. Leonard Creek to guard the ammunition and "utensils" stored there. This was Carberry's only face-to-face meeting with his commander. Wadsworth never consulted Carberry about troop movements or the plan to attack the British.[1]

Wadsworth and Barney met again on June 25 on board the *Scorpion* to discuss their final plan for the breakout attempt. Wadsworth did not have enough men to properly serve his 18-pounders and asked Barney if he could spare any of his flotillamen. The commodore promised to send Sailing Master John Geoghegan, whom he called one of his best officers, and twenty sailors.[2] Wadsworth wanted to ensure that he had control over the land aspect of the assault, so he asked the commodore to have Miller's company ready in the morning to support the Army troops. Barney's answer stunned him. He had no authority over Miller, Barney explained. The Marines were an independent command, and Wadsworth would have to work out any concerted effort with

Miller on his own. It was the first in a series of command breakdowns that would have serious implications as the attack unfolded. Wadsworth, in fact, had believed he was to command all of the infantry and Marines as well as the overall attack, and appeared miffed that it was to be a cooperative effort.[3]

Wadsworth returned to his headquarters, still determined to control the attack on the British blockaders. He spent much of the day developing a plan for the location and erection of his battery and shot furnace. Miller, meanwhile, set out from his camp overlooking the flotilla at 3 p.m. and began hauling his three guns to Petersons Point near the mouth of St. Leonard Creek, which he had selected as his battery site. Two hours later he ran into Wadsworth's aide, Capt. J. S. Marsteller, who told Miller the colonel wanted to borrow some Marines to help build a gun platform for the 18-pounders. Marsteller brought Miller to Wadsworth to work out the details. Miller agreed to provide fifteen Marines to protect the work parties as soon as Wadsworth asked for them.[4]

Sailing Master John Geoghegan and his flotillamen marched out of the anchorage about 5 p.m. to join Wadsworth. Shortly after 6 p.m. they encountered Marsteller, who told Geoghegan the colonel was down the road near a plantation house. The flotillamen hurried forward and arrived at Miller's camp around sunset. Wadsworth arrived soon afterward and, after detailing a sentry guard of ten men to watch the Marines' equipment, the force totaling 117 moved out in the darkness to set up their batteries. Wadsworth galloped ahead, scouting the ground while the marching men collected wood for the shot furnace. After finding a good location near Petersons Point for the furnace, the column halted at 11 p.m. at the spot Geoghegan thought best for the 18-pounders. He reported his position to Wadsworth and asked the artilleryman what he thought of the emplacement. Wadsworth sent Geoghegan a curt reply: "You are to command and fight them, place them where you please."[5]

While the ground forces mustered, Barney's barges silently moved out of their anchorage. The lack of masts and spars made the boats much lighter and easier to row, and the vessels quickly moved to a position about a mile from the mouth of the creek. The sailors muffled their oars with cloth to keep noise to a minimum, "that [they] might be near the enemy at the appointed hour next morning." Although the barges were lighter, the wet cloths made the oars heavier, and the sailors had to strain at their work. As they moved down the creek, Barney again divided his forces into red, white, and blue divisions under the same officers as on June 10. Once in position, the flotillamen settled down to grab some sleep before the coming battle.[6]

Barney might not have had his men exert themselves to remain quiet had he known that the British were not only aware of his reinforcements but also expected the breakout attempt. Newspapers had broadcast word of Wadsworth's movements almost as soon as he set out. Inhabitants of Calvert and St. Mary's Counties also provided the British with valuable intelligence.

What nobody could tell Capt. Thomas Brown, the commander of the two-ship blockading force off St. Leonard Creek, was when the Americans would strike. "Should the enemy possess a decent proportion of spirit and enterprise I imagine from the thick woods near the entrance of the creek, and on the opposite bank of the River, they might get guns that would oblige us to drop further out, and perhaps eventually out of the river," Brown wrote to Cockburn. "I learn also that at a place about five miles below, called Point Patience, they are beginning to erect batteries."[7]

To counter the Americans' breakout attempt Brown had the frigates *Loire* and *Narcissus*, several barges and ships' boats, and a rocket barge. He could land slightly more than one hundred Royal Marines and appealed to Cockburn for reinforcements, warning "all further attempts on Commodore Barney" would be "hopeless, without a considerable land force, as well as vessels calculated to carry long Guns, and not to draw more than eight feet water."[8]

Sailing Master Geoghegan and his twenty flotillamen began work on their gun emplacements slightly after midnight on June 26. A company of the 36th Infantry under Capt. Thomas Carberry (no relation to the colonel) stood by and watched as the mariners started digging. Several times Geoghegan asked the soldiers to help because they appeared to have an abundant supply of shovels, planks, pickaxes, and equipment for building shot furnaces. "I got seven spades and the same number of pick axes and commenced heaving up a breast work," Geoghegan reported. "My men continued digging without any assistance from the soldiers, although frequent application was made for help and for more shovels, but without effect." The flotillamen had been working for three hours when Wadsworth arrived with the cannon. The emplacement, Geoghegan said, "Was not so deep as intended . . . for want of assistance. The guns came soon after and the necessary preparations were made."[9]

Geoghegan had selected a position atop the hill from which he could sweep the creek and river. When Wadsworth walked the position, however, he disapproved of the spot. Apparently forgetting his earlier refusal to advise the sailor, Wadsworth told Geoghegan the site was "too much exposed to the enemy's fire." He ordered Geoghegan to move the guns several feet behind the emplacement he had already dug, where they would be on the reverse slope of the hill. Geoghegan protested, pointing out that the position Wadsworth selected was not only in soft sand but would make it impossible to engage the British with any accuracy. Wadsworth, however, was adamant and ordered Geoghegan to change the position. The sailing master quelled his misgivings and obeyed.[10]

The weary flotillamen once more started digging, and once more received little help from the Regulars stationed nearby. Barney's sailors could see similar frustration in the Marines, who were also hard at work and who were now somewhat exposed by the move of the 18-pounder emplacement. Some of the soldiers milling around near the Marines belonged to Maj. George Keyser's 2nd Battalion, 38th U.S. Infantry. Raw recruits made up most of the 260-man unit, and after a 30-mile forced march to get to the creek they were in no shape to do much of anything. They joined up with Captain Carberry's soldiers and took up a position on a flat field behind the batteries. To Keyser's horror, the plain was completely exposed to fire from the river. Lt. Thomas Harrison arrived with his three 12-pounder field guns from the District of Washington and began unlimbering next to Keyser's position, but the guns did little to allay the major's concern.[11]

Nor did Colonel Carberry do much to boost Keyser's confidence. Carberry sent Lt. Marcus Latimer to find Wadsworth and ask him to confirm the soldiers' position on the plain. But when Latimer found Wadsworth, the colonel was busy setting up the shot furnace and dismissed him with a wave of the hand, telling the young officer, "The 36th must take position behind that hill." Latimer had no idea which hill Wadsworth meant, and when he reported back to Carberry, the colonel decided to move his men away from the battery and into a small ravine near the river where a thick copse of woods would conceal them from the British. Keyser asked Carberry where he should put his men. He pointed out the Marines' position and asked for permission to move to that spot. Carberry agreed. By then it was 3 a.m., and Latimer again went in search of Wadsworth, who ordered Carberry to move to a position astride the road that led to the battery. This position, too, was wide open to possible enemy fire, and Carberry decided, on his own, to move to the original proposed battery site, where the slope would protect his soldiers.[12]

Capt. Samuel Miller and his Marines were the last to arrive on the battlefield. Miller and his men broke camp at 1 a.m. and began marching toward Petersons Point but ran smack into Keyser and the 38th, which was moving very slowly down the only road that led toward the battlefield. Miller decided to ride ahead to his chosen position, leaving Capt. Alfred Grayson, his quartermaster, to lead the Marines. The column, numbering ninety-four officers and men, included the fifteen men Miller had agreed to loan Wadsworth for guard duty.[13]

The slow-moving infantry prevented the Marines from reaching the battery site as quickly as Miller wanted. When Carberry decided to shift his position, the move brought the Marines to a complete halt. At 3:30 a.m. they finally reached the battery site, where Miller, who had scouted the position in daylight, pointed to the spot where he wanted to emplace his guns.[14]

By then, Wadsworth was incensed with Miller and his men. The colonel had expected the Marines to arrive much earlier and had never received the fifteen guards he had asked for—although he never sent orders for them to report to him. Wadsworth wanted Miller to set up his guns in a position to cover the 18-pounders because he did not believe the two battalions of Regulars, in

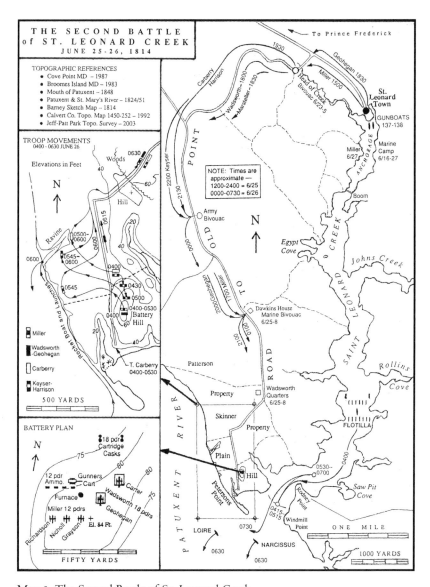

Map 3. The Second Battle of St. Leonard Creek

This map, taken from an original drawing by Stanley Quick, names St. Leonard Creek without the possessive. During the War of 1812 the creek was always called St. Leonard's Creek, and that spelling was used until the U.S. Geological Survey decided to drop possessives from topographical maps. Most state highway maps followed suit, and today most maps spell the name St. Leonard Creek although historians use both versions. The map also uses an alternative spelling of the names of Sailing Master John Geoghegan and Lt. William Nicoll (perhaps confused with Maj. Edward Nicolls of the Royal Marines).

whom he admitted to having no confidence, would hold their ground if the British landed troops. Because Miller had an independent command, however, Wadsworth had no authority to give him orders. Miller, knowing that Secretary Jones expected his Marines to aid the flotilla, ignored Wadsworth's "suggestion" and decided to place his cannon next to Geoghegan's position.

Miller set his men to work, racing to place the guns before dawn. He had Grayson set up his cannon immediately adjacent to Geoghegan but slightly forward, on the top of the hill. Lt. Benjamin Richardson and Lt. William Nicoll placed their guns to the right of Grayson, spaced about eight yards apart. Thanks to an almost herculean effort, the Marine battery was ready in the space of half an hour.[15]

On board the *Loire* the watch was striking the bell to mark 4 a.m. Belowdecks, sailors, Royal Marines, and officers were still asleep, resting up for what they thought would be another long, tedious day on blockade duty. The situation was the same on the *Narcissus*, which swung easily at anchor at the confluence of St. Leonard Creek and the Patuxent River, about one hundred yards from the *Loire*. The light of a waning moon sparkled off the river and silhouetted the two British ships against the background.

On Petersons Point, Sailing Master Geoghegan sighted his big 18-pounder cannon. The two British frigates were perfect targets as they lay some six hundred yards away. Satisfied, Geoghegan prepared to fire his first salvo. He touched his portfire—a paper tube filled with powder that smoldered for thirty minutes—to the vent hole on his gun. It was slightly after 4 a.m.[16]

On board the *Narcissus*, the cannon blast from the American battery atop Petersons Point came as a complete surprise. The sleeping sailors stumbled to their stations, reacting more by instinct than any awareness of what exactly was happening. The log of the frigate noted, "At 4:10 a.m. battery on top of a hill opened fire on us."[17]

Geoghegan fired the first round, and the 18-pounder under Master's Mate William Carter fired the second. Then the Marines opened fire. Each American gun fired in sequence rather than in unison as the gunners adjusted their fire. There were also safety concerns. If the gunners, who were trained to fire up to three rounds per minute, fired too quickly, the vent in which the gun commander inserted the firing tube could become too hot, prematurely igniting the primer and cooking off the round, which could kill or injure the crew. The flotillamen fired methodically, sending one round per minute per cannon at the British warships.

The crewmen of the *Loire* and the *Narcissus* were now fully awake and scrambling to bring their ships into position to reply to the fire coming from the point. Both ships had anchored and set spring lines that kept their guns aiming up the creek in expectation of Barney attacking. The fire from the hill forced them to haul in the springs, reset the lines, and shift the frigates by hand so they could engage the hidden batteries. It took the British more than fifteen minutes to open fire, and even then they could not see their enemy. Instead, Brown instructed his gunners to "fire where the smoke issued from."

The Marine gunners, manning lighter cannon than the flotillamen, quickly found their rhythm and began pumping round shot at the British. Miller proudly reported that his men fired four shots for every one that came from Geoghegan's battery. Nevertheless, Miller could see that the batteries had yet to score any hits. The heavier guns, Barney bitterly recalled, "being placed on a declivity, must either fire directly into the hill, or be elevated so high in the air, after the matter of bombs [mortars], they were rendered useless. At the very first, the guns recoiled halfway down the hill and in this situation they continued to fire in the air at random."[18]

Despite the ineffective fire of Geoghegan's battery, Wadsworth refused to admit that his placement of the guns was faulty. Each time the flotillamen fired, the heavy 18-pounders rolled downhill from the recoil and Geoghegan's weary men had to haul them back into place. Wadsworth defended his place-ment of the guns, saying, "In every respect it answered admirably. The enemy found it impossible to hit us; every shot either fell short and struck the bank or flew clear over us."[19]

On the *Loire*, Captain Brown watched as his shots slammed into the hill-side, causing no damage to the American battery. When he elevated his guns, his shots sailed over the hill. He ordered his gunners to use the ship's car-ronades with a reduced powder charge and watched with satisfaction as his rounds began landing on top of the hill. The gunners on the *Narcissus* quickly followed suit.[20]

Wanting an unobstructed view of where his gunners' rounds were land-ing, Captain Miller rode down to the river's edge, ordering several men to trail him. From this vantage point he could see that his shots were falling short while those of the 18-pounders were overshooting. He sent word to Geoghe-gan about the heavy guns and ordered his own gunners to elevate their cannon slightly. The file of Marines relayed Miller's directions to Grayson, Richardson, and Nicoll, who quickly found the mark. One shot from the Marine battery carried away the mizzen topgallant mast of the *Loire* while others smashed into the frigate's hull. As the Marine gunners bored in on the British ship, they scored more hits, crushing the *Loire*'s bridle ports and forward chain plates.[21]

Meanwhile, Wadsworth ordered Geoghegan and Carter to concentrate their fire on the *Narcissus*. Because the Marines maintained a faster rate of fire than the flotillamen, smoke soon obscured Wadsworth's line of sight and he was unable to adjust his fire. He obstinately refused to ask Miller for help; nor did he copy Miller's example of posting a line of messengers to relay information. Wadsworth also had the handicap of working with crews who had never handled hot shot. Early in the engagement, a round cooked off in Carter's gun, injuring Carter and severely wounding Seaman William "Billy" Monday. Carter was able to remain in action, but Monday lost both of his arms below the elbow. The flotillamen applied tourniquets and laid him down out of harm's way.[22]

As American shot whistled around his vessel, Capt. Thomas Brown on the *Loire* ordered his men to form a landing party. He filled his ships' boats with marines and sent them upriver along with the rocket barge to flank the Americans' position. Two barges carrying the Royal Marines also carried 18-pounder carronades, which opened fire as the sailors rowed them around the point.

Joshua Barney stood on the deck of his barge roughly a mile from the mouth of St. Leonard Creek. He was running late. Barney and Wadsworth had set the time for the attack at 4 a.m., but Wadsworth had sent him a note late in the night saying he did not think his guns would be ready at the agreed-upon time. The opening salvo of Wadsworth's cannon was supposed to signal the attack, so Barney was surprised when Geoghegan fired his first round at 4:10 a.m. His flotilla took another forty-five minutes to get into position to attack.[23]

The flotilla moved quietly toward the mouth of the creek. The knowledge they would soon engage their enemy seemed to propel the men on the oars, and "the barges now seemed to fly under the rapid strokes." Just before 5 a.m. Barney signaled his barges to open fire. Although the delay cost the Americans the ability to coordinate their attacks, the opening salvos from the flotilla completely surprised the British. The fire from the barges was dead on target, with seven rounds piercing the hull of the *Loire*. The flotilla advanced to within four hundred yards of the two enemy frigates, the guns continuing to pour shot after shot into the warships. The closer the Americans advanced, however, the more exposed the barges were to deadly grape and canister fire from the British frigates. As they rowed down the creek, the Americans lost their formation when the waterway narrowed to a point at which only eight barges could advance abreast.[24]

The sudden appearance of the Chesapeake Flotilla caught Brown completely off guard. Once more, sailors hauled on lines to swing the frigates so gunners could direct broadsides at the new threat. The British ceased firing on the land batteries and reloaded with grape and canister. The moment they could train their cannon on the approaching barges, they opened fire, unleashing a hail of lead that struck boats and water, churning the creek into a froth.[25]

The strength of the British fire stunned Barney. "They poured it into us, seeming to have just waked," he said. "It was a scene to appall the inexperienced and the faint hearted; but there were few of these among the daring spirits of the flotilla." The lack of bulwarks on the barges exposed the flotillamen to the brunt of the enemy fire, and the losses mounted with each successive broadside.[26]

Miller and Geoghegan maintained their bombardment when the flotilla joined the engagement, but the fire soon slackened because the Marines had used up their supply of round shot. Geoghegan's men began to use hot shot, trying to set the two frigates on fire. Once more, faulty aim cost the Americans as their rounds whistled harmlessly past the *Loire* and the *Narcissus*. As Carter, who remained at his gun despite his wounds, fired a shot, a chance 32-pounder carronade shot smashed into the American ball, sending red-hot shrapnel flying. One piece set an ammunition box on fire, which sent splinters scattering everywhere. Geoghegan went down with a knee wound but stayed with his gunners.[27]

As his men used the last of their solid shot, Miller spotted the rocket barge and two barges full of Royal Marines in the river and decided to move his guns to a position where he could engage the new threat. He consulted briefly with Geoghegan and for the first time saw the effect of the fire from the British barges and frigates on the infantry massed behind the hill. Nearly every shot that arced over the hill hit the area in which the men of the 36th and 38th Regiments stood. Miller also saw that the three 12-pounders from the Washington Artillery under Lieutenant Harrison were "injudiciously permitted to remain in a distant part of the field, without orders for firing a single shot, or instructions to be placed in a battery to resist an attack from the barges."[28]

Miller decided his best course of action was to limber his guns and move to the plain so he could engage the British barges, telling Geoghegan that he only had grape and canister rounds remaining in his ammunition chests and there was nothing more he could do to engage the frigates. Miller ordered his horses forward and began to limber his guns.[29] Unknown to Miller, however, the plan for the land force to coordinate its action with the flotilla had already unraveled.

Commodore Barney noticed the slackening in fire from the hill as his barges continued to blast away at the *Loire* and the *Narcissus*. He was "surprised and mortified to observe that not a single shot from the battery fell with assisting effect, and that the whole fire of the enemy was directed against his boats: shortly afterwards the battery, from which so much had been expected, became silent altogether." Barney was certain the storm of British grape and canister had cut his force apart and expected to learn that his flotilla had suffered more than a hundred casualties. He ordered his barges to pull back, for "it would have been an act of madness in such a force, unassisted, to contend against two frigates, a brig, two schooners, and a number of barges, in themselves equal to the force that could be brought into action from the flotilla." As his men rowed to a position roughly three quarters of a mile from the mouth of the creek, Barney received the pleasant news that his force had lost just six men dead and four wounded. Among the dead was a young midshipman, George Asquith, who had just joined the flotilla.[30]

As the Marines began moving from the hill to the plain to thwart a British landing, Miller realized his intended position was dangerously exposed to fire from both the British landing barges and the frigates. "I was compelled once more to seek a position sanctioned by military propriety," Miller reported. "One presented itself to my rear, near the defile which entered upon the road."[31]

Colonel Carberry's battalion of the 36th Infantry was almost completely exhausted. The foot soldiers had moved three times since midnight, and their position behind Geoghegan's battery had exposed them to overshots from the frigates. Although the shots caused no casualties, Carberry's officers deluged him with requests to move. As the British guns found the range and more shots careened toward their position, Carberry's battalion was "more exposed to severe cannonading than I ever saw troops [endure] in my life before." He ordered his men back to the ravine they originally occupied, the same ravine in which Miller wanted to place his guns.[32]

The 260 men of Maj. George Keyser's 38th Infantry also suffered under the British fire. Keyser finally received the opportunity to do something when Wadsworth, who was shuttling from position to position, ordered him to move his battalion closer to the river to meet any British landing. Keyser complied. Why Wadsworth gave Keyser the order instead of Carberry, who was senior in rank and had a larger force, is unknown. Wadsworth, however, completely ignored Carberry, who had already decided to act on his own and shift his men from their "exposed" position.[33]

Wadsworth was oblivious to the Carberry's predicament or his subsequent movements. So was Miller, who found to his surprise that Keyser's men were gathered at a gate in a fence and unable to deploy while Carberry's men were apparently in retreat. Miller had no idea what was happening. Carberry claimed the Marines precipitated his retreat when they began marching toward the river to repel a British landing. Carberry's men had already started to leave the field before the Marines shifted position.[34]

The British barges maintained their fire, sending rockets, grape, and canister toward any cluster of troops they could see. One of those clusters was the column of Marines making their way toward the river. The British gunners raked the Marines, killing at least one and wounding several others. It was one of the last acts of the flanking party. Slightly before 6 a.m. the three British boats received orders to withdraw, most likely to help counter the flotilla's attack.[35]

Commodore Barney had no idea what was happening on land. He knew fire from the battery had stopped and the British were giving his barges their full attention. As he withdrew, using a bend in the creek to cover his boats, he conferred with his commanders. Sailing Masters Henry Worthington, James Sellers, and John Kiddall all reported heavy but reparable damage to their barges. Barney was momentarily unsure of what to do. Smoke still obscured the creek. He expected Brown to attack with his force of barges and ships' boats, and decided to ready a defense for when the British came.[36]

The sailors on the *Loire* had more than the flotilla on their minds. The combined American attack, especially of the flotilla, had hit the frigate hard. American fire pierced the *Loire*'s hull at least fifteen times; other rounds peeled away some of her copper sheathing; and other shots smashed her whaleboat, gig, and yawl. The crew was "hard at work pumping, in plugging the shot holes to keep her from sinking and painting them over as fast as plugged." The story was similar on the *Narcissus*, which had also suffered from the American fire and was "very much cut up below the bends."[37] The *Narcissus*' crew was kept busy pumping the ship out to keep her afloat. After assessing the situation, Brown decided he had just one course of action. "The ships having been frequently hulled, and part of the rigging shot away, I thought it most prudent to weigh and drop down the river."[38] Slowly, the two British warships began to withdraw.

It was now fully daylight, and Wadsworth and Miller could see the confusion all around them. Carberry's men, whether prompted by the Marines' imaginary retreat, British fire, or both, were now marching away from the field, taking with them Keyser's battalion. "Every description of troops were leaving the field and the battery was abandoned," Capt. Alfred Grayson later testified. Miller returned to Geoghegan's battery, where he found Wadsworth and just sixteen men. Carter's gun had rolled all the way down the hill from the recoil of one shot, leaving only one 18-pounder left to fire. Wadsworth, seeing what looked like the beginnings of a rout, wanted to withdraw his guns, but he could not find his horse teams and decided to spike them instead.[39]

Several of Geoghegan's flotillamen now joined in the retreat and ran into the withdrawing infantry. They found the horse teams for the heavy guns and returned with the limbers for their cannon. Wadsworth had already left. He rode ahead of his gunners to stop the retreating Regulars and managed to halt at least some of Keyser's men to form a rearguard, and then was able to stop the entire column in some woods. There he ran into Miller, who had gone in search of the colonel. "I have saved my guns but you have lost yours," Miller yelled at Wadsworth, who bristled. Miller spun his horse and organized sixty Marines to return to the hill to help save the 18-pounders.[40]

Sailing Master Carter, suffering from multiple wounds, was among the last men to leave the battery site. As he painfully made his way down the hill, Carter ran into Miller and told him Seaman Billy Monday lay wounded in the bushes near the cannon. Miller ordered several Marines to collect Monday and bring him to the Marines' surgeon, who was set up at Miller's headquarters, and then took his men on to the battery to limber the 18-pounders.[41]

Carter continued on his way down the hill and met Midn. T. P. Andrews, Barney's aide-de-camp, who had volunteered to go ashore from the *Scorpion* to assist in repelling any British attack. Carter asked Andrews to help him return to the flotilla, which was still in the creek. Seeing the British were not planning to land, Andrew took Carter by the arm, and together they returned to the flotilla and boarded Barney's barge. Only then did Barney learn of the breakdown in command and the confusion among the land forces.[42]

Capt. Thomas Carberry's company of the 36th Infantry spent most of the battle in the woods on Petersons Point. The young officer was able to hear the battle but could not see what was happening. When the battery stopped firing, he decided to move his company to the field. As he ascended "Battery Hill," Captain Carberry found the position deserted except for Seaman Monday. Carberry commandeered a cart and put Monday on it and, with his infantry, limbered the artillery and carried the guns from the field. He caught up with Miller and Wadsworth just as the Marines were about to march to the battery site. Wadsworth cried out ecstatically, "I make you a colonel on the spot!" but never mentioned Captain Carberry in his official report.[43]

Barney was digesting the news of the confusion among the land forces when he heard a lookout say he thought the British were retreating. The commodore watched as the British pulled away from the creek and Petersons Point, and he also noticed the list of the *Loire*. The wind, which had allowed the British to maneuver the ships, suddenly died. The only way to move now was by oar, and Barney seized his chance. He ordered the entire flotilla—except for the two useless gunboats—including the *Scorpion*, the *Lookout Boat*, and the *Vigilant*, to move forward. The mariners pulled at their oars as hard and as fast as they could, and the flotilla quickly exited the creek and rounded Petersons Point, heading up the Patuxent. Barney had finally broken out.[44]

Capt. Thomas Brown of the Royal Navy could only watch in mounting frustration as the American flotilla, oars frothing the water around each boat, pulled away from his two frigates. He had the "mortification to observe them rowing down the creek, and up the river," knowing he had failed in his mission to either keep the Chesapeake Flotilla bottled up or destroy it.[45]

Triumph reigned on board the boats of the Chesapeake Flotilla. No one was happier than Barney, who once again had outthought and outfought his old adversary, the Royal Navy. "We have again beat them and their rockets, which they did not spare," Barney wrote to his brother Louis. "You see we improve. First, we beat a few boats which they thought would make an easy prey of us, then they increased the number, then they added schooners, and now behold the [two] frigates, all, all, have shared the same fate, I next expect, ships of the line; no matter we will do our duty."[46]

Six of Barney's men were killed in the battle, including Midshipman Asquith, and four were wounded, including Monday, who survived the loss of both of his arms. Brown reported just one man wounded on the *Narcissus*.[47]

CHAPTER 16

Retribution and Recrimination

OMMODORE BARNEY led the flotilla eleven miles upriver to Notting-ham, one of the few towns Barrie had not ravaged during his efforts to draw the Americans out of St. Leonard Creek. The commodore viewed the action as a victory. He had escaped the British blockade of the creek, inflicted severe damage on two enemy warships, and, at least for the time being, was able to operate on the upper tidal portion of the Patuxent. Others were not so sure about his victory. The press immediately criticized the manner in which Wadsworth and Barney had coordinated their attacks. Miller, Colonel Carberry, and Wadsworth engaged in a nasty and very public argument over who was to blame for the sudden retreat and near rout of the Army infantry as well as just how much damage each battery had inflicted on the British. By July 10 Secretary Jones had had enough of reading the various charges the officers hurled at another or planted in the *National Intelligencer*.[1] He ordered a hearing to examine Miller's role in the battle that dragged on into August before fully exonerating the Marines.[2]

Barney also received some criticism because he and his flotilla were not as free as he first reported. The British controlled the mouth of the Patuxent River, and while Barney could certainly move upriver, he had little chance of getting into the bay, especially after the long-awaited British reinforcements began to arrive from Bermuda. Jones ordered Barney to report to Washington, and the two hashed out the future of the flotilla. Should the British move on Washington via the Patuxent, Barney would be in a position to fight them. If the British went up the Potomac, however, they could keep the flotilla bottled up in the Patuxent and still go where they pleased. The two came to an agreement. Barney would remain at Nottingham and send his second in command, Lt. Solomon Rutter, to take command of the flotilla at Baltimore. If the British moved on Baltimore, Barney and his men would march there. If Washington were the target, Rutter would lead the Baltimore flotillamen to Barney's aid.[3]

Barney's move upriver was also less than popular with the inhabitants of Calvert County, most of whom blamed him for the British raids that left their homes, plantations, and farms in ruins. The local militia refused to turn out,

which Barney viewed as a blessing in disguise because he placed no faith in
them. The locals hated Barney for bringing the war to their doorstep, and their
anger knew no bounds. "It has enraged them so that a great many that were in
favor of him are now abusing him every day," wrote one Calvert County resident. "I think when I tell the mischief the British have done it will be enough
to make you and every man abuse Jim Madison and old Barney in Hell if you
could."[4] Barney could thus expect no real help from the people he was trying to defend, and the antiwar sentiment in southern Maryland was about to
increase because the British were ready to unleash a new campaign of terror.

The escape of the flotilla infuriated the British, who took out their anger on
St. Leonard Town. On July 3 a party of Royal Marines went ashore and completely leveled the town, burning every building except the home of the town
doctor. Although it had no impact on the American flotilla, the action signaled the start of Cockburn's burning season.

The admiral was eager to wreak havoc on Tidewater Virginia and southern Maryland, but he needed more soldiers to do it. On June 24 the 56-gun
frigate *Severn* arrived carrying dispatches from Admiral Cochrane in Bermuda. Cockburn decided he so needed the ship that he countermanded the
orders of her commander, Capt. Joseph Nourse, to proceed to blockade duty
off New York and ordered him to remain in the Chesapeake. He also ordered
Capt. Robert Barrie and the *Dragon* to remain in Lynnhaven Bay to keep an
eye on the *Constellation* rather than head to Halifax for a much-needed refit.

The admiral put most of his small tenders to work as store ships and was
able to augment his force of schooners and sloops through occasional forays. On July 1 the *Albion* made a move up the Patuxent, where her gig and
tender captured the 100-ton schooner *Flora*. Cockburn immediately armed
her. Two weeks later the *Loire* and the *St. Lawrence* returned from a cruise
on the upper Chesapeake with a dozen prizes. On the same day, Cockburn
received his long-awaited reinforcements when five ships—the 74-gun ship
of the line *Asia*, 44-gun frigate *Regulus*, 38-gun frigate *Brune*, 12-gun sloop
of war *Manly*, and 8-gun bombship *Aetna*—arrived in the bay. The five warships escorted a pair of transports that had traveled from Bermuda *en flute*
(with their guns stowed as ballast): the 38-gun troop ship *Melpomene* and the
12-gun brig *Thistle*. On board the transports were 350 Royal Marines and a
full company of Royal Marine Artillery. Although not enough men for Cockburn to attack Annapolis or Baltimore, the Royal Marine battalion gave the
admiral more than enough troops to execute his plan to bring the inhabitants
of the Chesapeake to their knees.

In addition to troops, the transports brought several letters from Admiral Cochrane. The British commander of the North America Station wanted Cockburn's ideas on where he should strike. Cochrane said he expected to receive up to 20,000 battle-hardened troops from Europe, with which he expected to easily defeat the Americans. The question was where to make the main thrust. Cochrane was considering targets ranging from Portsmouth, New Hampshire, to Newport, Rhode Island, to Philadelphia, Baltimore, and Washington and asked for Cockburn's input.[5] Cockburn had a ready answer for his commander.

> I therefore most firmly believe that within forty eight hours after the arrival in the Patuxent of such a force as you expect, the City of Washington might be possessed without difficulty or opposition of any kind. An Army landing at Benedict might possess itself of the Capitol—always so great a blow to the government of a country as well on account of the resources, as of the documents and records the invading army is almost sure to obtain thereby, must strongly I should think urge the propriety of the plan here proposed, and the more particularly as the other places you have mentioned.[6]

The idea of destroying the American seat of government was one Sir George Prevost, commander in Canada, had advanced after American troops burned York (now Toronto) in 1813 and Dover in 1814. He wrote to Cochrane demanding that the admiral exact revenge for "American depredations," and Cochrane was only too happy to oblige. On July 18 he issued an order to all units on the North America Station to "destroy and lay waste such towns and districts upon the coast as you may find assailable; you will hold strictly in view the conduct of the American Army towards His Majesty's unoffending Canadian subjects."[7]

It was all Cockburn needed to put his plan into motion. He ordered Captain Nourse and the *Severn* to take command of the blockade of the Patuxent, along with the *Aetna*, *Brune*, and *Manly*. He sent the *Asia* to Lynnhaven Bay to finally relieve the *Dragon* and took the rest of the squadron to the Potomac. His plan was simple. Cockburn intended to ravage both sides of the Potomac River while sounding the waterway as high up as Kettle Bottom Shoal, a major impediment to deep-draft traffic heading toward Alexandria and Washington. The two flotillas were to cause enough alarm in the national capital to spread fear but not enough to give away the plan to attack the city. It would also just about force Cochrane to commit to Cockburn's idea of attacking Washington, something to which Cochrane had yet to agree.[8]

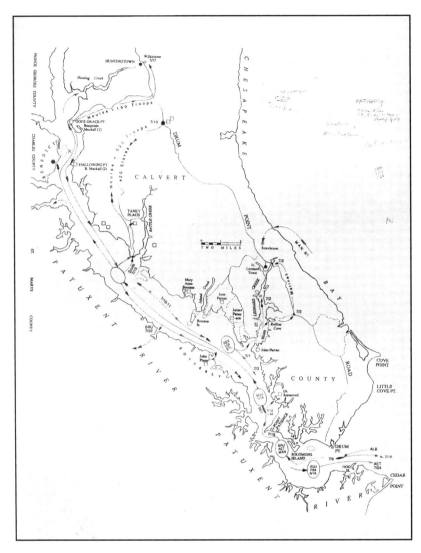

Map 4. British Operations in the Patuxent, Summer 1814
TAKEN FROM AN ORIGINAL DRAWING BY STANLEY QUICK

Cockburn put his forces into motion on July 15 when he ordered Nourse to take his squadron up the Patuxent. Two days later Cockburn entered the Potomac with the *Albion, Loire, Narcissus, Regulus, Brune,* and *Melpomene* and 500 Royal Marines. His first target was Leonardtown, the county seat of St. Mary's County. Cockburn had information that Colonel Carberry had moved the 36th Infantry to the town, and on July 18 sent in the *Loire* and his ships' boats to engage him. Leonardtown sat at the head of a small waterway called Breton Bay. The Royal Marines, under Maj. George Lewis, set off at 8:30 p.m.

along with a large force of sailors. The marines landed on both sides of the bay and marched overland to Leonardtown while Cockburn personally led the seamen in the boats. The three prongs converged on the town at dawn.

After the Royal Marines reconnoitered the outskirts of the town and encountered no opposition, Cockburn quietly took possession of the hamlet of sixty buildings and dwellings just as its inhabitants began to wake. The British searched for Carberry's soldiers, but they had fled at the first inkling of Cockburn's advance on the town. The landing party seized twenty barrels of flour and ten barrels of beef the Americans had left behind along with forty stand of muskets, which Cockburn's men destroyed. The British also carried off seventy hogsheads of tobacco, loading it onto two schooners they seized at the town dock. They refrained from putting private residences to the torch when the female inhabitants of the town quietly remained indoors. Cockburn wanted to burn the county courthouse but decided against it when Eliza Key, a relative of Francis Scott Key, told the admiral the townspeople often used the courthouse as a place of worship. The almost tame behavior of the invaders left a favorable impression on Eliza Key, who said the British were "very civil and vastly polite" toward the inhabitants.[9]

Cockburn next moved to Nomini Creek on the Virginia side of the Potomac. Around noon on July 20 Cockburn again led the ships' boats, organized in three divisions under the command of Capt. Robert Rowley of the *Melpomene*, Capt. Robert Ramsey of the *Regulus*, and Lt. George Urmston, the first lieutenant of the *Albion*. As the British rowed up the creek, they saw a force of mounted militia gathered in front of a large house on a hill near a ferry slip. The militia opened fire with muskets and a fieldpiece, killing one seaman and wounding four others before galloping off into nearby woods and "hiding" the cannon.[10]

The British sailors landed and raced up the hill after the Americans. Lt. James Scott of the *Albion* and an officer from the *Regulus* entered the house and found numerous bottles of wine and liquor and drinking glasses set out on the porch. Scott, acting on information from one of the black servants at the house, warned his fellow officers the liquor was likely poisoned. He told Cockburn, who ordered Scott to burn the house and its outbuildings in retaliation. The British also left a note explaining why they burned the house, accusing the militia of poisoning the liquor. Lt. Col. Richard E. Parker, commander of the 37th Militia Regiment, sent a note to Cockburn refuting the charge. Scott's account claims Cockburn had his ship's surgeon analyze the wine and sent a note back to Parker with the results—someone had laced the wine with arsenic.[11]

Cockburn and his sailors continued up Nomini Creek to the village of Mount Holly while the Royal Marines pursued the militia. The chase lasted four miles but the British managed to grab only a few stragglers. By the time the Royal Marines returned to Mount Holly it was almost dark, and Cockburn made camp. In the morning, his sailors and marines carried off everything they could, including tobacco, cattle, and livestock—even the silver communion set of Mount Holly Church—before they set fire to the buildings. As they rowed back down the creek, Cockburn stopped off on a point of land that jutted into the waterway on which he saw militia. The Americans fired a ragged volley at the invaders and then ran away. Cockburn landed his force, which again burned every building in the vicinity. They also carried off 135 slaves who were, he reported, "anxious to join us."[12]

Lieutenant Urmston took charge of the refugees and used the *Thistle* to take them to Tangier Island. James White of the *Thistle* took command of the *Albion* and on July 23 led an expedition into St. Clemens Bay on the Maryland side of the river, an estuary similar to Breton Bay. He ran into no opposition and captured four schooners and burned a fifth. On July 26 he probed Lower Machodoc Creek on the Virginia shore and again ran into no opposition. He burned six schooners he found anchored in the creek and carried off one hundred head of cattle before returning to the main squadron.[13]

On July 15 Capt. Joseph Nourse moved into the Patuxent with a squadron based on the 56-gun frigate *Severn*. His first action was to burn the town of Calverton, also known as Battle Town, at the head of Battle Creek. Calverton was the former county seat of Calvert County and dated back to 1669. After plundering everything they could carry, Nourse's sailors and marines put the town to the torch. On July 16 they moved upriver to Sheridans Point. From there the invaders fanned out across the countryside, burning everything that hinted of having value. On July 17 they landed at a plantation called God's Grace and marched seven miles to Huntingtown at the head of Hunting Creek and burned a warehouse containing 130 hogsheads of tobacco. Winds spread the fire to nearby houses, and soon the entire town was aflame. The British returned to God's Grace and demanded twenty hogsheads of tobacco from the workers. When the workers refused, the sailors and marines destroyed the plantation.[14]

On July 19 Nourse landed his troops and marched nine miles inland to Prince Frederick, the new county seat of Calvert County. A large force of militia guarded the town, but its men fled as soon as the British sailors and marines marched into view. Nourse set his men to work burning the town and returned to his boats by 4 p.m. The following day Nourse went ashore two miles south of Benedict and burned several tobacco warehouses. He then turned his ships south toward the mouth of the river.[15]

Nourse's raids—especially those inland—sowed panic in Calvert and St. Mary's Counties. Militia flittered about from town to town, never really trying to intercept the British incursions or oppose them. Property owners fled at the mention of red-coated invaders. Commodore Barney, who moved his flotilla out of his anchorage at Nottingham several times based on reports of British actions, was astonished at the way the inhabitants reacted. "The people," he said, "are all frightened out of their senses running about the country like so many mad people."[16] Eventually Barney ceased placing any faith in anything the county residents told him. "There are so many individuals that make it their business to give false and alarming news," he wrote to Jones, "that we cannot believe anything we hear."[17]

Nourse plundered numerous homes along the Patuxent on his return trip. He proudly wrote to Cockburn, "The people on either side of the Patuxent are in the greatest alarm and consternation many are moving entirely away from both Calvert and St. Mary's, and I think in a short time they will be nearly deserted, those that remained at home all their slaves have left them and come to us." Nourse was disappointed that he had been unable to engage Barney's flotilla, but he took pride in the knowledge that the Americans had no idea where or when to expect the next attack. "Jonathan I believe is so confounded that he does not know when or where to look for us and I do believe that he is at this moment so undecided and unprepared that it would require but little force to burn Washington, and I hope soon to put the first torch to it myself."[18]

Cockburn spent two days distributing supplies before moving farther up the Potomac. He dropped anchor off the mouth of the Wicomico River on July 28. A heavy rainstorm delayed disembarking troops until the next day, when Cockburn led a force of five hundred marines and sailors up the estuary. Cockburn had received information that Brig. Gen. Philip Stuart and a force of militia were ready to contest his advance. He deployed flanking parties to scout both sides of the estuary and also sounded Kettle Bottom Shoals on the Potomac, then pushed up the estuary and entered Chaptico Creek. Cockburn had his sailors and Royal Marines scour the area for opposition throughout the night, but they encountered none.[19]

At daybreak on July 30 the British landed at what the inhabitants called the "Hamburg Warehouse." The landing party met no opposition and set the warehouse alight after picking it clean of everything of value. From there they marched to and seized the town of Chaptico. They allegedly entered a burial vault at Christ Church, where, according to Stuart, they stripped the burial shroud off the body of a woman only recently laid to rest.[20]

Cockburn remained on the *Loire* and, with six schooners and several ships' boats, pushed up the Potomac another sixteen miles to Lower Cedar Point as he searched for a passage around Kettle Bottom Shoals. A landing party from the *Loire* went ashore and ran into pickets guarding Stuart's camp, but after a brief exchange of musket fire the British withdrew. Nevertheless, Cockburn concluded he could in fact maneuver even his largest warships around the shoal, making Washington vulnerable to a direct attack from the river. Satisfied, he turned his ships back down the Potomac to Tangier Island.

The squadron fought headwinds and calms for two days before arriving off the mouth of the Yeocomico River, a tributary of the Potomac, on August 3. In a now familiar pattern, Cockburn sent out mapping crews while the sailors and Royal Marines set ablaze farmhouses, barns, and other outbuildings. The wanton destruction pleased Cockburn but came as a shock to some of his junior officers.

"And so well did we act up to the very spirit of our orders, that if the Americans who bounded the shores of Virginia and Maryland do not entail upon their posterities the deepest hatred and the loudest curses upon England and her marauders, why, they must possess more Christian charity than I give them credit for," wrote Midn. Frederick Chamier. "The ruin, the desolation, the heartless misery, that we left them to brood over, will forever make the citizens of the United States, in spite of the relationship of the countries, hate us with that hatred which no words can allay, or time eradicate."[21]

And still the destruction continued. After anchoring off the Yeocomico River in Virginia, Lieutenant Scott of the *Albion* led a force of sailors and Royal Marines toward Mundy Point. As Scott's force neared the shore, a battery of artillery under the command of Capt. Stephen Henderson opened a devastating barrage. Henderson, a native of Ireland, commanded the artillery attached to the 37th Virginia militia. He lived near Mundy Point and had spent considerable time improving his position, having built a barrack, storehouse, smokehouse, and stable, as well as erecting breastworks to protect his position. He had placed two 4-pounder field guns behind a log breastwork and another behind a sand-and-dirt fortification and had issued standing orders to man the guns whenever the enemy threatened.[22]

Unlike their neighbors in Maryland, the Virginia militia turned out in strength as Cockburn sailed up the Potomac. Governor James Barbour ordered the entire 4th Division to gather just a few miles away from Henderson's position at Mundy Point, and at least a full brigade was present at the camp under Maj. Gen. Alexander Parker. Henderson had orders to fall back on the divisional camp should the British come ashore in force.[23]

Lieutenant Scott had no idea American artillery was guarding the shore. His first inkling was Henderson's opening salvo, which decapitated a Royal Marine sitting next to Scott, splattering him with blood and brains. The gruesome death did not even slow down the oarsmen. "'Hurrah, my lads! Stretch out—hurrah! hurrah!' was repeated by the crew, and an extra tug at the oars evinced their anxiety to come to close quarters," Scott wrote. A second salvo from Henderson's battery killed two more men in Scott's boat, but still the British pulled for the shore. When the boat grounded on a sand spit, several men jumped overboard to free it just as Henderson's guns fired another blast that killed two more marines and wounded two.[24]

The concentrated fire on Scott's boat allowed Maj. George Lewis to sweep in and, avoiding the sandbar, land his force so rapidly that Henderson had to limber his guns and flee. Henderson's men stopped briefly to engage Lewis' Royal Marines with muskets but fled again when the entire British force landed. The British stopped to set fire to all of the buildings at the battery, a pause that granted Henderson a mile head start over his pursuers.[25]

The sun had risen by the time Henderson and his men entered some woods three miles from Mundy Point. The artillerymen were fatigued after the long run, and the 90° temperature further sapped their strength. With the enemy so close on their heels, they decided not to head to Parker's camp for fear the militia gathered there were unaware of the British incursion. Instead, they turned toward the village of Lottsburg and jettisoned one of their two cannon. Scott and Lewis pursued the retreating Americans by following the wheel tracks of the cannon. When they came upon the abandoned gun they decided to manually push it back to their landing spot. As they marched back to Mundy Point, the two officers ran into Cockburn leading the main force of Royal Marines. A runaway slave had told Cockburn about a large stash of military stores hidden on a nearby farm, and rather than pursue Henderson, the admiral ordered his men to head to the farm.[26]

The Royal Marines arrived at the farm after a four-mile march. It belonged to Henderson, who used it as a secondary supply depot. The residence and several outbuildings were stuffed with military stores, and Cockburn ordered his men to burn all of the buildings. The British used several barrels of captured powder to destroy a storehouse on the farm, and Cockburn reported hearing a satisfactory blast as his men marched back to Mundy Point.[27]

Major General Parker, the commander of the 4th Division of Virginia Militia, decided to find out for himself the exact whereabouts of Cockburn and his invaders and left his camp along with his son and an aide, Maj. John Taylor Lomax. The three officers were mounted and moving through a patch of rough terrain when they ran into Scott and a group of skirmishers. The British opened fire, scaring the horses, which dumped their riders to the ground. The horses galloped off while the three Americans scrambled into the brush to avoid capture. Parker suffered a broken collarbone and his son had some bruises; Lomax was unscathed. Parker's absence, however, had far worse consequences than a broken bone and three lost horses.[28]

Cockburn, again on advice from runaway slaves, found Parker's camp in a large field shielded by dense woods. A large contingent of militiamen had gathered there and, in the absence of their leader, were standing in formation facing to the west while a mounted unit was set up facing south. The Royal Marines, along with the captured cannon, quietly moved into the woods near the cavalry unit. The moment they opened fire with musket and grapeshot, the Americans' horses bolted into the massed infantry. The main Royal Marine force advanced with fixed bayonets, and the militia fled the field. Cockburn had routed an entire division of militia without suffering a single casualty. He immediately ordered his men back to Mundy Point in hope of preventing the Americans from crossing the Yeocomico to the town of Kinsale.[29]

The Royal Marines, sweltering in their wool uniforms, marched double-quick back to Mundy Point and threw themselves on the beach. Cockburn allowed a two-hour rest before he ordered three companies to board the boats and row across the river to attack Kinsale. When Cockburn had first entered the Potomac, Brig. Gen. John Hungerford had established a strong force of militia infantry, backed with cannon, to defend the town. His men built a blockhouse on a height that commanded the river, then settled in to wait.[30]

Cockburn ordered a rocket barge to engage the Americans and drive them off, but the militia withstood the initial barrage. Scott jumped into the barge and, with only two rockets remaining, directed the fire. His first rocket hit the blockhouse, and his second demolished one of the gun positions. Cockburn then personally led a frontal assault on Hungerford's position. The Americans melted before the Royal Marines' onslaught. Hungerford, despite his best efforts, was unable to rally his troops. Cockburn again had no casualties while the militia lost eight dead and five captured.[31]

The battle over, the Royal Marines deployed howitzers and fieldpieces for defense while sailors loaded sixty-eight hogsheads of tobacco and twenty barrels of flour onto five schooners they had captured in the town harbor. The landing party reembarked at 2 a.m. on August 4. The only casualties the British suffered came in the first landing when artillery raked Lieutenant Scott's boat.[32]

Parker's division simply disappeared. The militiamen likely returned to their homes, although some probably joined with Hungerford's men, who rallied after fleeing Kinsale. For the British, the flight of yet another strong force of militia was proof that Jonathan would not and could not stand up to the king's forces, no matter what the Yankee press might say. Scott, in a derisive analysis of American newspaper pronouncements of imminent defeat for the marauding Royal Navy force, openly wondered what the local press would make of the swath of destruction Cockburn's men had wrought as well as the poor showing of the Virginia militia. "The military achievements of the gallant general with the whole assembled militia of Virginia, Spotsylvania, etc., are best left to the imagination," the lieutenant wrote, "the Government doubtless considering the publication of them as a work of supererogation."[33]

The raid up the Yeocomico left the Coan River as the only marginally navigable tributary of the Potomac on the Virginia shore that Cockburn had yet to pillage. That changed on August 6 when the admiral learned militiamen were erecting a strong battery there. The squadron arrived at night, and at daybreak the next morning Lewis led a landing party in the ships' boats to destroy the battery. The Americans fired one volley, then fled at the sight of the bayonet-brandishing Royal Marines, dragging their three fieldpieces with them. Cockburn, Lewis, and Urmston pushed ahead to the top of the tortuous estuary where they found five schooners at anchor. The British stripped the warehouse where the schooners were anchored and loaded the ships with twenty-eight hogsheads of tobacco before returning to the squadron.[34]

On August 6, while Cockburn was plundering along the Coan River, the vanguard of Admiral Cochrane's main force arrived from Bermuda. The supply ship *Tucker*, loaded with four months' provisions; the 38-gun frigate *Menelaus* under Capt. Sir Peter Parker; and the 36-gun frigate *Hebrus* under Capt. Edward Palmer joined the squadron just as Cockburn was pushing up the Coan River. On board the *Hebrus* was Lt. Col. Sir James Malcolm, who had gained ample experience in Cockburn's operations in 1813. Malcolm assumed command of all the Royal Marines, assembling them into a full battalion. After hearing about Cockburn's planned raid on the Coan, Parker, Palmer, and a group of sailors rowed up the river and joined the raiders. Both officers were enthusiastic about the value of their experience, and Cockburn decided to conduct a "training" expedition on the St. Marys River in Maryland.[35]

On August 8 Cockburn embarked the newly assembled Royal Marine battalion under Malcolm and all of his small-arms-armed sailors before dawn and led them into the St. Marys River with the *Aetna* and tenders following close behind. He divided the land force into two divisions and put Parker and Palmer in charge of them. The divisions landed on either side of the inlet and marched toward the head of the river, where they found a "factory" for making cotton fabric. The British met no opposition on their march. The locals readily complied with whatever orders they received and furnished any supplies Cockburn demanded. After burning the factory, the admiral turned his force around and marched back to the boats while the *Aetna* remained anchored to collect the requisitioned supplies.[36]

His work complete, Cockburn returned to the Potomac. Six days later, Cochrane arrived with his main fleet and another four thousand soldiers. The question for the British was where to strike next.

CHAPTER 17

Prelude to Disaster

*T*HE ABILITY OF THE BRITISH essentially to strike anywhere their boats could reach was a painful fact to President James Madison and his administration. Even before Cockburn began his campaign of subjugation along the Potomac, Madison had concerns about the final British target. On July 1, 1814, he convened a special meeting of his cabinet. Attorney General Richard Rush, Secretary of State James Monroe, Secretary of the Navy William Jones, Secretary of War John Armstrong, and Secretary of the Treasury George Campbell duly arrived at the executive mansion at noon to discuss one topic: Was Washington, the national capital, the next British target?[1]

Most of the cabinet members had already voiced their thoughts on the subject. Armstrong, a surly, nearly universally disliked New Yorker, believed the British would thrust toward Baltimore, which in his mind was far more important than the Federal District—"this sheep walk," as he called it. Washington had no military significance, he argued time and again when panic swept through the city over Cockburn's raids. He believed there was simply nothing in Washington that would entice the British to attack, and nothing could convince him otherwise.[2]

Jones was almost as sure as Armstrong that Cochrane would hit Baltimore rather than Washington. He put Miller's Marines on alert when Cockburn made his thrust up the Patuxent, but beyond that Jones did nothing to strengthen the defenses around the Washington Navy Yard, which was a legitimate military target. Rush, Campbell, and Monroe apparently said nothing at the meeting, although Monroe had vacillated somewhat regarding British intentions at previous meetings. He could see the merit to both arguments: Washington might be a target, or it might not.[3]

Madison apparently was not really interested in what his cabinet thought. He believed Washington was in danger of a British attack precisely because it was the national capital, and to deal with the threat he summarily created a new military district. Up to that point the city had been part of the Fifth Military District, which included Maryland and portions of Virginia and Pennsylvania. Henceforth the city and its immediate environs would comprise the Tenth

Military District. To give his new district teeth, Madison ordered the creation of a force of up to three thousand men to cover Washington and Baltimore and wanted them stationed at a point from which they could march rapidly to either city. The president also "suggested" establishing an additional force of 10,000–12,000 volunteers and militia to reinforce that unit in case of attack.[4]

Madison selected newly minted brigadier general William Henry Winder to command the new district. Winder was thirty-nine and recently returned from captivity in Canada. A political appointee, his military career had started only two years before as the lieutenant colonel of the 14th U.S. Infantry. He fought in one battle—at Stoney Creek on the Canadian border in 1813, where he was wounded and captured. Winder was the nephew of Maryland governor Levin Winder, the powerful Federalist on whom he would have to rely for the bulk of his troops. Although he shared Madison's concerns about Britain's intentions, Governor Winder remained cool at best to the war. Madison saw William Winder as a way to bring the Maryland governor more into the conflict.[5]

The new Tenth Military District looked good on paper. Neither Madison nor Armstrong, however, ordered the construction of trenches, redoubts, or any other type of fortification to protect the city. Fort Washington, twelve miles south of the city and the main fortification guarding the Potomac approach to the capital, had a garrison of just seventy-nine Regular Army artillerymen. There were not even enough muskets to equip the militia in the Tenth District. The Regular Army units within the district—the 36th Infantry under Colonel Carberry and the 38th under Major Keyser—were on their way north toward Annapolis, thirty miles from the capital, because several British warships had anchored in the Severn River off the Maryland capital. Finally, the soldiers assigned to Winder's command were not on active duty because the government lacked the funds to pay them. The militia and volunteers would report only if and when the British moved.[6]

It was a difficult situation for Brigadier General Winder, who had no staff, no flints for the few weapons he had, and no real idea of how he was supposed to defend Washington or Baltimore with a mere three thousand men. On July 9 he wrote to Armstrong, "What possible chance will there be of collecting a force after the arrival of the enemy. He can be in Washington, Baltimore, or Annapolis in four days after entering the Capes."[7] Armstrong never replied. In fact, the secretary of war wanted nothing to do with Winder's or Madison's plans and dragged his feet at fulfilling any directive regarding the city's defense. In early August, as Cockburn was burning his way up and down the Potomac, Winder finally got permission to call up the Maryland militia. The turnout was predictably small, just 250 of the 3,000 men called actually reported for duty.[8]

Alexander Inglis Cochrane, Vice Admiral of the Red, commander of the North America Station, arrived off the mouth of the Potomac River on August 16 with a squadron of twenty-four warships, including his flagship, the 80-gun *Tonnant*, and the 74-gun ship of the line *Royal Oak*. Cochrane, Cockburn, and Maj. Gen. Robert Ross, the land forces commander, held a conference on August 17 to decide exactly where to strike. Cockburn remained committed to an attack on Washington, and the ease with which he had been able to strike along the Potomac and Patuxent convinced Cochrane to agree. The only senior officer Cockburn failed to convince was Ross.[9]

The veteran of the Peninsular campaign in Portugal and Spain pointed to Cochrane's orders from the Admiralty to avoid marching deep into enemy territory where he could be cut off from naval support. The Chesapeake was supposed to be a sideshow, Ross insisted, a way of easing pressure along the Canadian frontier while also serving as a backdrop to the real prize: New Orleans. He viewed an attack on Washington, at least when he first arrived in the Chesapeake, as an unnecessary risk.[10]

Cochrane eased Ross' worries when he revealed his plan. The British would strike using a three-pronged attack, two prongs of which would mask their final destination. Capt. James A. Gordon would ascend the Potomac with the frigates *Seahorse*, 38 guns, and *Euryalus*, 36 guns, as well as three bomb ships (brigs converted to carry mortars) and a rocket barge. His target was Fort Washington, although his main role was diversionary. Capt. Sir Peter Parker with the 38-gun frigate *Menelaus* and two tenders was to sail up the bay toward Annapolis to prevent the Americans from sending reinforcements by way of the Eastern Shore. The main land force, under Ross, was to land at Benedict, move to Upper Marlboro, and from there march on Washington. Cockburn, with his sailors and Royal Marines deployed in ships' boats, would parallel and support Ross' movements from the Patuxent.

Maj. Gen. Robert Ross, commander of the British army that defeated the American forces at Bladensburg, captured Washington, D.C., and tried to take Baltimore. He was killed in the Battle of North Point on September 12, 1814. NATIONAL MARITIME MUSEUM, GREENWICH, ENGLAND

The British force available to Cochrane was much smaller than the one he had at first envisioned. As late as June he had written to Cockburn that he expected 20,000 of Lord Wellington's finest troops. Although he did receive some of Wellington's best men, the actual number was only slightly more than 4,000. In addition to the battalion of 500 Royal Marines that had arrived several days before Cochrane, Ross had a second battalion formed from the ships' Royal Marines. For British army units he had the 4th King's Own Lancashire; the 21st, 44th, and 85th Regiments of Foot; about 250 Colonial Marines; and support troops. He did not have horses. The British force would advance without a cavalry screen and would also have to leave most of its artillery behind because there were no horses to pull the guns and limbers. Ross' troops would instead take Congreve rockets, which were man portable.

The British set their plan in motion on August 18 when Gordon hoisted sail for the Potomac and Parker for the middle bay. Cockburn and the main force entered the Patuxent, where their first target was a cagey enemy who had so far eluded them.

Commodore Joshua Barney had no illusions when his lookouts spotted Cochrane's force off Benedict on the morning of August 19. He immediately sent a courier to Washington, thirty-five miles away, telling his superiors that the British were coming ashore. He received a reply that afternoon from Navy secretary Jones:

> Appearances indicate a design on this place, but it may be a feint, to mask a real design on Baltimore[.] If however their force is strong in troops, they may make a vigorous push for this place. In that case they probably would not waste much time with the flotilla. If you can impede and retard his movements, time will be gained which is all important, but should he advance upon you, with an overwhelming force, you will effectually destroy the flotilla by fire, and with your small arms, retire as he advances, towards this place.[11]

It was a blow for Barney, who had handed the British a bloody nose on two occasions with the ragtag flotilla he had built and trained. Now the fifty-five-year-old Baltimore native would have to preside over its destruction.

Barney, who had a reputation for action, did not suffer from the indecision that seemed to plague his superiors in Washington. As Ross' ground forces assembled at Benedict, the commodore sent a terse note to Jones. "No doubt their object is Washington, and perhaps the flotilla," he wrote.[12] It was all Jones needed to act on his own. He issued orders to Barney to

> retire before the enemy toward this place opposing his progress as well by your arms, as by felling trees across the road,

removing bridges, and presenting every other possible obstacle
to his march. Tomorrow morning the detachment of Marines
with three twelves and two long light 18-pounders with everything complete will march to join you and will be placed under
your command. When combined your men will man the guns
and the Marines under the command of Captain Miller will act
as infantry under your command.[13]

That was the first positive step any government official had taken for the
defense of the national capital. Jones did not stop there. He sent orders to Capt.
David Porter to ready sailors and Marines and transport them by water to
the Chesapeake, and also ordered Capt. John Rodgers in Philadelphia to send
three hundred men to aid in the defense of Washington.[14]

The British landing so close to Benedict sent the capital into a frenzy.
Many of the district's 8,100 residents had already left the city, not from fear of
the British but because of Washington's notoriously humid, mosquito-filled
summers. Many of those who had stayed home now began packing, looking
over their shoulders all the while to see whether a dust cloud from the south
signaled the arrival of the British.

Brigadier General Winder, who had been a whirlwind of energy since
taking command of the city's defenses in July, began issuing orders calling
out more militia. His problem was that he had no idea where to position his
troops if and when they arrived. The dispatches of James Monroe were his best
source of information. As soon as word of Ross' landing reached Washington,
the former cavalryman had volunteered to act as a scout for President Madison. Monroe rode down toward Benedict to see for himself just what was happening. Although he forgot to bring a spyglass, he could see the British fleet
assembled off the town. Monroe had eleven dragoons with him as an escort,
and he sent several galloping back to Washington with his observations.

Ross moved out of Benedict the afternoon of August 20 as soon as his men
were assembled. They tramped unopposed for five miles along a mostly uphill
sandy road to a crossroads with one fork leading north toward Nottingham.
The oppressive heat and humidity made even that short distance wearying
for the British troops. Each man carried sixty pounds of equipment and wore
a wool uniform. It was an entirely new experience for Wellington's "Invincibles," who had fought in the dry heat of the Iberian Peninsula but were unprepared for the sauna-like conditions of a Maryland summer.

Ross was also wary of an ambush. American sympathizers had warned
him of the presence of rifle companies ahead of him, and he moved his column
deliberately to avoid being surprised. Ross' target was the thorn in Cockburn's
side—Barney's flotilla. After bivouacking for the night at a crossroads the
British resumed their march on August 21, walking fourteen hot, miserable

miles to Nottingham. When they arrived late that afternoon they found the town nearly empty of American forces. Barney and his flotilla had already left. The commodore had moved his barges farther upriver to Pig Point, where the Patuxent narrowed so much it was almost unnavigable. The only other American troops in town were a small force of dragoons the British spotted as they approached the village, but the Americans quickly withdrew after firing a few shots. With Barney gone, Ross again vacillated on his target. He was twenty miles from the fleet and forty miles from the Chesapeake. Washington was still thirty miles away, a hard two-day march, and the lack of opposition worried the general. The Americans had to be up to something.[15]

Cockburn hurried ashore to allay the general's misgivings. The Americans, Cockburn told Ross, had not attacked because they lacked the resources to do so. The local militia was completely useless militarily and would never stand up to His Majesty's troops. Moreover, Washington was undefended and ripe for the picking. Ross was convinced. First, though, the British had a closer target. During the morning on August 22 the naval forces moved to attack Barney.

When Cockburn's amphibious forces reached Pig Point east of Upper Marlboro they could see the mastheads of Barney's flotilla sticking up behind a small hill. Cockburn immediately embarked his Royal Marines, ordering an overland attack. The admiral himself led the ships' boats in a final dash at his elusive foe. As he rounded the point, he could see the *Scorpion* flying Barney's pennant along with sixteen barges and thirteen merchant schooners. He could also smell smoke. Before his sailors or Royal Marines could make a move, flames shot out of the *Scorpion*'s gun ports, followed by a massive explosion that destroyed the cutter. The gun barges and merchant schooners went up next. Barney had again eluded capture, but this time Cockburn no longer had to worry about the threat of the flotilla.[16]

On receiving orders to scuttle the flotilla if threatened by the enemy, Barney had ordered the bulk of his crews to march to join Winder's troops, leaving behind a skeleton contingent to destroy the flotilla. He marched his flotillamen overnight to Winder's camp at Wood Yard, arriving just in time to see Winder and Secretary of State James Monroe conferring. Within minutes of their arrival the flotillamen were on the move once more, this time toward Washington.[17]

Brigadier General Winder had his hands full trying to organize his disparate troops into a unified command. His call for militia had so far netted barely 1,500 soldiers, although he knew more were on the way. Wood Yard sat astride the main roads leading both to Baltimore and to Washington at a point midway between the two possible targets. Winder had two regiments of militia from Washington: the 1st Regiment under Col. George Magruder and the 2nd Regiment under Col. William Brent. With the British now clearly favoring Washington, Winder sent orders to Maj. Gen. Samuel Smith in Baltimore telling him to send Brig. Gen. Tobias Stansbury's brigade. Brig. Gen. John Stricker received orders to send his elite 5th Maryland militia, a Baltimore City unit, his rifle battalion, and "two of your most active artillery companies." Requests for militia also went out to Virginia and Pennsylvania as Winder tried his best to collect enough armed men to face the British.[18]

Winder had more problems than finding troops. He had asked Armstrong to send one thousand flints to his camp but received just two hundred. He needed axes to fell trees to block the roads and slow the British advance; he had none. He needed horses to haul artillery, limbers, and ammunition wagons, and tents for his solders. One company of riflemen under Capt. John Stull arrived in camp without rifles. Winder sent a constant stream of messages to Armstrong begging for help or advice. He received no replies. The secretary of war remained convinced the British would not attack Washington, telling Maj. Gen. John Van Ness, commander of the district's militia, "Oh, yes! By God they would not come with such a fleet without meaning to strike somewhere but they certainly will not come here—what the devil will they do here?"[19]

With Armstrong convinced the British would strike elsewhere, Winder was all but on his own as he frantically tried to cover the approaches to the city as well as maintain mobility in case Ross turned toward Annapolis or Baltimore. He ordered the militia marching from Baltimore to head for Bladensburg, just northeast of Washington. Winder had a hodgepodge of units at Wood Yard—250 Maryland militia, the Federal District regiments, a composite battalion of 300 Regulars from the 36th and 38th Infantries, a troop of 125 dragoons from Virginia, plus Barney's 400 sailors and 120 Marines under Capt. Samuel Miller. Additionally, Winder had 20 pieces of artillery.[20]

Winder wanted this force to move to Upper Marlboro, where it could cover roads leading both to the capital and to Baltimore. Ross beat him to it. As the British marched north from Nottingham they had two choices: turn left and head directly for Fort Washington and possibly the two lower bridges over the Eastern Branch of the Potomac (now the Anacostia River) that led to the capital, or continue straight and move toward Upper Marlboro, from which they could strike at either Washington or Baltimore. Ross first turned his force left to attack some American forces he saw there but then turned around and marched north, forcing Winder to again try to decipher just where the British would strike.

Secretary of State Monroe had no illusions or doubts about Ross' intentions. Monroe and his little band of dragoons had been shadowing the British advance. After arriving at Winder's camp late on August 21, the exhausted secretary collapsed in a bed. At 9 a.m. the next day at Bellefields, the home of

Maj. Benjamin Ogden, Monroe saw the British march toward him down the road leading toward the capital. He sent a message to President Madison: "The enemy are in full march for Washington. Have materials prepared to destroy the bridges." He added ominously, "You had better remove the records."[21]

Indecision continued to plague Winder. At 2 a.m. on August 22 he woke his soldiers and ordered them to head toward Nottingham, where he wanted to strike at the van of Ross' force. When the British changed direction and marched toward Upper Marlboro, Winder canceled the order and told his troops to march to Long Old Fields, near Forestville. Information was coming into the camp, but much of it was unreliable and contradictory, with reports of the British moving toward both Baltimore and Washington. Winder received no help from Armstrong, who remained utterly convinced that Ross had no designs on the capital other than what he called a "Cossack hurrah"—a minor raid. When solid information came into the American camp that the British were still in Upper Marlboro, Winder concluded the target was Annapolis. He had always believed the Maryland state capital was Ross' goal because of its excellent harbor, which could act as a base from which to attack Baltimore.[22]

After news arrived that the British were moving toward Washington rather than Annapolis, Armstrong again pronounced the information wrong. "They have no such intention," he insisted. "They are foraging I suppose, and if an attack is meditated by them upon any place, it is Annapolis."[23]

Winder decided he had to act. He designed a three-pronged attack on Ross at Upper Marlboro. He now had nearly 3,000 men at Long Old Fields. He also knew Stansbury was either on his way or at Bladensburg with 1,400 Baltimore militia while Lt. Col. Joseph Sterrett was on his way with another 800. Winder sent orders to both to meet with the main force on the road to Upper Marlboro. Col. William Beall was somewhere south of Annapolis with an 800-man force of militia. Winder sent gallopers looking for Beall's command with orders for it to head for Upper Marlboro too.[24] Winder's math told him he had 6,000 men with which to strike. His scouts estimated Ross' army at 4,000 to 6,000 men.[25]

What Winder did not know was that Ross was already moving toward the American camp at Long Old Fields. Maj. George Peter knew. His detachment of infantry and artillery was on the road from Long Old Fields to Upper Marlboro when it ran into Ross' column. The sight shocked the Americans. Winder had said Peter would, at most, meet scouting parties. Instead the major found Ross' entire force bearing down on him.

The British had set out toward the American capital on August 23 at 2 a.m. They had been tramping along for more than twelve hours when they ran into Peter's reconnaissance party. Among Peter's men were Captain Stull's riflemen, still without rifles. Instead, Winder had issued them muskets. The riflemen cursed their weapons when they fired on the British from two hundred yards and failed to hit anything. Ross ordered his light companies to attack, and the British charged after the Americans. Stull's men fired a couple more volleys and then retreated, the redcoats in hot pursuit. Lt. Col. Jacint Laval, with 120 Regular Army dragoons, came galloping up but refused to cover Peter's withdrawal, complaining his horses were not trained.[26]

The British chased Peter's men from the road but then stopped to camp instead of following them. Wellington's Invincibles had yet to acclimate to the heat and humidity, and they could not continue.[27] Monroe and Thomas McKenney, a dry goods store clerk turned volunteer scout, watched Ross' men pitch camp, and then Monroe galloped for Bladensburg while McKenney rode to Long Old Fields to tell Brig. Gen. Walter Smith, whom Winder had left in charge, of the approaching British. Smith ordered his militiamen to form a line of battle across the road and waited. He sent McKenney off in search of Winder while he went to look for Stansbury and Sterrett. McKenney met Winder on the road to Bladensburg, and his news changed everything. Winder rode back to Long Old Fields and ordered Smith to break camp and head for, of all places, Washington.[28]

Winder later defended his decision by pointing out that his militia would have been no match for the British had they attacked at night, which he greatly feared they would do. A move to Bladensburg would have left the capital wide open—unless someone managed to destroy the two lower bridges that spanned the Eastern Branch. There was nothing to do, the general reasoned, except fall back on Washington.[29] He gave the orders and his weary, dispirited soldiers moved out around sunset, marching the eight miles back to Washington at such a brisk pace that one artilleryman called it a "run of eight miles." The first elements of the army crossed the bridges into the city around 8 p.m. and collapsed exhausted in fields around the navy yard.[30]

Confusion reigned in both the American and the British camps throughout the night of August 23. Winder still had no real handle on either his army or the British. He believed Ross planned to strike Washington but had no idea which route the British would take. The general spent a sleepless night blundering about the darkened capital, tracking down officers, issuing orders, and, most of all, worrying. His latest concern was the two bridges that spanned the Eastern Branch from Maryland on the road leading directly into the city. Around 1 a.m. he roused young Capt. Benjamin Burch of the Washington Artillery and ordered him to take thirty men and a pair of 6-pounder cannon to cover the southernmost of the two bridges.[31]

Burch and his men had covered the retreat of Winder's army into Washington and were dead tired. Nevertheless, he roused himself and his men and set off for the lower bridge. The upper bridge was still completely unguarded. Winder had an answer for that. He ordered a party of soldiers to burn it, and by 4 a.m. both the British around Upper Marlboro and Stansbury's men in

Bladensburg could see the glow of the blaze. Stansbury had arrived in Bladensburg earlier that night, along with Sterrett. The 2,200 men of the combined brigade were also dead tired, having force-marched from Baltimore. About 1 a.m. Stansbury received orders from Winder to prepare for a possible night attack from the British. Stansbury had his men formed in a battle line by 2 a.m., but except for a few shots that nervous sentries fired at nothing, the night was peaceful. At 4 a.m. Winder ordered Stansbury to march his men into Washington. Soon after that he sent new orders telling Stansbury to remain in place in Bladensburg. By then Stansbury could see the glow of the burning bridge near Washington but had no way to know that Winder had destroyed only one of the bridges. As far as the Baltimore militia general knew, the bridge at Bladensburg, which his brigade now guarded, was the only standing bridge over the Eastern Branch. If Ross planned to attack Washington, he would have to cross this bridge or ford the river a short distance upstream.[32]

Major General Ross could also see the glow of the burning bridge. Like Stansbury, he believed it meant the Americans had destroyed both of the nearest bridges to Washington. Ross awoke about 4 a.m. on the morning of August 24 at the breathless summons of Lt. James Scott, Cockburn's tireless aide. Scott had delivered messages to Cochrane down on the Patuxent and returned with new orders for Ross and Cockburn. Cochrane expressly forbade an attack on Washington. The news shook Cockburn especially hard. Ross was ready to turn around, but Cockburn argued that they had come too far to turn back now. He assured the general that no matter how big the force that lay ahead of them, it was just militia. Experience had taught Cockburn that militia could not and would not stand up to British Regulars. Washington, he said, was just a few miles away and ready for conquest. All Ross had to do was to march down and take it. Although it was in direct contradiction to Cochrane's orders, Cockburn told Ross no would argue with success once he had seized the American capital.[33]

The British commander thought for a minute and then began issuing orders. If the Americans had destroyed the southern bridges that led to their capital, he would march to Bladensburg if necessary and ford the shallow river there. The column pushed out at 5 a.m. Ross had committed himself to taking the city.

CHAPTER 18

The Bladensburg Races

BRIG. GEN. TOBIAS STANSBURY felt more than slightly isolated as he ordered his men to take positions covering the bridge over the Eastern Branch just west of Bladensburg. Stansbury was already tired after spending all of August 23 marching to, then preparing to leave, and then finally pitching camp, at Bladensburg. He went to sleep around 2 a.m. only to awaken a half hour later when a messenger arrived with news of Winder's retreat into Washington. He roused his men and clattered over the bridge, taking up a defensive position on the west side of the river opposite Bladensburg. The militia moved slowly, and it was nearly daybreak by the time the Baltimore brigade was across the river. Stansbury sent a messenger to Winder to find out what was happening and ordered his men to cook their rations and "refresh themselves."[1]

Bladensburg was an obvious access point to Washington. Not only was the bridge over the Eastern Branch of the Potomac there, but just upstream the river was shallow enough to ford. The town also sat at a crossroads. Its prominence came not just from being the uppermost deepwater port on the Eastern Branch but also from the roads that snaked through the town—roads that led to Georgetown and Washington to the southwest, Baltimore to the north, and Annapolis to the east.

The first sliver of daylight was already visible when Major General Ross ordered his army to move out. Their destination was Bladensburg, about seven miles to the north. The marching was easy as the British moved along shaded roads in the early morning. As the sun rose higher in the sky, however, the column began to show signs of exhaustion. The march slowed to a crawl, then came to a complete halt "to give time for the stragglers to overtake the column."[2]

News of the British advance soon reached Washington, although Winder continued to vacillate over just where Ross was headed. He still believed the target was Annapolis or possibly Fort Washington. Because he wanted to cover every possible contingency, however, he agreed to let Secretary of State Monroe ride to Bladensburg to tell Stansbury the British were on the move. Uncertain of his next move, Winder turned to Secretary of War Armstrong for advice, sending him a note at about the same time Ross ordered his men to move out. "I should be glad of the assistance of counsel from yourself and government," Winder wrote to Armstrong. "If more convenient, I should make an exertion to go to you the first opportunity."[3] The note actually went to Madison—the courier could not find Armstrong—and the president himself rode over to Winder's headquarters to see what had the general so vexed.[4]

He arrived to find confusion rampant. No one had any coherent idea of what was happening. Rumors abounded. Some claimed the British were headed to Bladensburg, others said toward Washington, and still others toward Fort Washington. Winder was worried about the remaining southern bridge into the city, which young Captain Burch and his thirty artillerymen currently guarded. He had yet to hear from Capt. Thomas Tingey, commander of the Washington Navy Yard, who was supposed to provide explosives to destroy the bridge. Winder sent a frantic note to Tingey asking him to send powder to the bridge and decided to send Commodore Barney and his force of four hundred tough flotillamen to guard it as well.[5]

The entire city was awake before daybreak. Couriers dashed from place to place while the few residents still in town tried to find wagons and horses to cart their belongings to the countryside. Winder still had no idea where Ross was headed. Armstrong wanted to take a force of three thousand men and hole up in the Capitol building.[6] Madison was already arranging where government officials should meet if the city fell. He decided on Frederick, Maryland. By 8 a.m. the situation was bedlam. Rumors, conjecture, and outright guesses completely paralyzed command and control. At 10 a.m. a courier arrived with definitive news. Ross was headed for Bladensburg.[7]

Winder finally made his decision. He ordered Burch and Maj. George Peter to take their artillery to Bladensburg along with Laval's dragoons, Brig. Gen. Walter Smith's District of Columbia militia, the battalion of 350 Regulars under Col. William Scott, and Captain Stull's riflemen, who were still armed with muskets. He left behind only Col. George Minor and his eight hundred Virginia militiamen. Minor had arrived late on August 23 with no weapons or equipment and spent much of the day on August 24 trying to find Colonel Carberry of the 36th Infantry, who was supposed to equip the Virginians. His unit would play no part in the day's events.[8]

Also left behind, guarding the bridge into Washington near the navy yard, were Barney and his 400 flotillamen and Miller and 113 Marines. Barney was livid. He knew his men and the Marines were the best and most experienced fighters at Winder's disposal, and yet they were guarding a bridge. When Madison rode to the bridge to inspect its defenses around 11 a.m., Barney exploded.

U.S. Marines under the command of Capt. Samuel Miller making a last stand during the Battle of Bladensburg. The Marines and a force of four hundred sailors under Joshua Barney held off the British while the remainder of the American army fled in disarray. Painting by Col. Charles H. Waterhouse.
NATIONAL MUSEUM OF THE MARINE CORPS, TRIANGLE, VIRGINIA

Why, he demanded to know, should his tough sailors and Marines—"500 of the precious few fighting men around," as he put it—stay put at the bridge to "do what any damned corporal could do better with five men?"[9]

Madison agreed. He ordered Barney, Miller, the sailors and Marines, and their two 18-pounder and three 12-pounder artillery pieces to head for Bladensburg. It would prove an especially difficult march for the sailors, who had just been issued new shoes.[10]

Armstrong's obstinacy continued to impede General Winder's efforts. Madison suggested that Armstrong speak with Winder and offer some advice before the general issued his men their marching orders. Armstrong went to Winder's headquarters but apparently did nothing to help plan for the coming battle. "I took it for granted that he received the counsel he required," Armstrong told the president, "for to me he neither stated doubt nor difficulty nor plan of attack nor defense."[11]

Armstrong's attitude stunned the president. Pushed by Treasury secretary George Campbell, Madison begged Armstrong to ride to Bladensburg. Winder needed all the advice he could get, the president said, and Armstrong's help was vital to the success of the defense of the city. At first, Armstrong resisted. Madison promised to resolve any disputes over command if they arose. Believing that Madison had just given him command of the army, Armstrong immediately set out for Bladensburg. The president, Benjamin Rush, and a few aides followed soon afterward.[12]

Stansbury and his Baltimore militia could see the dust cloud of the approaching reinforcements but had no idea whether they or the British would arrive first. He decided to set up his defenses on the west side of the Bladensburg bridge, using an emplacement Col. Decius Wadsworth had built the previous day as the centerpiece of his line. He ordered his artillery, composed of six 6-pounder field guns, into the emplacement. To their right he placed Maj. William Pinkney's battalion, and on their left he put Stull and Capt. John Doughty and their companies of riflemen. Doughty's men, like Stull's, had muskets instead of rifles.[13] The position was a strong one, bordered by a ravine on the left and a large tobacco warehouse on the right, which would act as a funnel. The British would likely cross the bridge in front of the emplacement, where the cannon and supporting infantry could sweep the field.[14]

About fifty yards behind this first line Stansbury ordered Col. Jonathan Schutz's five-hundred-man regiment to take up a position on the left flank in a field that bordered an apple orchard. Stansbury put Col. John Ragan's regi-ment on the right flank, also covered by the orchard. He placed Lt. Col. Joseph Sterrett and his 5th Baltimore on the right. The positions would allow the infantry to easily support the front line while the orchard would shield them from view.[15] Stansbury wanted to place Col. William Beall and his eight-hundred-strong contingent of Annapolis militia on his far left flank, where they could cover a ford over the river and protect the soldiers in the orchard. Unfortunately, he never got the chance.

Secretary of State Monroe, just back from another scouting mission, arrived in the camp around the time Beall's footsore militia came jogging onto the field. Monroe rode along the lines Stansbury had established and decided, on his own authority, to change the positioning of the troops. He ordered Schutz and Ragan to move their men to a hill five hundred yards behind the riflemen and artillery—much too far back to offer any kind of cover to the gunners.[16] The change completely exposed the right flank of Stansbury's position and unnerved the militiamen, who had to leave the cover of the orchard to stand in the open on top of a hill that was in plain view of the enemy.[17]

Monroe was not finished playing general. Realizing Schutz and Ragan were exposed, he ordered Sterrett to take the 5th Baltimore and join the other two regiments on the hill. As Beall arrived after a sixteen-mile forced march—before Stansbury even knew the Annapolis regiment was on the field—Monroe grabbed the militia colonel and ordered him to take a position not on the left but on a hill to the right of the front line and nearly a mile behind the Baltimore units at the gun emplacement. Finally, Monroe buttonholed Laval as he and his troopers rode up and ordered him to take a position in a small ravine to the left of the new militia emplacement on the hill. Satisfied, he went in search of Stansbury and Winder.[18]

Stansbury was looking for Monroe as well. The general, after inspecting the artillery and Pinkney's and Stull's positions, looked in horror at the now deserted orchard and wondered where his men were. He quickly spotted the three regiments on the hill and raced to move the men back to their original positions. Just then Brig. Gen. Walter Smith rode up with his district militia, as did Winder. The army commander had arrived around noon and, like Stansbury, was inspecting the positioning of the troops. Stansbury and Monroe reached Smith at about the same time, but before the Baltimore general could complain about Monroe's meddling, the secretary of state rather proudly told Winder he had been "aiding" Stansbury with arranging the defense. Stansbury was about to demand that Winder do something when a cloud of dust on the horizon drew their attention.[19] Time had run out. The British had arrived.

Ross' column moved into Bladensburg hot, tired, and incredulous. The British had expected to run into opposition throughout their march. Eighteen-year-old Lt. George Robert Gleig of the 85th Foot was especially surprised that American riflemen had not taken up positions among the buildings in the town. Ross sent in his advance guard to reconnoiter, and the light infantrymen came under fire from the emplacement across the river. The British halted to decide on their plan of attack.[20]

While the British planned, Winder's army continued to stream onto the field. Benjamin Burch came pounding up with his artillery and looked for a place to set up his five guns. One of his men spotted Winder, who gave the unit a rather grim order, "When you retreat, take notice you must retreat by the Georgetown road."[21] Winder had Burch place three guns near the now-abandoned orchard in a last-ditch effort to support the front line of troops. Colonel Wadsworth, who arrived on the field with Winder, grabbed the other two cannon and set them up on the Washington road to cover the Baltimore artillery at the emplacement. What Wadsworth did afterward is a mystery. No reports mention him being on the field during the battle.[22] Remarkably, no one in the first line of defense had any idea that Winder's army had arrived. Stansbury said the first time he realized he was not alone on the field was when Commodore Barney's flotillamen, who were the last units to arrive, opened fire on the British.[23] Major Pinkney was also under the impression that his were the only troops on the field and said he did not know the rest of the army was behind him until the battle was nearly over.[24]

The soldiers from Washington were now arriving en masse. General Smith began placing the units as each came onto the field. Maj. George Peter's six-gun artillery unit went into a battery near a small bluff about a mile from the bridge. Smith put a six-hundred-man Maryland militia unit to the right of Peter's guns and ordered Colonel Scott with his battalion of Regulars to take up a position to the left of the cannon. George Magruder's 1st District of Columbia militia took station 100 yards behind Scott. Col. William Brent and the 2nd District militia, and Capt. John Davidson's company of riflemen moved to a ridge to the left of Peter's guns. Well off to the right were Beall's men, still without orders, standing on their hill and watching the commotion from 250 yards away.[25]

Winder did his best to take control of the army, but Monroe's meddling in the placement of the front line all but doomed the Americans. Now, Winder had Madison, Armstrong, and Rush as well as several congressmen converging on the scene. Armstrong had one final chance to work with Winder but again refused when he realized he would not command the army. His ego bruised, Armstrong peremptorily left the field, leaving Winder to his own devices. Madison and his party made their way to the front line and settled in to watch until the first British volley sent them scurrying for the rear.[26] His precipitous retreat aside, Madison, who had no military experience, was the first chief executive to take the field with an army in a position to execute his duties as commander in chief. Madison, however, demurred from exercising command, telling Armstrong and Rush "it was proper" to leave such matters to military men. (Abraham Lincoln helped orchestrate the recapture of Norfolk during the Civil War, but he was not present when Union troops went ashore to retake the city.)

Confusion remained rampant. None of Stansbury's men knew that the bulk of the army was behind them. They could see the heavy column of British just across the river and even let out a cheer when the first volleys of cannon fire sent the red-coated scouts running for cover among the buildings of the town.[27] It was short-lived bravado.

Col. William Thornton, commander of the 85th Foot and the first brigade of Ross' army, led his men across the bridge and was greeted by a blast of grape and canister. Thornton urged his men on as a group of Royal Marine artillerymen set up the launchers for their Congreve rockets. A second volley from the Baltimore artillery momentarily stopped the advance, but Thornton quickly had his men moving "at the double quick toward the head of the bridge." As the light infantry crossed the wooden structure, the American infantry and Wadsworth's two guns opened fire. The effect was "tremendous," Gleig reported. "For at that first discharge, an entire company was swept down."[28]

The British kept coming. The infantrymen of the 85th fanned out as they crossed the bridge, using the shrubs and bushes along the riverbank as cover. At the same time, the Royal Marines launched their first salvo of rockets, which whooshed well over the American line but clearly startled the defenders. The next salvo was much better aimed and streaked through the line. The rockets unnerved the riflemen and gunners, whose next volley was far less effective.[29] Wadsworth's pair of guns, deployed on the road to the left of the emplacement, opened fire and again drove the British back. Thorton, however, urged his men forward, with the 85th in the van while the light companies of the 4th, 21st, and 44th Foot followed. The heavy column continued to envelop the right and left flanks of the first American line and also bore down on Wadsworth's little battery. They were the first to break, abandoning their guns before the British could get within bayonet reach.[30]

On the right of the emplacement, a company of skirmishers fled as the redcoats approached, causing a domino effect on the line. The Baltimore artillery suddenly ceased firing and began limbering their guns with a speed few had ever seen the unit execute. Major Pinkney's riflemen, stationed adjacent to the artillerymen, were next. As the gunners fled, the riflemen simply began to run toward the orchard and the hill on which Sterrett and the 5th Baltimore stood. It was the first inkling Winder, who was also on the hill, had that his front line was disintegrating. He ordered Sterrett to move to support the now-fleeing Baltimore artillery.[31] Winder wanted the 5th to retake the orchard, which would secure the far right flank of the position, but after marching just fifty yards Sterrett could see that the British were already among the apple trees and halted his men. His unit now held the right flank of the army while Burch's battery, which continued to engage the redcoats, held the far left.[32]

At this stage Winder actually saw opportunity. Despite the huge gap in his line, he still had two full regiments at his immediate disposal and all of the District militia. If he could move Ragan's and Schutz's men into the now vacant center to support Sterrett and link up with the two companies still supporting Burch, he might just be able to salvage the battle.[33] He did not factor in the rockets. Lt. John Lawrence and his Royal Marine artillerymen found the range, and Congreve rockets streaked over the battlefield. After unnerving the center, Lawrence concentrated on the American units he could see on the hill—the regiments of Sterrett, Ragan, and Schutz. Sterrett moved his men before they came under fire. The other two regiments took one salvo and ran madly down the hill to escape the rockets.[34]

The 5th Baltimore held its ground, briefly. The British in the orchard opened fire on the Americans and, despite the efforts of Burch's artillery, continued firing on the militiamen, who returned fire but could not see their assailants. Winder ordered the 5th to fall back, then countermanded the order. He quickly reversed that decision and again ordered the Baltimoreans to withdraw. The series of orders, as well as the increasing fire from the orchard, was too much even for the "elite" men of the 5th, and they broke and ran for the rear, following the other two city units.[35]

There was no stopping the panic now. Winder, Stansbury, and Sterrett all tried to stem the flight of the frightened militia, only to become engulfed in the tide of fleeing men. Winder attempted to funnel the mass toward the troops still pounding up the road from Washington, but the militiamen nearly all turned down the Georgetown road instead, which led in a different direction.[36] The horde of panicked troops ran so fast the day would become known as the "Bladensburg Races."

The stampede signaled to President Madison and his party that it was time to leave, and they rode past a bewildered Winder and headed back toward the city. Winder got a boost when Commodore Barney rode up at the head of his sailors and Miller's Marines. Winder had him take up a position in the center of the third defensive line, on the road to Washington.[37]

The British now moved to exploit their rout of the Baltimore militia. They first attacked the Maryland militia positioned near Beall. After receiving one volley the Marylanders broke and joined Beall on his isolated hilltop position. The British advanced and ran smack into the concentrated fire of Peter's six-gun battery and Barney's five guns. Peter's battery fired a volley that staggered the redcoats, and Barney unleashed a salvo from his 18-pounders that swept them from the road. The light infantry regrouped and tried again, only to run into a second hail of fire. They tried a third time and were again driven back, this time into a field near the road, which gave Miller and his Marines their chance. Miller opened up with his 12-pounders, and his Marines poured volleys of musket fire into the clump of men. With cries of "Board 'em," the flotillamen and Marines charged and sent the 85th Foot reeling. Colonel Thornton went down with a thigh wound. His replacement, Lt. Col. William Wood of the 85th, was also wounded. The entire British first brigade reeled from the combined Marine-flotillamen charge and looked ready to break.[38]

Ross and Cockburn, observing the battle from the east bank of the river, immediately ordered Col. Arthur Brooke to push forward with the second brigade, made up of the battalion companies of the 4th and 44th Foot. Brooke was to lead the 4th around the American left flank while Ross himself took command of the 44th and attacked on the right. The reinforcements stiffened the light infantry, which again surged forward. Brooke and the 4th slammed into Beall's men, who crumpled from the blow. The Annapolis militia melted away, running, a flotillaman said contemptuously, "like sheep from dogs."[39]

On the left, Colonel Magruder's 1st District militia exchanged fire with Ross and the advancing 44th Foot. The district regiment stood its ground until receiving an order to withdraw. At first the militiamen refused, but when a second order came they moved back about sixty yards and turned to engage the British once more. Another order came in to retreat still more. The 1st moved back another six hundred yards before receiving an order to withdraw all the way to Washington Heights.[40]

All over the field, American units were running. On the far left, Lieutenant Colonel Laval and his dragoons found themselves nearly crushed by the Baltimore artillery. "They poured in torrents by us," he reported. "An artillery [battery] drove through. . . . [S]everal of my men were crushed down, horses and all and myself narrowly escaping, my thigh broken by one of the wheels, which shook me off my horse."[41] Major Peter and his battery and Colonel Scott and his Regulars held their ground until Winder ordered both, along with the 2nd District militia, to join the retreat. All three at first refused. The Regulars were just about to engage the 4th Foot when the order came to withdraw, and they howled with rage at being told to pull back. The men of the 2nd were equally outraged, but they did not know that the American left flank had disintegrated in a panicked mass of men and horses. Winder wanted to save as many men as he could before the British could turn their flank yet again. Reluctantly, Peter limbered his guns while Scott's Regulars and the 2nd District militia joined the general retreat. The infantry never fired a shot.[42]

The retreat left only Barney and Miller to face the entire British army. Neither the Marines nor the flotillamen flinched. Each time the British attacked, concentrated artillery and musket fire greeted them. Ross' favorite mount, the Arabian charger he rode during the Peninsular War, was shot out from under him. He barely escaped capture as the Marines and sailors counterattacked with vicious efficiency.[43] The British regrouped and charged again, the Marines meeting them with the bayonet, the sailors with cutlasses. Their valor earned them the praise of their enemies. "It would be an injustice not to speak of them in the terms which their conduct merits," said Gleig. "They were employed as gunners, and not only did they serve their guns with a quickness and precision which astonished their assailants, but they stood till some of them were actually bayoneted with fuses in their hands."[44]

The sheer weight of numbers was against Barney and Miller. The Marines slowly began giving ground as more of them fell dead or wounded. Miller engaged in personal combat with one British soldier, who fired at him and missed. Miller fired back and also missed. Before he could reload, the redcoat snapped off another shot that shattered Miller's arm. He dropped wounded onto the field and was eventually captured. Despite spending ten months in the hospital, he never regained full use of the arm.[45]

The flotillamen too were now hard-pressed. Barney remained at the guns, directing fire. When a sharpshooter killed his horse, he fought on foot. Another round struck the fifty-five-year-old in the thigh. He dropped to the ground and saw the British now working their way into his rear.[46] The flotillamen and Marines fought on, stubbornly holding their positions. The Marines were down to about seventy men; the sailors continued to work the big guns. Barney watched as one gunner fought hand to hand with a British officer, slashing at the Englishman with his cutlass only to die at the officer's hand.[47] The British closed in, and the non-flotillamen in charge of Barney's ammunition trains scampered off, taking the sailors' last rounds with them.

There was nothing left to do. Barney ordered his men to spike their guns and withdraw. Unable to walk because of his wounds, he told his men to leave him on the field. Three of his senior officers tried to carry him but were unable to move him. He told the trio of sailing masters to leave him behind, but they refused. He ordered them to leave; two reluctantly complied while the third stayed with him. That officer, Sailing Master Jesse Huffington, remained with Barney and helped flag down a young officer for help.[48] Barney thought the young man was a midshipman, but he was actually Cockburn's aide, Lt. James Scott. The lieutenant assured Barney he had nothing to fear and immediately fetched Vice Admiral Cockburn and General Ross. Both British officers were extremely gracious to their fallen enemy. Barney quipped to Cockburn, "Well, Admiral, you have got hold of me at last." Cockburn quickly replied, "Do not let us speak of this state now, Commodore; I hope you are not seriously hurt." Cockburn and Ross granted Barney and Huffington paroles and gave permission to move the commodore to any abode he chose. Ross' personal physician tended to Barney's wound. Barney would remain grateful for the kindness Ross and Cockburn bestowed, while the affection the flotillamen showed for their commander moved the redcoats.[49]

The British officially reported losses of 64 dead and 185 wounded. The Americans reported 30 dead and 41 wounded, most of them Marines and flotillamen.[50] Dr. Hanson Cartlett, regimental surgeon of the 1st District militia, had the chance to survey the battlefield before burial parties cleared it and put British losses at 180 dead and 300 wounded.[51]

Barney's capture brought the battle to a close. The British, already tired from their march to Bladensburg, needed a rest. The American force had vanished. Only the flotillamen and Marines maintained their cohesion as they headed for Washington. The Baltimore militia units were, for all purposes, gone. Most of the men from Stansbury's line took the road leading to Baltimore and never looked back. The cavalry and Regulars, along with the district units, were on their way to Georgetown, although they straggled through Washington throughout the night of the twenty-fourth. Winder was also on his way Georgetown. He had decided to abandon Washington rather than risk his remaining soldiers in a slugfest within the city. He conferred with both Armstrong and Monroe before making the decision, and later reported, "Both men concurred it would subject the whole of my force to certain capture" had he attempted to defend the capital.[52] Washington, D.C., and the few people still in the city were on their own.

CHAPTER 19

Fire and Ruin

*T*HE DAY'S EXERTIONS had taken a heavy toll on the British army that was now poised to enter Washington. The battle at Bladensburg ended around 5 p.m., when the heat of the day was still at its fiercest. Many British soldiers simply collapsed from heat exhaustion on the fields they had recently conquered. Ross allowed his men to rest for three hours. The soldiers buried their dead, tended their wounded, and readied for the final push.[1]

In the city, people grabbed whatever belongings they could carry and joined the bedraggled stream of militia and fellow citizens running from the city. First lady Dolley Madison oversaw the removal of belongings from the executive mansion. She was particularly insistent on saving the full-length portrait of George Washington by Gilbert Stuart. The first lady was a for-midable presence. Unlike nearly everyone else in Washington, Dolley Madison remained calm, almost defiant, toward the impending occupation of the nation's capital. She carefully managed the packing of the president's valuables and removed as much silverware as she could carry and her personal copy of the Declaration of Independence. Then she took one look back at her home and boarded a carriage that would take her to Virginia and relative safety.[2]

Capt. Thomas Tingey, commander of the Washington Navy Yard, had no idea whether he should leave or remain at his post.[3] The navy yard was full of supplies and housed two warships—the 44-gun frigate *Columbia* and the new sloop of war *Argus*—that were nearing completion. Three barges—two 75-foot boats and one 50-foot vessel—also bobbed at anchor. The workshops at the yard had sails, ropes, and lumber—everything needed to build and equip warships. Tingey had orders to ensure that none of the supplies fell into Brit-ish hands.[4] Just past 4 p.m. Tingey saw a portion of the Eastern Branch bridge blown up into "splintery fragments" as Captain Creighton and his small party of sailors blew up the second of the three bridges over the Eastern Branch lead-ing to the city. Clerk Mordecai Booth volunteered to act as a scout to deter-mine where the British were and to provide warning if they headed for the navy yard. Tingey agreed, and Booth rode off toward Bladensburg.[5]

Ross began rousing his tired soldiers as the last rays of sunlight faded. The British commander left his first two brigades, which had seen the bulk of the combat during the afternoon, at Bladensburg, where they could continue to rest and follow once Ross had secured the city.[6] He pushed forward with Col. William Patterson's third brigade of Patterson's 1st Battalion, 21st Foot, and the Royal Marine battalion under Lt. Col. James Malcolm. Ross himself led an advance guard of two hundred men to the outskirts of the city. He met no resistance, nor did anyone answer his calls for parley as he apparently sought someone who could officially surrender the city.[7]

As Ross and his advance party approached a large, stately house within view of the Capitol, a group of unseen gunman opened fire on the British, killing one man and wounding two. The volley dropped Ross to the ground when a round killed his horse. Ross immediately ordered a squad from the 21st to envelop and attack the house, which had once belonged to Albert Gallatin. Although the soldiers found the house empty, Ross ordered them to burn it down as a warning to those still in the city.[8] The flames were the first of the evening in the capital that the British started, but not the first flames. A glow from the southwest signaled the destruction of the Washington Navy Yard.

Tingey waited until Mordecai Booth returned to the navy yard around 8 p.m. with word that the British were in the city before he gave the order to set the yard ablaze. He and the few men left at the yard lit fuses leading to warehouses, sail lofts, and rope lockers. Tingey raced along the dock, setting the fuses to the *Columbia* and the *Argus*. Fire licked at every bit of wood in the yard, adding to the growing glow in the night sky. Within minutes the navy yard was burning brightly. The frigates *New York*, *Boston*, and *General Greene* were also at the yard, essentially rotting at the wharf. All three went up in flames, adding to the heat.[9]

Ross and Cockburn led their column toward the Capitol, which was clearly visible in the fading light atop its hill. Although it did not yet have a distinctive dome—that would not be built for another fifty years—the building was the centerpiece of the still-new city. Soldiers broke down the doors and Lt. James Scott entered the building. "It was an unfinished but beautifully arranged building," Cockburn's aide reported. "The interior accommodations were upon a scale of grandeur and magnificence little suited to pure Republican simplicity. We might rather have been led to suspect that the nation, whose councils were held beneath its roof, was somewhat infected with an unseemly bias for monarchial splendor."[10]

That "grandeur" made perfect kindling. Soldiers and Royal Marines dragged furniture, books, papers, and anything else that would burn into large piles and set fire to them. The Library of Congress, then housed within the Capitol, provided even more fuel. When the flames had completely engulfed the Senate and House wings, the British moved to the Supreme Court. The court building was still new and had little furniture, but the redcoats made do. They hauled in furniture from other rooms and made another pile of kindling before setting it alight. The fires completely gutted but did not destroy the Capitol.

After setting fire to the Capitol, the British troops under Ross and Cockburn marched to the President's House, a mile down Pennsylvania Avenue from the Capitol. The executive mansion was eerily quiet when they entered it sometime after 10 p.m. In the dining room, the table still held the sumptuous feast Madison had planned to serve that evening. Famished after the day's exertions, the British gorged themselves. "Never was nectar more grateful to the palates of the gods than the crystal goblet of Madeira and water I quaffed at Mr. Madison's expense," Scott recalled.[11]

After eating, the British fanned out through the house to find souvenirs. Cockburn snatched up a cushion and a hat he believed belonged to President Madison. Someone took an ornate medicine chest. Scott grabbed clean shirts from the president's bedroom while an officer from the 85th Foot spirited away an ornate sword. Another "saved" a portrait of the first lady. Their rummaging finished, the British turned to the business of setting the house on fire. As they had done at the Capitol, the redcoats used drapes, papers, and furniture for kindling. The fire quickly moved through the house, gutting the building.[12]

Cockburn's next target was the Treasury Department building, which stood next to the executive mansion. Soldiers smashed the windows of the brick edifice then tossed in torches. Flames quickly engulfed the building. Cockburn wanted to continue the destruction by burning the War Department and State Department buildings, but Ross scuttled the idea, saying the soldiers and marines needed to rest. The British bedded down for the night with plans to continue the destruction of the city in the morning, although the vandalism continued.

When Cockburn passed by the offices of the *National Intelligencer*, he wanted to burn the building but stopped when neighbors begged him not to do it. Instead Cockburn ordered a party of sailors to literally tear down the building by passing ropes through windows and around the walls. Neighbors again pleaded, claiming the building did not belong to the newspaper's owner and the British would be destroying private property. Cockburn again relented, and then ordered soldiers to remove all the furniture, type, and presses and burn them in the street.[13] The redcoats finally settled down to sleep after they set the offices of the State Department on fire.

Soon after sunrise the redcoats went back to work. A party of sailors went to the War Department building and very quickly set it ablaze. Lieutenant Scott led a detail to the Tench Ringgold, John Chalmers, and Heath and Company ropewalks, private businesses that supplied rope and cordage to the military. The huge, long buildings contained bundles of hemp, which the British

A contemporary engraving showing the executive mansion, now called the White House, following the British occupation of Washington, D.C.
NATIONAL ARCHIVES AND RECORDS ADMINISTRATION

covered with tar and used as fire starters. Within thirty minutes the ropewalks were brightly burning.[14]

A column of eighty men marched to the Greenleaf Arsenal, where they destroyed cannon and shot. They spiked unmounted artillery barrels and tossed them into the Potomac along with cartridges and grenades. The destruction went according to plan until the men came across 130 barrels of gunpowder, which they began tossing one by one down a well. A freak spark triggered a massive explosion that killed or injured nearly every sailor, Royal Marine, and soldier at the arsenal. Thirty men died, buried beneath tons of dirt and debris, and forty-seven more were wounded. The blast presaged an even bigger explosion, this one natural.[15]

Just hours after the explosion at the arsenal, a storm blew in from the west. Summer thunderstorms were normal, but this storm packed tornadoes. Bolts of lightning lit the sky as the winds tore through the city, toppling trees, knocking over chimneys, and spreading terror. Rain came down in torrents, extinguishing any embers that remained from the fires and soaking exposed troops, who cowered in open fields. The storm raged for two hours. When it finally subsided, Ross and Cockburn determined their work was done and began to collect their troops on Capitol Hill. Just after nightfall the British began to leave the city, setting campfires first to make any American soldiers in the area believe they were still present. The British returned to their ships by marching first to Bladensburg, where they spent several hours resting before marching to Benedict to reembark.[16] The invasion fleet spent two more days on the Patuxent before joining up with the Patuxent and Upper Chesapeake squadrons.

[Editor's note: Stanley Quick created a daily diary for Royal Navy captain James A. Gordon describing his push up the Potomac River that coincided with Cockburn's and Ross' attack on Washington, D.C., and the subsequent American efforts to trap Gordon on the river on his return trip. Mr. Quick went into great detail about the British use of kedges and hawsers to literally pull their vessels up the Potomac as well as the numerous times the British grounded on shoals in the river. He provided no sources, although he did reprint the reports of the principal officers involved, from which his account apparently derives. The following is a condensed version of his chapter on Gordon.]

The same storm that hammered Ross' troops as they left Washington lashed the squadron of Capt. James Gordon in the Potomac River. Gordon commanded one of the two diversionary forces that Cochrane set in motion when Ross set out for Washington. Gordon's mission was to ascend the Potomac and either act in concert with Ross and Cockburn in reducing Fort Washington before attacking the capital city or act alone in running past the fort to attack Alexandria.

Capt. James Gordon led an epic Royal Navy expedition up the Potomac as a diversion from the main thrust at Washington, D.C. Gordon brought his squadron as far as Alexandria, Virginia, which he captured before engaging in a running battle back down the river to the Chesapeake. NATIONAL MARITIME MUSEUM, GREENWICH, ENGLAND

Gordon entered the Potomac in command of seven ships: his own 38-gun frigate, the *Seahorse*; Capt. Charles Napier's 36-gun *Euryalus*; the bomb ships *Aetna*, *Devastation*, and *Meteor*; the rocket ship *Erebus*; and the tender *Anna Maria*. He started the one-hundred-nautical-mile journey toward Alexandria on August 17 and for a week worked his way up the river, dodging shoals, oyster banks, and sandbars. Each night Gordon placed a cordon of guard boats around his ships to prevent both attack and desertion.[17] On August 24, the day Ross routed Winder at Bladensburg, Gordon and his squadron anchored off Maryland Point, about twenty-five miles south of Fort Washington. He was still preparing his ships to pass the shoals off Maryland Point when the storm struck.

"The squall thickened at a short distance, roaring in a most awful manner, and appearing like a tremendous surf," Napier later wrote. The Potomac churned as the full force of the storm swept over the British ships. Lightning struck one of the guard ships of the *Euryalus*, sinking the boat. The *Euryalus* lost her bowsprit, jib boom, topmast, fore topgallant mast and foremast head, many sails, blocks, lines and running rigging. The *Seahorse* lost her mizzenmast and all of her cross trees and trestle trees. The *Meteor* grounded and lay on her side after the storm, losing her topgallant mast.[18]

After assessing the damage the following morning, Gordon was ready to abandon his mission and return to the Chesapeake. He believed the *Euryalus* was beyond repair, and the damage to his other ships was clearly extensive. His captains, however, assured him they could make the necessary repairs while under way, and Gordon agreed to continue. By the early afternoon on August 26 Gordon's flotilla was again in motion, including the *Meteor*, which had been righted and pulled off the shoal with brute force.[19] On August 27 the squadron arrived off Fort Washington.[20]

The fort should have presented a major impediment to Gordon's so-far-unchallenged ascent of the river. On paper, at least, Fort Washington had a pair of 52-inch Columbiads, two 32-pounders, eight 24-pounders, five 18-pounders, and a collection of 12- and 6-pounder field guns. The magazine contained more than 3,000 pounds of powder, 899 cannon cartridges, several hundred rounds of grape and canister, muskets, flints, musket cartridges, and bayonets.[21] What the fort's commander, artilleryman Capt. Samuel Dyson, lacked was soldiers to man all that ordnance. Dyson had fewer than sixty men to work the more than twenty cannon at the fort and stave off a land attack.[22] It was a nearly impossible situation.

As he retreated from Bladensburg on August 24, Winder, as commander of the military district that included Fort Washington, sent Dyson orders that "in the event of his being taken in the rear of the fort by the enemy," he was "to blow up the fort and retire across the river."[23] Dyson apparently needed little urging. As the British squadron hove into view, he called a council of war with his officers to decide whether to fight or flee. In his official report Dyson claimed he had information that a two-thousand-man British brigade "was on their march to cooperate with the fleet."[24]

Gordon ordered his mortar vessels to take up positions "just out of gunshot" from the fort at 5 p.m. At 6:30 the British lobbed their first shots. Gordon planned to shell the fort all night and attack with his frigates on the morning of August 28. Dyson, however, sped up that timetable. Within minutes of the first bombs landing, Napier, on the *Euryalus*, reported, "The garrison, to our great surprise, retreated from the fort." Dyson had his men spike all the cannon and set a fuse in the magazine. At about 8 p.m. Fort Washington exploded.[25]

"We were at a loss to account for such an extraordinary step," Napier later said. "The position was good, and its capture would have cost us at least fifty men, and more, had it been properly defended; besides, an unfavorable wind, and many other chances, were in their favor, and we could only have destroyed it had we succeeded in the attack."[26]

The next morning Gordon sent ashore a party of sailors and Royal Marines, who wrecked the carriages of the spiked cannon and destroyed everything the explosion had missed.[27] Dyson faced a court-martial for his actions and was eventually cashiered out of the Army.[28]

Gordon next set his sights on Alexandria. He set sail after completing his work at Fort Washington, and at 9 p.m. that night the bomb ship *Aetna* anchored off the town. Her captain, Lt. Thomas Alexander, reported finding several merchant vessels either dismantled or scuttled in the harbor. Officials in Alexandria were quick to seek terms from the British and offered to surrender the city. Gordon arrived with the remainder of the squadron at daylight on August 29 and dictated harsh terms: Alexandria and its merchants were to deliver to the British "all naval and ordnance stores, public or private"; surrender "all shipping, and their furniture must be sent on board by the owners without delay"; refloat the vessels either scuttled or dismantled; and, finally, hand over "merchandise of every description."

Gordon spent the next two days stripping Alexandria of anything and everything of value, including slaves. His sailors raised the scuttled vessels so that Gordon could use them to haul off his booty. The British took twenty-one prize vessels—schooners and sloops of varying sizes—and stuffed them full of the material they took from Alexandria. On September 1 Gordon received information that the Americans were establishing batteries on both sides of the Potomac to oppose his return to the Chesapeake. While protecting private property as per the agreement, Gordon destroyed any military supplies and goods he could not load and, with his prize ships in tow, began to make his way back down the river.

The surrender of Alexandria without a shot upset Americans almost as much as the burning of their capital. Howls of anger arose, and Navy secretary Jones turned to three naval heroes who had just arrived in Washington to prevent either a second attack on the capital or an attack on Georgetown. Oliver Hazard Perry, David Porter, and John Rodgers were all in Baltimore at the end of August. Perry was assigned to ready the new frigate *Java* for sea, while Porter and Rodgers were tasked with assisting in the defense of Baltimore. Jones ordered the three captains to Washington to take on Gordon's squadron, with Rodgers, the senior officer, in overall command.[29] Jones asked Rodgers to rush to Washington with "650 picked men or more" who were to attack the British ships in small boats.[30] He ordered Porter to the Virginia side of the river to take command of a party of sailors and Marines and five 18-pound guns.[31] Perry received orders to set up a battery on the Maryland side of the Potomac.[32]

For the next week the Americans engaged the British squadron in a running battle from just below Alexandria down to Kettle Bottom Shoals. Porter twice came close to sinking enemy vessels when his big cannon blasted the brig *Fairy* and the rocket ship *Erebus* while both ships were guarding other vessels in a convoy that had run aground. Rodgers, who arrived in Alexandria on September 1, twice attempted to use fire ships to destroy the enemy flotilla. On September 3 Rodgers led fifty men in four boats in an effort to take both the bomb ship *Devastation* and a prize vessel. Rodgers had three fire ships, but boatloads of Royal Marines arrived from the squadron in time to beat off the attack.[33]

Porter had a chance the same day to attack the *Erebus* and the *Euryalus* when the British attempted to disrupt construction of his battery at White Horse, Virginia. Porter's Marines and militia drove off a landing attempt while his big guns pounded the enemy rocket ship with grape and canister. Rodgers made a second attempt to attack with fire ships that night, but again without success.[34] By September 8 the convoy had cleared Kettle Bottom Shoals, and the last chance to intercept the British in the Potomac was gone. The weeklong ordeal cost the British seven dead and thirty-five wounded, most of them on the *Euryalus*, which bore the brunt of Porter's barrages on September 3.[35]

Gordon rejoined Cochrane's main fleet on September 9, and the combined force set sail for Kent Island, where Cochrane planned to meet Sir Peter Parker and the second diversionary force before setting out for the ultimate target, Baltimore.

[Editor's note: Stanley Quick wrote at length about the events surrounding Parker's brief forays along the Eastern Shore of the Chesapeake. He went into great detail about the lives of the owners of the farms the British burned and even named the slaves who ran away to join the British. The following is a greatly condensed version of Mr. Quick's account of the small battle at Caulk's Field.]

Capt. Peter Parker, commander of the second diversionary force, and his ships, the frigate *Menelaus* and the tenders *Mary* and *Jane*, arrived off Rock Hall on the Eastern Shore on August 27 after reconnoitering Baltimore Harbor. Parker placed buoys and tested the city defenses, battling several gunboats before heading toward Annapolis. The *Mary* swamped during a storm, carrying with her muskets and ammunition.[36] After anchoring off Poole Island, Parker reported to Cochrane that he observed "the Enemy's Regular Troops and Militia in Motion along the whole coast," and that they "had taken up a strong Position close to a large Depot of stores."[37]

The storehouse was actually the farm of Henry Waller. When he saw the *Menelaus* at anchor off the farm, the local militia commander, Lt. Col. Philip Reed, marched three companies of the 21st Maryland militia to the farm to contest any landing that might occur. The presence of the militiamen convinced Parker the farm harbored war materiel, and "this induced me instantly to push on shore with the small arms men and Marines."[38] He dispatched all of his ships' boats and covered the assault with gunfire from the *Menelaus*. Reed, who had stationed his men along a fence on the farm about eight hundred yards from the main house, decided not to contest the landing in the face of superior firepower. The British landed, took possession of the farm, and set fire to all of its buildings. Reed's militia opened fire as they were leaving and wounded an officer.[39]

Waller recovered the casing of a spent Congreve rocket the British fired at his home that is now on display at the Fort McHenry museum. Years later, with the help of their attorney, Francis Scott Key, the family received full compensation from the federal government for the loss of their home.[40]

On the morning of August 30 Parker decided to make another landing, this time with the goal of rooting out the militia. Parker was particularly glum that day because his cocked hat had fallen overboard while he was inspecting rigging on the *Menelaus*. "My head will follow this evening," he remarked to those around him. He prepared his will, destroyed his personal papers, and acted very much like a man going to his death.[41] At 9 p.m. a force of 104 armed sailors and 30 Royal Marines embarked, bringing with them a Congreve rocket launcher.[42]

The boats moved with muffled oars under the protection of the *Jane*. On landing just after 11 p.m., Parker divided his sailors and Royal Marines into two sections and began to move inland. The advance guard moved out rapidly and within a quarter of a mile came upon three mounted pickets under a large tree, fast asleep astride their horses. The seamen approached within ten paces, took deliberate aim, and—foolishly breaking silence—fired, hitting neither man nor horse. The pickets, startled awake, fired back and headed off into the nearby woods. One of the fleeing sentries fired a pistol, and the British could hear answering volleys as the sentries alerted the militia.[43]

Nevertheless, Parker decided to press on. He had another chance to use secrecy when his guide told him he had arrived on the outskirts of the American camp and could use a nearby wood to come up on the rear of the militia. Parker, however, decided to launch an all-out frontal attack. He led his men into a defile of felled trees that allowed five men to march abreast. The defile led right to Caulk's Field. The British nearly caught the Americans by surprise because Lieutenant Colonel Reed was expecting Parker to attack a nearby farm, not his camp. A sentry warned the militia just in time, and Reed set his men to greet the invaders.

He posted a company of twenty riflemen about sixty yards from where the defile met the field and established his main line two hundred yards behind the riflemen. His force numbered around three hundred men and included three artillery pieces.[44] Reed completed his defensive preparations at 1 a.m. on August 31, just as Parker ordered his column to move out from the defile. The rash British advance showed the contempt Cockburn had instilled in his officers for militia. As the head of the column emerged, the American riflemen opened fire with a well-aimed and rapidly delivered fusillade. Seven attackers were hit. The first man killed carried the staffs for the rockets, which prevented the British from using them in the battle.[45]

Capt. Sir Peter Parker, Royal Navy, commanded a second diversionary campaign during the British drive to capture Washington, D.C. NATIONAL MARITIME MUSEUM, GREENWICH, ENGLAND

Unable to back down or turn aside, the British had no option but to charge. They burst into the "open field" surrounded by a thick wood. At the summit of a gentle slope the three American fieldpieces pointed directly at the opening of the defile. As the British surged forward, Reed raced along the line and sent the riflemen to his right flank. The British headed right at the center of the line. A volley from the cannon killed a midshipman, forcing the British to change tactics.[46]

Lt. Henry Crease, second officer on the *Menelaus*, led his seamen and attacked Reed's right while Parker, leading the Royal Marines, tried to turn the left flank. The marines fired with great speed, advancing at the double quick to close with the militia and finish the battle at bayonet point. The American left began to bend but did not break. At this instant Parker, who had been cheering on his marines with his ornate Turkish sword, suddenly collapsed into the arms of one of his officers, saying, "I fear they have done for me. . . . [Y]ou had better retreat, for the boats are a long way off." A bugle sounded and the British backed off, a group of Royal Marines carrying their dying leader on their shoulders. Parker died from a thigh wound that cut his femoral artery.[47]

The British retreated to their boats, leaving the field in Reed's hands. They suffered 11 dead, 24 wounded, and 6 missing out of a force of 136 men. The

Royal Marines took the brunt of the casualties, with 7 dead and 11 wounded out of 32 officers and men.[48] Reed's force suffered just 3 wounded.[49]

The British flotilla rejoined Cochrane's main fleet. After considering several options, including an attack on Rhode Island, it was decided to "make a demonstration" against Baltimore. The fleet set sail for the Patapsco River and Baltimore.

CHAPTER 20

Baltimore

MAJ. GEN. SAMUEL SMITH KNEW, as every citizen in the city knew, that the British were heading for Baltimore. He did not know when the masts of the enemy armada would appear off the Patapsco River, but he knew it would be only a matter of days, if not hours, especially after the news reached Baltimore of the British occupation of Washington, D.C. Only forty miles separated Washington from Baltimore, and Smith expected the British to strike at any moment.

Smith was a political powerhouse in Maryland—a veteran of the Revolutionary War, a U.S. representative, interim secretary of the Navy, and most recently a U.S. senator. He also commanded the 3rd Division of the Maryland militia, and when Cockburn had first appeared off Baltimore in 1813, the mayor had turned to Smith to organize the city's defenses. The city leaders again turned to Smith, who had the backing of Brig. Gen. John Stricker, who commanded the 3rd Brigade of Smith's division; Capt. Oliver Hazard Perry; Capt. Robert T. Spence, commander of the sloop of war *Erie*; and Maj. George Armistead, commander of the city's Regulars stationed at Fort McHenry. Smith agreed to command the defenses with one caveat: his authority was to be absolute. He was not going to allow the breakdown in command and control that had doomed Winder. The city leaders agreed, as did Governor Levin Winder, who gave the sixty-two-year-old Smith direct command of the Baltimore area, putting him in charge of Winder's nephew, Brig. Gen. William Winder, the luckless loser at Bladensburg.[1]

The command question settled, Smith set about preparing to meet the British. He called in troops from everywhere. Militia streamed in from Pennsylvania, Virginia, and Maryland. There were some very familiar faces. Col. James Hood, commander of the Annapolis militia at Bladensburg, showed up with 500 of his once 800-man-strong battalion. William Pinkney reported with his riflemen, all of whom now had rifles. Lt. Col. Joseph Sterrett and the 5th also reported. All of them were itching for redemption after Bladensburg. The units that probably pleased Smith the most, however, were the sailors and Marines who began to report back to Baltimore after attempting to destroy

Gordon's flotilla on the Potomac. Commodore John Rodgers had pulled nearly 1,200 of the tough fighters out of Baltimore on August 24 to help in the defense of Washington. Now, two weeks later, they began to return.[2]

By September 10 Smith had more than 15,000 men guarding the city.[3] The linchpin was Fort McHenry, the masonry-and-earth fortress that dominated the approaches to the inner harbor. A French military engineer had designed the star-shaped bastion so that each gun emplacement covered the others. Smith, since the invasion scare of 1813, had beefed up those defenses. The fort sat on a spit of land called Whetstone Point, where the Patapsco split into the Northwest Branch, which led directly to the inner harbor, and the Ferry Branch, which curved to the west before arcing back to within a mile of the city. The Lazaretto, Commodore Barney's former headquarters, sat across from McHenry. Smith strung a massive wooden chain-linked boom across the Patapsco from the Lazaretto to Fort McHenry. He put Navy lieutenant George Budd in command of Fort Look Out, which mounted seven 24-pounder cannon, and told the sailors to ready a group of old merchant vessels for scuttling behind the boom if necessary. On the Northwest Branch he positioned Chesapeake Flotilla veteran Lt. Solomon Rutter with the city's barges and a handful of Navy gunboats to defend the boom.[4]

In a shrewd tactical move, Smith put naval officers in charge of every harbor defensive point except for Fort McHenry. Navy lieutenant Henry Newcomb and eighty sailors manned 10-gun Fort Covington, which sat a mile west from McHenry on the Ferry Branch. Five hundred yards east of Covington, Sailing Master John Webster and sixty-five flotillamen manned 6-gun Fort Babcock. At the Lazaretto, Lt. Solomon Frazier of the flotilla set up three 12-pounder field guns behind an earthwork while Sailing Master Solomon Rodman and still more flotilla veterans manned five big 32-pounder cannon at the water battery at Fort McHenry. Smith "borrowed" the guns from a French warship stranded in the harbor and sent two militia artillery units to the water battery as well, swelling the number of cannon in the battery to twenty-six.[5]

At Fort McHenry, Maj. George Armistead commanded a garrison that now numbered nearly one thousand men. In addition to his Regular Army artillerymen Armistead had several volunteer units assigned to his post and six hundred Regular Army infantry poised to attack any landing the British might attempt. Depending on the weather conditions, floating over the fort was either the massive American garrison flag or the smaller American storm flags that Armistead had commissioned from local seamstress Mary Pickersgill the year before.

Smith concentrated his land defenses east of the city, fortifying Hampstead Hill, which would protect the city from an attack coming from the most logical direction. Smith anchored the line north of the city hospital and ran it right to the edge of the harbor. He posted 10,000 men and 63 guns in the

An 1814 painting shows Gen. John Stricker and his staff, center, placing troops on the field near North Point, outside Baltimore. MARYLAND HISTORICAL SOCIETY, BALTIMORE

U.S. Army artillery officer
Maj. George Armistead com-
manded the garrison and guns
at Fort McHenry. Painting by
Rembrandt Peale. MARYLAND
HISTORICAL SOCIETY, BALTIMORE

trenches, putting his best force, the 700
sailors and Marines under Rodgers, in
a redoubt in the center of the line. The
militiamen dubbed the redoubt "Rodgers
Bastion."[6]

There was little more Smith could
do. He, along with his soldiers, settled
in to wait. The masts of Cochrane's fleet
hove into view on September 11. Among
the many vessels was an American truce
ship that followed behind the British
flagship, the 80-gun ship of the line *Tonnant*. On board the *Tonnant* were two
Americans, John S. Skinner and Francis
Scott Key, whom President Madison had
sent to negotiate the release of an American doctor captured by the British. They
succeeded in obtaining the release of Dr.
William Beanes, but Cochrane detained
the Americans after they overheard the
admiral and his staff planning the attack on Baltimore. Before beginning the
bombardment he had all three transferred to the American truce boat under
guard by Royal Marines. Nevertheless, they were in the middle of the British
fleet as it began its bombardment of Fort McHenry.

Ross began disembarking his land troops at 3 a.m. at North Point, some
fourteen miles southeast of Baltimore's eastern defenses. His army of about
4,700 men included a battalion of 600 Royal Marines and small-arms-trained
sailors. "It was seven o'clock before the whole army was disembarked and in
order for marching," reported Lt. George Robert Gleig of the 85th Foot.[7] The
British were in high spirits as they set off toward Baltimore. The only opposition they expected to meet was militia, and Wellington's Invincibles knew how
to deal with American citizen-soldiers. Ross had declared he did not care if it
"rained militia," and this same attitude infected his army.[8]

The British advanced about three miles before stopping to regroup and
rest. Once again the summer heat and humidity quickly sapped the redcoats'
stamina. Ross and Cockburn took over a farm belonging to Robert Gorsuch
and enjoyed a leisurely breakfast while waiting for Col. Arthur Brooke, second in command of the army, to push forward with the bulk of the troops,
including six artillery pieces. Brooke, however, had orders not to advance
until the entire army had disembarked and could move as a single unit. A
delay of several hours ensued as the British rowed ashore, assembled, and
began moving out.[9]

Waiting for the British were Brig. Gen. John Stricker and his brigade of 3,200 Maryland militiamen. Stricker's men had received a warm reception when they marched from Baltimore to the Patapsco Peninsula, where they took up a position to block Ross. Stricker arranged his brigade in a line at a narrows between two creeks astride the road leading to North Point. He placed the 5th Maryland on the right side of the road and the 27th Maryland on the left, and put the 51st and 39th Regiments in line behind them. He held the 6th Regiment in reserve. An artillery battery of seventy-five men and six 4-pounder field guns held the center of the front line. Stricker placed the rifle corps—companies under Maj. William Pinkney and Capt. Edward Ainsquith—forward of the line in a dense wood to slow down Ross' advance. The general gave his militia officers clear, concise orders. If the first line had to fall back, the units were to filter through the second line and regroup with the reserves.

As the morning wore on, scouts brought Stricker word that the British were still enjoying their rest at the Gorsuch farm. He decided to push a force of 230 men and a cannon forward to literally pick a fight with Ross and goad him into an attack. Among the units Stricker sent forward was a small company of riflemen under the command of Ainsquith.

Ross and Cockburn, meanwhile, had finished breakfast and were pushing forward with their advance party. They were roughly five miles from the landing beach when they encountered resistance in the form of Stricker's advance party. Ainsquith's riflemen opened fire on Ross' party from the cover of the woods, and the two sides traded volleys. Several of the riflemen fell and others fled. A few held their position. Ross turned to Cockburn and shouted, "I'll return and order up the light companies." As he started to ride back toward his advancing columns the riflemen fired again. Ross slumped over in his saddle, then fell off his horse. Officers advancing with the column came upon their wounded leader lying on the ground attended by his aide de camp, Lieutenant Gleig. The advance party of the first British brigade reported, "We were already drawing near the scene of the action when another officer came at full speed towards us, with horror and dismay on his countenance, and calling loudly for a surgeon. . . . In a few moments we reached the ground where the skirmishing had taken place and saw General Ross laid by the side of the rode under a canopy of blankets and apparently in the agonies of death."[10]

Ross' death dampened but did not destroy the spirits of his men. Brooke rode forward on hearing the news of the general's death and found his light infantry drawn up facing the American line. Brooke brought up the remainder of his troops just as the American artillery began to bark. He ordered his own artillery and rocket battery to engage the Americans while he deployed his infantry. The light infantry of the 85th, bolstered with elements of the 44th Foot and some of the Royal Marines and sailors, moved to attack the

American left flank. Brooke had the 4th and 21st arrayed to strike on the right flank, with support from the remaining naval forces.[11]

The American riflemen who had fired on Ross ran back to Stricker's line, and he placed them on his far right flank. His artillery tore into the advancing columns of invaders, but the British artillery took an equal toll on the American line. Stricker had his guns cease firing, hoping to draw the British into canister range. He saw Brooke massing for a punch at his left flank and ordered the 39th and two cannon to take a position on the line. He ordered the 51st into a support position at a right angle to the line, but the raw militiamen were unable to execute the maneuver cleanly. Stricker wanted the seven-hundred-man regiment to run their line from the 39th back toward the rear, from which they could engage any flanking parties, but their slowness in moving into position left them exposed to British cannon and musket fire.[12]

On the right, the 5th was taking everything Brooke's men could give them and giving it right back. The casualties piled up on both sides as the 5th obstinately held its ground. The militiamen's stand earned the respect of their enemies, with Gleig calling them "the flower of the enemy's infantry."[13]

Brooke's men had far more success on the left flank. The 51st had barely fired off one volley when the British replied. The idea of being fired on from the flank was too much for the Americans and they broke, taking with them the 39th Regiment. Brooke ordered his army to charge, and the entire left flank collapsed. The 5th fought on, but the rout of the left flank put them in danger of being surrounded and either wiped out or captured. Stricker, after trying unsuccessfully to rally his fleeing militia, ordered the units still on the field to fall back to Hampstead Hill.[14]

The British, worn out from the march from North Point and the two-hour fight with Stricker's brigade, did not pursue, although Brooke lamented, "Had we had but 300 cavalry not a man would have escaped."[15] The battle, though short, was costly to both sides. The British reported 39 dead and 251 wounded; Stricker reported 24 dead, 130 wounded, and 50 captured.[16]

Brooke drew his army up in front of Smith's earthworks, which extended for roughly a mile. Winder came pounding up with a brigade of Virginia militia and joined forces with Stricker on the left flank of the defensive line while Stansbury and his brigade moved slightly forward on the right. Smith believed Brooke planned a night assault on his position with bayonets, and in his report said he wanted advance elements ready to flank the British depending on where they attempted to strike.

The battle between Stricker and Brooke ended around 3 p.m. Brooke spent the rest of the day scouting the defenses on Hampstead Hill, searching for a soft spot. He decided his best chance for success lay in cooperating with Cochrane's fleet. After receiving a note from Cochrane that the squadron

American militiamen fire on advancing British troops in the opening stages of the Battle of North Point, September 12, 1814, in this oil on canvas painting by Thomas Ruckle. Although a tactical defeat for the United States, the action at North Point prevented the British from advancing directly on Baltimore. MARYLAND HISTORICAL SOCIETY, BALTIMORE would attempt to break into the harbor the next morning, Brooke settled in for the night of September 12 to await developments on the water.[17]

In the forts and batteries dotted around Baltimore Harbor, sailors, soldiers, and Marines watched as the British fleet slowly moved into attack position. Cochrane ordered a squadron of seventeen frigates, brigs, bomb vessels, and his single rocket ship to move up the Patapsco to a spot where they could bombard the fortifications. The warships carefully made their way toward Fort McHenry, anchoring about two and a half miles from the fort's nearest guns. Cochrane, on board the frigate *Surprize*, commanded the advance squadron.[18] Just after sunrise on September 13, the bomb ship *Volcano* fired a pair of ranging shots that fell short of the fort. Her captain inched the vessel closer, with the *Terror*, *Devastation*, *Aetna*, and *Meteor* following behind. The little tender *Cockchafer* and the rocket ship *Erebus* also moved in closer. Before the bomb and rocket ships could anchor in a firing position, the *Cockchafer* let loose a broadside that did little to disturb Armistead's defenders.[19] At 7 a.m. the *Meteor* opened fire, lofting a 200-pound shell at the fort. The other bomb ships also opened fire, as did the *Erebus*.[20] Shells and rockets whizzed over Fort McHenry. Armistead gamely returned fire, but his 24- and 36-pounder guns simply did not have the range. After a three-hour exchange, Armistead ordered his gunners to cease firing.[21]

For Colonel Brooke, the commencement of the bombardment signaled the next phase in the plan to take Baltimore. Brooke and his army were camped about a mile in front of the American line on Hampstead Hill. He had no intention of hitting the center. He could see the strength of the redoubt Rodgers had built, although he did not know he had veteran sailors and Marines facing him. Instead, he looked to the flanks. He was counting on Cochrane getting past the harbor defenses so they could give fire support to his attack. Brooke moved troops northward to flank the American left, believing this would cause the militia to flee and open the road to Baltimore for his army.[22] Smith saw the maneuver and repositioned his troops to protect his flank.

The bombardment went on hour after hour. The five bomb ships could hurl between forty-five and fifty shells an hour, giving the British an overwhelming and essentially unchallenged edge in firepower. After two hours little had changed, other than that the Americans had stopped firing back. By 11 a.m. Cochrane was growing ever more pessimistic about his chances of smashing through the defenses and aiding Brooke's land attack. Despite his misgivings, Cochrane continued to pound the fort. At 2 p.m. a shell landed squarely on the crew of a 24-pounder, killing the gun officer and two others and dismounting the gun. As artillerymen struggled to remount the gun another shell burst, killing yet another defender. More shells slammed into the fort, one of them penetrating the main magazine. Luckily for the defenders, either the fuse fizzled or a soldier was able to douse the fuse before it could explode. Armistead ordered his men to empty the magazine and place the powder along the rear wall of the fort.[23]

Lieutenant Frazier at the Lazaretto had a clear view of the British squadron, yet for hours he was powerless to do anything about the bombardment. All he and the other commanders around the harbor wanted was the chance to hit back. They got their chance around 3 p.m. when the silence from Fort McHenry induced Cochrane to send the bomb ships, the *Erebus*, and a frigate in closer to finish off the Americans. It was exactly the opportunity for which Frazier, Lieutenant Rutter, and Major Armistead had been waiting. Every gun the Americans could bring to bear opened fire.[24]

At the Lazaretto, Frazier took aim with the one 12-pounder, sighting in on the *Erebus* and opening fire. Lieutenant Rutter on the barges also opened fire, as did the big 36-pounder cannon and 42-pounder carronades at Fort McHenry. The volley staggered the British.[25] The *Volcano* took five hits. A cannonball tore through the *Devastation*'s bow and another took out her topmast. As the Americans reloaded, Cochrane frantically raised signal flags ordering the vessels back to their original position. The British limped out of range and once more began lobbing shells.[26]

Once back in their former position, the bomb ships renewed their attack with new intensity. As though to punctuate the assault, a late summer storm blew in from the Chesapeake. Peals of thunder and flashes of lightning joined in with the red streaks of Congreve rockets and orange shellbursts. The storm

John Bower's iconic print shows a view of the British bombardment of Fort McHenry on September 13, 1814. MARYLAND HISTORICAL SOCIETY, BALTIMORE

added to the misery of Fort McHenry's defenders because there was limited shelter for them from either the rain or the storm of British fire.

In front of Hampstead Hill, Colonel Brooke found himself in a quandary. He had yet to receive Cochrane's note telling him not to expect naval support, but he knew he lacked enough men to launch a direct assault. He had initially expected to attack the American defenses that morning, but delay after delay had scuttled that plan. His letter to Cochrane, which he sent around midnight, told the admiral he expected to be in Baltimore sometime between noon and 1 p.m. That plan too fell apart when Brooke got a better look at the defensive works in front of him. The continuous downpour that afternoon further delayed the assembly of his troops in an assault formation.[27]

After scouting the American line, Brooke was surprised to find Stricker's and Winder's troops positioned on the left flank he had thought was open. A daylight attack was now out of the question. Brooke and Cockburn believed that a night attack, however, when American artillery would be less effective (because the gunners would not be able to see the attackers), might allow the British to turn the American left flank and smash their way into Baltimore. He sent a note to Cochrane asking the admiral if he could conduct some sort of diversion on the Ferry Branch that would draw off some of the defenders while he attacked what he believed was the weak left flank.[28] He set the time for the attack at 2 a.m. and ordered Cockburn's aide, Lieutenant Scott, to carry a message to Cochrane asking him to set up the diversion.

Scott arrived on board the *Surprize* with Brooke's note around 3:30 p.m.[29] Cochrane looked toward Baltimore and saw no signs of fighting, then gave way to caution. He sent Cockburn, who was with Brooke, a curt order all but canceling the land attack. "It is impossible for the Ships to render you any assistance—the town is so far retired within the Forts. It is for Colonel Brooke to consider under such circumstances whether he has force sufficient to defeat so large a number as it [is] said the enemy has collected; say 20,000 strong or even a less number and to take the town: without this can be done it will be only throwing the men's lives away and prevent us from going upon other services."[30]

Scott raced back to Brooke and Cockburn with Cochrane's glum assessment, arriving at the army's camp around 6 p.m. After reading the admiral's letter, Brooke called a council of war with his officers. Cockburn, as always, was for the original plan. He believed the land forces could push through the militia with or without naval support. The other officers, however, were not so sure, and neither was Brooke. The debate lasted until midnight.[31] When he finally made a decision, Brooke wrote to Cochrane: "I called a council of war, though I had made all my arrangements for attacking the Enemy at three in the morning the result of which was that from the situation I was placed in, they advised I should retire. I have therefore ordered the retreat to take place tomorrow morning, and hope to be at my destination the day after tomorrow that is the place we disembarked from."[32]

Brooke's message did not reach Cochrane until 7:30 the next morning. The admiral, unaware that Brooke had canceled the attack, had decided to move forward with the diversion. At 9:30 p.m. on September 13, Cochrane sent Capt. Charles Napier orders to make an attack on the Ferry Branch. Cochrane told Napier to take "an additional quantity of blank cartridges to fire for the intention of drawing the notice of the enemy." He was to take twenty boats of Royal Marines and sailors under muffled oars and row along the riverbank until he came to a point where he could make enough noise to make the Americans believe the British were launching a new offensive. Cochrane told Napier to begin his diversion at 1 a.m. and continue it until he could hear "the army is seriously engaged," at which time he was to return to the fleet.[33]

All during this time, the bomb ships continued to loft shells at Fort McHenry. The fire slackened then ceased around 9 p.m. Thirty minutes later Napier and his men boarded their boats and began pulling for Ferry Branch in a driving rain. The night was pitch black, and they had nothing on which to get bearings because both the warships and the fort were silent. Napier and nine boats made the turn up the Ferry Branch, but the other eleven boats missed the turn and instead rowed directly toward the line of gunboats stationed between the Lazaretto and the fort. The men manning the guns were dead tired; otherwise they probably would have spotted the eleven boats filled with British mariners. The men in the eleven boats realized their mistake and turned around before they had ventured too far up the Northwest Branch and returned to the *Surprize*.[34]

Napier and his nine boats continued on their way. They silently rowed past Fort McHenry and, keeping to the shoreline, had nearly passed Fort Babcock when Sailing Master Webster heard the sound of oars. He peered into the darkness and after personally aiming each of his big 18-pounders, ordered his men to open fire. Lieutenant Newcomb at Fort Covington also heard Napier's rowers and opened fire at the same time.[35] Minutes later the gunners at Fort McHenry opened up, as did the British bomb ships, which launched their fiercest bombardment yet.

Napier held his position for nearly two hours, miraculously escaping injury amid the storm of grape and canister coming from Fort Babcock and Fort Covington. But he could neither see nor hear any signs of battle coming from Baltimore. Brooke's attack was supposed to kick off at 2 a.m., but at 3 a.m. there was still no sign of a land attack. Napier decided to head back to the flotilla. His men set off, hugging the far shore from the forts. As they passed Fort McHenry one officer fired a signal flare to alert the squadron the boats were returning. The flare also alerted the gunners in Fort McHenry, who opened a massive bombardment on the boats. Napier reported just two men wounded, but Armistead reported finding three bodies and two smashed boats.[36]

The British bombardment came to a final end around 4 a.m. Key and Skinner, on board the truce ship, tried to determine whether the cessation meant that Fort McHenry and Baltimore had fallen or that the defenders had managed to beat them off. Nearly three hours would pass before they knew. In accordance with regulations, the garrison of Fort McHenry assembled in front of the tall flagpole inside the fort and ran up the garrison flag at 9 a.m. The sight of the Stars and Stripes unfurling in the morning breeze was an indelible moment for Francis Scott Key.

The British fleet withdrew downriver to North Point to embark Brooke's troops. Cochrane released Key, Skinner, Dr. Beanes, and the American truce boat and crew, and the British fleet slowly made its way down the Chesapeake. The battle for Baltimore was over. The American defenders suffered twenty-eight casualties, including four dead, in the bombardment. British casualties were likely about ten dead or wounded.

As the truce boat passed Fort McHenry on the way to Baltimore everyone on board saw the large garrison flag flying over the fort. Emotions must have been keenly felt. That evening, in a hotel in Baltimore, Key put pen to paper and wrote down the lyrics he had been constructing in his mind all day. "The Defense of Fort M'Henry," as he titled the song, set to the well-known tune "Anacreon in Heaven," soon became known as "The Star-Spangled Banner." The next day the lyrics were printed as a broadside and copies handed out to the defenders of Fort McHenry. The patriotic song and the lyrics quickly became popular throughout the United States.

The majority of the British ships left the Chesapeake for Halifax, Bermuda, or elsewhere. A greatly diminished blockade of the Chesapeake remained in force into the winter as the fighting around the bay continued. The British occupied Tilghman Island on the Maryland Eastern Shore and skirmished with local militia at Tracys Landing on October 27 and at Kirby's Wind Mill on October 31, both in Anne Arundel County. They raided St. Inigoes in St. Mary's County on October 30 and Tappahannock, Virginia, on December 2. The British finally abandoned their major base of operations at Tangier Island on December 13.[37]

Perhaps the least known post-Baltimore incident of the war occurred in Dorchester County, Maryland, on February 7, 1815, a month after the Battle of New Orleans. A raiding party from the tender of the British sloop *Dauntless* pillaged the area around Madison, taking sheep and burning several vessels. As the raiders began making their way back to the Patuxent River, the tender encountered considerable drift ice and became icebound off James Island. Members of the 48th Maryland militia engaged the raiders, and after a two-hour musket barrage the tender's crew of twenty surrendered, including a lieutenant, a midshipmen, thirteen crewmen, three Royal Marines, and a civilian black man and woman. This was the last engagement between the United States and Great Britain in the Chesapeake, although the British liberated eight slaves without opposition from Loker Plantation in southern Maryland on February 20. On March 10 the last British warship, the frigate *Orlando*, left the Chesapeake.[38]

The war along the Canadian border fizzled out as both sides dug in for the winter. The British built up their force in Canada to 30,000 soldiers, expecting to launch an offensive when the rivers and lakes thawed. The Americans had assembled more than 9,000 Regulars and 20,000 militiamen preparing for their own offensive.[39]

Across the Atlantic, in Ghent, Belgium, representatives of Great Britain and the United States opened talks to end the war. Eleven days later the two warring sides came to terms and signed the Treaty of Ghent. Cochrane, who had no idea of the talks or of the treaty, moved forward with his plan to attack New Orleans, arriving off Mobile Bay, Alabama, on December 13. He launched his attack on January 8, 1815. The American defenders, under Gen. Andrew Jackson, handed the British a bloody repulse. A month later, on February 17, 1815, both sides ratified the Treaty of Ghent, officially ending the war.[40]

Secretary of War John Armstrong resigned under pressure after the Battle of Bladensburg. Madison replaced him with James Monroe, who served simultaneously as both secretary of state and secretary of war. Secretary of the Navy William Jones tendered his resignation soon after the British attack on Baltimore but agreed to stay on until November 30. The Navy Department, however, was in disarray. Capt. Charles Gordon, who was still in Norfolk with the *Constellation*, sent letter after letter to Jones and his temporary replacement, Benjamin Homans, asking for permission to take the *Constellation* to sea. He never received it. In January 1815, new Navy secretary Benjamin Crowninshield sent Gordon orders to ready the *Constellation* to take part in Stephen Decatur's expedition against Algiers, which had allied itself with England during the war. For Gordon, it was scant consolation.

"During this war it has been my misfortune to be deprived all opportunity of performing my part in common with my brother officers," he wrote to Crowninshield. "And when the field for fame is to be again open, I must depend upon the next British war as I cannot conceive any other victory so brilliant as those obtained over a proud Briton."[41] Gordon never got his revenge. He spent 1815 and 1816 in the Mediterranean, but his exertions exacerbated the wound he had suffered in his duel with Hanson. Charles Gordon died on September 6, 1816, in Messina, Sicily.

NOTES

Chapter 1. Irreconcilable Differences

1. Charles J. Ingersoll, *Historical Sketch of the Second War between the United States of America and Great Britain* (Philadelphia: Lea and Blanchard, 1845), 1: 20–23.
2. Donald R. Hickey, *The War of 1812: The Forgotten Conflict* (Chicago and Urbana: University of Illinois Press, 1989), 20–21.
3. Edward Preble to Robert Smith, October 23, 1803, Letters and Papers of Edward Preble, Library of Congress, Manuscript Division. See also numerous reports from John Rodgers, Stephen Decatur, Isaac Hull, Jacob Jones, and David Porter to the secretary of the Navy regarding British attempts to lure or impress U.S. Navy sailors, in Letters Received by the Secretary of the Navy from Commanders, National Archives and Records Administration [hereafter NARA], Record Group [hereafter RG] 45, microfilm roll [hereafter MR] 147.
4. Ingersoll, *Historical Sketch*, 1: 36–38.
5. George C. Daughan, *If by Sea: The Forging of the American Navy—from the American Revolution to the War of 1812* (New York: Basic Books, 2008), 276–77.
6. Walter R. Borneman, *1812: The War That Forged a Nation* (New York: HarperCollins, 2004), 39–41. See also Lisa R. Morales, *The Financial History of the War of 1812* (Denton: University of North Texas Press, 2009).
7. Hickey, *Forgotten Conflict*, 17–19.
8. Ingersoll, *Historical Sketch*, 1: 23–27.
9. Timothy Pickering to Rufus King, October 26, 1796, Timothy Pickering Papers, Massachusetts Historical Society, Boston.
10. James Madison, Message to Congress, Declaration of War, June 1, 1812, *American State Papers, House Journal*, 456–58.
11. Resolution of Maryland Legislature, November 26, 1811, in William H. Marine, *The British Invasion of Maryland, 1812–1815* (Baltimore: Society of the War of 1812 in Maryland, 1913), 1–2.
12. Joseph H. Nicholson, quoted in Marine, *British Invasion*, 4.
13. Charles E. Trow, *The Old Shipmasters of Salem, with Mention of Eminent Merchants* (New York: G. P. Putnam and Sons, 1905), 12–13; Report of Albert Gallatin to Congress, February 27, 1812, 12th Cong., 1st sess., *American State Papers, Commerce and Navigation*, 1: 926–28.
14. Trow, *Shipmasters of Salem*, 13.

15. Hickey, *Forgotten Conflict*, 55.

16. J. Thomas Scharf, *The Chronicles of Baltimore* (Baltimore: Turnbull Brothers, 1874), 309–16.

17. Various historians have estimated the antiwar population as 35 percent to 45 percent of Americans. See Hickey, *Forgotten Conflict*; Daughan, *If by Sea*; and Everett T. Thomlinson, *The War of 1812* (New York: Silver Burdett and Company, 1906). The latter, although old, uses individual stories to detail Americans' and Canadians' views on the war.

18. William L. Calderhead, "A Strange Career in a Young Navy: Captain Charles Gordon, 1778–1816," *Maryland History Magazine* 72, no. 3 (1972): 373–74.

19. Ibid.

20. *Register of Officer Personnel United States Navy and Marine Corps and Ships' Data, 1801–1807* (Washington, D.C.: Government Printing Office, 1945), 21.

21. Ibid.

22. Department of the Navy, *Proceedings of the General Court Martial of Commodore James Barron, Captain Charles Gordon, Mr. William Hook and Captain John Hall of the United States Ship* Chesapeake *in June, 1808* (Washington, D.C.: Jacob Gideon Jr., 1822), 98–100.

23. Ibid.

24. Ibid., 6.

25. Ibid., 421.

26. Ibid., 422–23.

27. Ibid., 440.

28. Charles Gordon to Paul Hamilton, July 29, 1809, Letters of Masters Commandants to the Secretary of the Navy, NARA, RG 147, MR 2.

29. Paul Hamilton to Charles Gordon, August 19, 1809, Letters of Navy Secretaries to Officers, NARA, RG 149, MR 8.

30. Ibid., 57.

31. Marine, *British Invasion*, 2.

32. *Federalist Republican*, June 20, 1812, quoted in Marine, *British Invasion*, 7–8.

33. *Exact and Authentic Narrative of the Events That Took Place in Baltimore the 27th and 28th of July Last, Carefully Collected from Some of the Eyewitnesses* (Baltimore, Md., 1812) [hereafter *Events*], 4.

34. Ibid., 6.

35. Ibid., 5.

36. Ibid.

37. Scharf, *Chronicles of Baltimore*, 338–39.

38. *Events*, 8.

39. Scharf, *Chronicles of Baltimore*, 337–38.

40. Ibid., 339.
41. Calderhead, "A Strange Career," 382.
42. Charles Gordon to John Bullus, May 7, 1812, Charles Gordon Collection, Miscellaneous Papers, New York Public Library.
43. Calderhead, "A Strange Career," 386.
44. Scharf, *Chronicles of Baltimore*, 339.

Chapter 2. A Very Exposed Coast

1. *Historical Register of the Army of the United States* (Washington, D.C.: Government Printing Office, 1903) [hereafter *Army Register*], 48.
2. Ibid., 63.
3. Ibid., 65.
4. *Number of Troops in the Last War with Great Britain*, 35th Cong., 1st sess. (n.s.) [hereafter *Number of Troops*], 2.
5. Ibid., 4.
6. Ibid., 3.
7. John R. Elting, *Amateurs to Arms: A Military History of the War of 1812* (Chapel Hill, N.C.: Algonquin Books, 1991), 13–15, 136–39.
8. Ibid.
9. Ibid.
10. Report of Secretary of the Navy Paul Hamilton, December 14, 1811, *American State Papers, Naval Affairs*, 265.
11. Ibid.
12. See Chipp Reid, *Intrepid Sailors: The Legacy of Preble's Boys and the Tripoli Campaign* (Annapolis, Md.: Naval Institute Press, 2012).
13. Report of Secretary of the Navy Paul Hamilton, November 26, 1809, *American State Papers, Naval Affairs* [hereafter Hamilton Report to Congress], 202.
14. Howard I. Chapelle, *History of the American Sailing Navy: The Ships and Their Development* (New York: W. W. Norton, 1949), 189–91.
15. *Annals of Congress*, 9th Cong., 2nd sess., February 10, 1807, 460; Hamilton Report to Congress, 204.
16. Chapelle, *Sailing Navy*, 196–212.
17. Thomas Jefferson to Thomas Paine, September 6, 1807, Thomas Jefferson Papers, ser. 1, Library of Congress.
18. Albert Gleaves, *James Lawrence* (New York: G. P. Putnam and Sons, 1904), 57–58.
19. Ibid., 58.
20. Ibid., 56.
21. Hamilton Report to Congress, 204.
22. Jefferson to Paine, September 6, 1807.

23. James R. Jacobs and Glenn Tucker, *The War of 1812: A Compact History* (New York: Hawthorne Books, 1969), 197.

24. F. Edward Wright, *Maryland Militia, War of 1812* (Silver Spring, Md.: Family Line, 1979), 1: 16.

25. Ibid., 1: 20.

26. Jacobs and Tucker, *The War of 1812*, 197.

27. Robert Wirth and Thomas Pinder, unpublished research for Wells-McComma VFW Post, Edgemore, Md.

28. William James, *The Naval History of Great Britain from the Declaration of War by France in 1793 to the Accession of George IV* (London: R. Bentley, 1878), 4: 230.

29. James Scott, *Recollections of a Naval Life* (London: Richard Bentley, 1834), 3: 123.

30. Harold L. Peterson, *The Book of the Continental Soldier* (Harrisburg, Pa.: Stackpole, 1968), 42.

31. Oswald Tilghman, *History of Talbot County, Maryland, 1661–1861* (Baltimore: Williams and Wilkins, 1915), 2: 157–59.

32. Marine, *British Invasion*, 48.

33. Ibid.

34. Calderhead, "A Strange Career," 382.

35. John Warren to John W. Croker, January 9, 1813, Papers of Admiral Alexander I. Cochrane, Admiralty Letters to Admiral Sir John Borlase Warren, 1812–1814, Library of Congress, Manuscript Division, MS2340 [hereafter Warren Orders].

36. Christopher T. George, *Terror on the Chesapeake: The War of 1812 on the Bay* (Shippensburg, Pa.: White Maine Books, 2000), 12–13.

37. Ibid., 13.

38. John Philips Cranwell and William Bowers Crane, *Men of Marque: A History of Private Armed Vessels out of Baltimore during the War of 1812* (New York: W. W. Norton, 1940), 371–401.

39. See Edgar Stanton Maclay, *A History of American Privateers* (New York: D. Appleton and Company, 1899), for a complete story on privateers and their impact on the British economy. Maclay scatters statistics throughout the book.

Chapter 3. The Gathering Storm

1. Claude Berube and John Rodgaard, *A Call to the Sea: Captain Charles Stewart of the USS* Constitution (Washington, D.C.: Potomac Books, 2005), 66–68.

2. Ibid., 68.

3. Charles Stewart to William Jones, February 5, 1813, in *Naval War of 1812: A Documentary History*, ed. William S. Dudley, (Washington, D.C.: Naval Historical Center, 1985) [hereafter *Documentary History*], 2: 311.

4. Benjamin Bryan, *Constellation* log, February 3, 1813, in Dudley, *Documentary History*, 2: 393.

5. Charles Stewart to William Jones, February 3, 1813, in Dudley, *Documentary History*, 2: 311.

6. Log of HMS *San Domingo*, February 4–5, 1813, Public Records Office, London [hereafter PRO], ADM 512834.

7. Two books, both by Andrew Lambert, are invaluable for the study of Britain's admirals and the Royal Navy in the Age of Sail: *Admirals* (London: Faber and Faber, 2009), and *War at Sea in the Age of Sail* (New York: Collins, 2005).

8. *Dictionary of National Biography* (London: Smith, Elder, and Company, 1908–9), 20: 679–72.

9. Ibid.

10. James Pack, *The Man Who Burned the White House: Admiral Sir George Cockburn, 1772–1853* (Annapolis, Md.: Naval Institute Press, 1987), 265.

11. Hickey, *War of 1812*, 283.

12. John W. Croker to North American station captains, July 10, 1813, in Dudley, *Documentary History*, 2: 185.

13. Adm. John Warren to Admiralty Lord John W. Croker, October 5, 1812, in Warren Orders.

14. Adm. John Warren to Admiralty Lord John W. Croker, January 9, 1813, in Warren Orders.

15. Log of HMS *San Domingo*, February 4–6, 1813.

16. Pack, *George Cockburn*, 24–30.

17. Scott, *Recollections*, 2: 119.

18. Ibid., 1: 15.

19. John W. Croker to George Cockburn, October 31, 1812, Sir George Cockburn Papers, Library of Congress, Manuscript Division [hereafter Cockburn Papers].

20. Journal of George Cockburn, February 18, 1813, Cockburn Papers.

21. John Warren to George Cockburn, February 15, 1813, Cockburn Papers.

22. George Burdett to John Warren, February 9, 1815, in Dudley, *Documentary History*, 2: 271.

23. Ibid.

24. Ibid.

25. Ibid.

26. George Burdett to John Warren, February 14, 1813, Cockburn Papers.

27. Maclay, *History of American Privateers*, 225–29; Donald A. Petrie, *The Prize Game: Lawful Looting on the High Seas in the Days of Fighting Sail* (New York: Berkley, 1999), 9–11, 147–63.

28. Brian Lavery, *Nelson's Navy: The Ships, Men and Organization, 1793–1815* (Annapolis, Md.: Naval Institute Press, 1987), 116, 131.

Chapter 4. Lighting the Fuse

1. *Norfolk Herald*, February 5, 1813.
2. William F. Carson, "Norfolk and Anglo-American Relations, 1805–1815" (master's thesis, Old Dominion University, Norfolk, Virginia, 1965), 124.
3. Charles Stewart to William Jones, March 22, 1813, in Dudley, *Documentary History*, 2: 316.
4. Cockburn journal, March 11, 1813, Cockburn Papers.
5. James Fenimore Cooper, *History of the Navy of the United States* (New York: Singer and Townsend, 1856), 2: 157.
6. Scott, *Recollections*, 3: 74–75.
7. Charles Stewart to William Jones, March 17, 1813, in Dudley, *Documentary History*, 2: 315.
8. Charles Stewart to William Jones, March 22, 1813, in Dudley, *Documentary History*, 2: 316.
9. George Cockburn to John Warren, March 13, 1813, Cockburn Papers.
10. George Cockburn to Commissioners of Victualing, May 19, 1813, Cockburn Papers.
11. William James, *Naval History of Great Britain* (London: R. Bentley, 1878), 3: 227.
12. John Croker to John Warren, March 20, 1813, Cockburn Papers.
13. Charles Ball, *Fifty Years in Chains* (New York: Dover, 1970), 469.
14. George Cockburn to Kendall Addison, June 11, 1813, Cockburn Papers.
15. Frank A. Cassell, "Slaves of the Chesapeake Bay Area and the War of 1812," *Journal of Negro History* 57, no. 2 (1972): 144–55.
16. Ball, *Fifty Years in Chains*, 471.
17. Scott, *Recollections*, 3: 80.
18. Ibid., 81.
19. Ibid.
20. James Polkinghorne to John Warren, April 3, 1813, in Dudley, *Documentary History*, 2: 340.
21. Ibid.
22. Scott, *Recollections*, 3: 83.
23. Polkinghorne to Warren, April 3, 1813.
24. James, *Naval History*, 3: 225–26.
25. Log of HMS *Fantome*, April 8, 1813, PRO, ADM 51/2295; Scott, *Recollections*, 3: 92.
26. Elias Jones, *History of Dorchester County, Maryland* (Baltimore: Williams and Wilkins, 1902), 254.

27. Cockburn journal, April 12, 1813, Cockburn Papers.
28. Deposition of John Gibson, *American State Papers, Military Affairs*, 1: 363.
29. George Cockburn to John Warren, April 19, 1813, Cockburn Papers.
30. Ibid.
31. John Warren to John Croker, May 28, 1813, Cockburn Papers.
32. George Cockburn to John Warren, May 2, 1813, Cockburn Papers; Scott, *Recollections*, 2: 100.
33. Scott, *Recollections*, 3: 101–2.
34. Ibid.
35. *Niles' Register*, May 15, 1813.
36. George Cockburn to John Warren, May 3, 1813, Cockburn Papers.
37. Ibid.
38. Marine, *British Invasion*, 35.
39. Cockburn to Warren, May 3, 1813.

Chapter 5. By Land and by Sea

1. Elting, *Amateurs to Arms*, 116–27.
2. Ibid., 103–8.
3. Levin Winder to Thomas Foreman, May 28, 1813; and Levin Winder to Caleb Hawkins, May 28, 1813, Maryland Governor and Council Letterbook, 1796–1818, Maryland State Archives, Annapolis [hereafter Governor's Letterbook].
4. Winder to Foreman, May 28, 1813.
5. William Martin and Walter Dorsey to Levin Winder, May 25, 1813, Governor's Letterbook.
6. Ibid.
7. Marine, *British Invasion*, 49–51.
8. Winder to Foreman, May 28, 1813.
9. Scott, *Recollections*, 3: 118–19.
10. Ibid., 120–22.
11. Log of HMS *Mohawk*, May 5, 1813; George Cockburn to John Warren, May 6, 1813, Cockburn Papers.
12. Adm. George Cockburn's report to Adm. John Warren, May 6, 1813, in John Marshall, *Royal Naval Biography; or, Memoirs of the Services of All the Flag Officers, Superannuated Rear Admirals, Retired Captains, Post Captains and Commanders* (London: Longman, Rees, Orme, Brown, and Green, 1830), suppl. 3, p. 244.
13. George Johnston, *History of Cecil County, Maryland* (Elkton, Md., 1881), 420.
14. George Cockburn to John Warren, May 6, 1813, Cockburn Papers.

15. Johnston, *Cecil County*, 420.

16. Cockburn to Warren, May 6, 1813.

17. Deposition of Joshua Ward, *American State Papers, Military Affairs*, 1: 360.

18. Deposition of John Allen, *American State Papers, Military Affairs*, 1: 361.

19. Letter of Dr. Edward Scott, May 1813, Bryan Family Archives, Chestertown, Md.

20. Ibid.

21. Hulbert Footner, *Rivers of the Eastern Shore—Seventeen Maryland Rivers* (Cambridge, Md.: Read Books, 1944), 344–46.

22. Cockburn to Warren, May 6, 1813.

23. *Niles' Weekly Register*, May 15, 1813.

24. Cockburn journal, May 17, 1813, Cockburn Papers; *San Domingo* log, May 8 and May 13, 1814.

25. *San Domingo* log, May 11, 1813; Scott, *Recollections*, 3: 116.

26. George Cockburn to John Stackpole, May 18, 1813, Cockburn Papers.

27. Ibid.

28. William Jones to Charles Gordon, February 16, 1813, in Dudley, *Documentary History*, 2: 331.

29. Charles Gordon to William Jones, February 16, 1813, in Dudley, *Documentary History*, 2: 331.

30. William Jones to Charles Gordon, April 15, 1813, in Dudley, *Documentary History*, 2: 349.

31. Ibid.

32. Charles Gordon to William Jones, April 18, 1813, in Dudley, *Documentary History*, 2: 350.

33. Charles Gordon to William Jones, May 19, 1813, in Dudley, *Documentary History*, 2: 351.

34. Ibid., 2: 352.

35. Ibid.

36. Ibid.

37. Jones to Gordon, April 15, 1813.

38. Charles Gordon to William Jones, June 21, 1813, in Dudley, *Documentary History*, 2: 353.

39. Ibid., 2: 352.

Chapter 6. Target: Norfolk

1. Henry Earl Bathurst to Col. Thomas Beckwith, March 20, 1813, in Dudley, *Documentary History*, 2: 326.

2. Log of HMS *Barrosa*, 358–65; Paul Harris Nicolas, *Historical Record of the Royal Marine Forces* (London: Thomas and William Boone, 1845), 2: 242.

3. George Cockburn orders, July 12, 1813, Cockburn Papers.

4. Napier, *Life and Opinions*, 1: 222.

5. Stuart Lee Butler, *A Guide to Virginia Militia Units in the War of 1812* (Athens, Ga.: New Papyrus Publishing, 1988), 227–43.

6. John Cassin to William Jones, June 21, 1813, in Dudley, *Documentary History*, 2: 358–59.

7. Robert Taylor to John Armstrong, June 18, 1813, quoted in George, *Terror on the Chesapeake*, 42.

8. *Dictionary of Naval Biography* (London, 1909), 2: 191–92.

9. Ibid., 14: 41–43.

10. Napier, *Life and Opinions*, 1: 224.

11. George Cockburn journal, June 12, 1813, and June 16, 1813, Cockburn Papers.

12. Butler, *Virginia Militia Units*, 173.

13. James Saunders to George Cockburn, June 20, 1813, Cockburn Papers; Cassin to Jones, June 21, 1813.

14. John Warren to George Cockburn, June 21, 1813, Cockburn Papers.

Chapter 7. The Battle of Norfolk

1. James Faulkner, letter, June 10, 1813, James Faulkner Papers, Virginia Historical Society, Richmond.

2. Butler, *Virginia Militia Units*, 232, 242.

3. Ibid.

4. Thomas Crabbe, "Recollections of the Last War," *United States Nautical Magazine* 1 (1846): 341–44.

5. Henry Beatty to Moses Myers, undated letter, Henry Beatty Collection, Library of Congress, Manuscript Division.

6. Napier, *Life and Opinions*, 1: 223–25; Scott, *Recollections*, 3: 104–5.

7. Napier, *Life and Opinions*, 1: 217.

8. James Jarvis to Leopold P. C. Cowper, February 12, 1849, Report of the Select Committee on the Defense of Craney Island, Virginia General Assembly, House of Delegates, 1848 [hereafter Defense of Craney Island], 18.

9. Ibid., 20–24.

10. Ibid., 21; James Faulkner to Elisha Boyd, July 6, 1813, Faulkner Papers.

11. Robert Taylor to John Armstrong, July 4, 1813, printed in *Norfolk Gazette*, July 14, 1813.

12. Napier, *Life and Opinions*, 1: 228; Defense of Craney Island, 24.

13. Ibid., 25–26.

14. Scott, *Recollections*, 3: 141–43.

15. William James, *Naval History*, 6: 232.

16. Scott, *Recollections*, 3: 145.

17. Defense of Craney Island, 21, 24.

18. Sydney Beckwith to Robert Taylor, July 6, 1813, *American State Papers, Military Affairs*, 1: 378–79.

19. Log of HMS *San Domingo*, June 22, 1813.

20. Ibid.; Scott, *Recollections*, 3: 145.

21. John Warren to John Croker, June 24, 1813, in Dudley, *Documentary History*, 2: 360.

22. John Warren to Robert Dundas, Viscount Melville, June 23, 1813, unbound manuscript collection of the correspondence between Admiral Sir John Borlase Warren and Robert Dundas, Viscount Melville, First Lord of the Admiralty, National Maritime Museum, Greenwich, England [hereafter Warren-Dundas correspondence].

23. Defense of Craney Island, 21.

24. Butler, *Virginia Militia Units*, 231.

25. John Warren to Robert Dundas, Viscount Melville, June 26, 1813, Warren-Dundas correspondence.

26. Thomas Beckwith to John Warren, June 26, 1813, in Dudley, *Documentary History*, 2: 363; Log of HMS *San Domingo*, June 22, 1813.

27. Stapleton Crutchfield to James Barbour, June 28, 1813, printed in *National Intelligencer*, July 6, 1813.

28. Ibid.

29. Cockburn journal, June 24–25, 1813, Cockburn Papers.

30. Crutchfield to Barbour, June 28, 1813.

31. Ibid.

32. John Cooper to Charles Mallory, June 28, 1813, printed in *Niles' Weekly Register*, July 10, 1813.

33. Nicolas, *Royal Marines*, 2: 244.

34. Crutchfield to Barbour, June 28, 1813; Cooper to Mallory, June 28, 1813.

35. Ibid.

36. Nicolas, *Royal Marines*, 2: 245.

37. Beckwith to Warren, June 26, 1813.

38. Ibid.; Crutchfield to Barbour, June 28, 1813.

39. George Cockburn journal, June 25, 1813, Cockburn Papers.

40. *Niles' Weekly Register*, August 21, 1813.

41. John Warren to Robert Dundas, Viscount Melville, July 6, 1813, Warren-Dundas correspondence.

42. Beckwith to Taylor, July 6, 1813; Napier, *Recollections*, 3: 151.

43. Robert Taylor to Thomas Beckwith, July 5, 1813, *American State Papers, Military Affairs*, 1: 379.

44. George Cockburn journal, June 28, 1813, Cockburn Papers.

45. John Warren to Robert Taylor, June 29, 1813, *American State Papers, Military Affairs*, 1: 376.

Chapter 8. Off the Beaten Path

1. Marine, *British Invasion*, 52.
2. Ibid., 54.
3. John Warren to George Cockburn, March 6, 1813, Cockburn Papers.
4. John Farnum to Nathaniel Shaler, July 13, 1813, in Dudley, *Documentary History*, 2: 186.
5. *The War* (newspaper), July 20, 1813.
6. John Warren to Robert Dundas, Viscount Melville, July 6, 1813, Warren-Dundas correspondence.
7. Nicolas, *Royal Marines*, 2: 246–47.
8. Thomas Singleton to William Hawkins, July 24, 1813, Governor William Hawkins Letterbook, North Carolina State Archives, Raleigh.
9. Farnum to Shaler, July 13, 1813.
10. Napier, *Life and Opinions*, 1: 214.
11. George Cockburn to John Warren, July 12, 1813, Cockburn Papers.
12. Ibid.
13. Farnum to Shaler, July 13, 1813; Cockburn to Warren, July 12, 1813.
14. Nicolas, *Royal Marines*, 2: 248.
15. Singleton to Hawkins, July 24, 1813.
16. Ibid.
17. Cockburn to Warren, July 12, 1813.
18. Log of HMS *Sceptre*, July 14, 1813; Singleton to Hawkins, July 24, 1813.
19. Cockburn to Warren, July 12, 1813.
20. George Cockburn to John Warren, July 19, 1813, in Dudley, *Documentary History*, 2: 365–66.
21. Log of HMS *Diadem*, July 2, 1813.
22. John Warren to Robert Dundas, Viscount Melville, July 2, 1813, and July 22, 1813, Warren-Dundas correspondence.
23. Log of HMS *Junon*, June 28–29, 1813.
24. Logs of HMS *Barrosa*, HMS *Junon*, HMS *Mohawk*, and HMS *Narcissus*, June 30, 1813; *National Intelligencer*, July 9, 1813.
25. *National Intelligencer*, July 9, 1813.
26. Log of HMS *Junon*, July 3, 1813.
27. Robert F. Fulton, *Torpedo War and Submarine Explosives* (New York: William Elliott, 1810), 27.
28. James T. de Kay, *The Battle of Stonington: Torpedoes, Submarines, and Rockets in the War of 1812* (Annapolis, Md.: Naval Institute Press, 1990), 29.

29. Scott, *Recollections*, 3: 69–72.

30. Log of HMS *Plantagenet*, July 27, 1813; *Easton Star*, August 10, 1813.

31. William Jones to Elijah Mix, August 25, 1813, Letters of the Secretary of the Navy to Junior Officers, NARA, RG 45.

32. Log of HMS *Plantagenet*, July 24, 1813.

33. Jones to Mix, August 25, 1813.

34. Ibid.

35. John Warren to John Croker, July 29, 1813, in Dudley, *Documentary History*, 1: 368–69.

36. John Warren to Robert Dundas, Viscount Melville, June 1, 1813, Warren-Dundas correspondence.

37. Charles Morris, *Autobiography of Commodore Charles Morris* (Annapolis, Md.: Naval Institute Press, 2002), 61–63.

38. Henry McClintock to William Jones, July 19, 1813, in Dudley, *Documentary History*, 1: 368.

39. *National Intelligencer*, July 19, 1813.

40. Morris, *Autobiography*, 62–63.

41. Henry McClintock to William Jones, July 19, 1813.

42. Ibid.

43. Ibid.

44. Ibid.

45. Log of HMS *Barrosa*, July 20, 1813; Nicolas, *Royal Marines*, 2: 247.

46. Thomas Beckwith to Henry Goulburn, July 23, 1813, Warren-Dundas correspondence.

Chapter 9. *The Long, Hot Summer*

1. Cockburn journal, July 26, 1813, Cockburn Papers.

2. *National Intelligencer*, July 29, 1813.

3. Charles Morris to William Jones, July 18, 1813, in Dudley, *Documentary History*, 2: 370.

4. William Jones to Charles Morris, July 18, 1813, in Dudley, *Documentary History*, 2: 372.

5. John Warren to Robert Dundas, Viscount Melville, July 22, 1813, Warren-Dundas correspondence.

6. John Warren to Robert Dundas, Viscount Melville, August 23, 1813, Warren-Dundas correspondence.

7. Cockburn journal, August 6–7, 1813, Cockburn Papers.

8. Scott, *Recollections*, 3: 159–60.

9. Oswald Tilghman, *History of Talbot County, Maryland* (Baltimore: Williams and Wilkins, 1915), 2: 161.

10. Charles Morris to William Jones, August 13, 1813, Letters of Captains to the Secretary of the Navy, NARA, RG 45.

11. Morris, *Autobiography*, 63.

12. Tilghman, *Talbot County*, 2: 161.

13. Maine, *British Invasion*, 54.

14. Tilghman, *Talbot County*, 2: 161.

15. Ibid., 2: 157–60.

16. Ibid.

17. Ibid., 2: 164.

18. Henry Baker to George Cockburn, August 10, 1813, Cockburn Papers.

19. Ibid.

20. Ibid.

21. Tilghman, *Talbot County*, 2: 166.

22. J. C. Adams, undated letter in Samuel A. Harrison Manuscript Collection, Maryland Historical Society, MS 432.

23. Interview with Thomas Auld, James Harrison Manuscript Collection.

24. James Polkinghorne to Henry Baker, August 10, 1815, Cockburn Papers.

25. George Cockburn to John Warren, August 10, 1813, Cockburn Papers.

26. Cockburn journal, August 10, 1813, Cockburn Papers.

27. Wright, *Maryland Militia*, 1: 46.

28. John Warren to John Croker, August 23, 1813, Warren-Dundas correspondence.

29. Wright, *Maryland Militia*, 1: 49–50.

30. William Nicholson to Thomas Wright, August 13, 1813, Maryland Historical Society, Manuscript MS 1846 [hereafter Nicholson Report].

31. Ibid.

32. Ibid.

33. Ibid.

34. Napier, *Life and Opinions*, 1: 215.

35. Ibid.

36. Ibid., 1: 216.

37. Nicholson Report.

38. William Nicholson, letter to the editor, *Easton Star*, August 23, 1813.

39. Nicholson Report.

40. Wright letter to the editor, August 23, 1813.

41. Napier, *Life and Opinions*, 1: 220.

42. Ibid.

43. Ibid.

Chapter 10. Bay Blues

1. John Warren to Robert Dundas, Viscount Melville, September 6, 1813, Warren-Dundas correspondence.

2. Logs of HMS *Mohawk* and HMS *San Domingo*, August 28, 1813.

3. John Croker to John Warren, November 4, 1813, Papers of Sir Alexander Cochrane—Admiralty Letters Addressed to Admiral Sir John Borlase Warren and Delivered to Admiral Cochrane on His Assuming Command, MS 2340, Library of Congress, Manuscript Division.

4. Napier, *Life and Opinions*, 1: 230; Nicolas, *Royal Marines*, 2: 250.

5. Cockburn journal, October 21, 1813, Cockburn Papers.

6. Robert Barrie to Mrs. George Clayton, September 4, 1813, in Dudley, *Documentary History*, 2: 384–85.

7. Samuel Jackson to Robert Barrie, September 23, 1813, in Dudley, *Documentary History*, 2: 385–86.

8. Robert Barrie to George Cockburn, October 12, 1813, Cockburn Papers.

9. Ibid.

10. Log of HMS *Dragon*, November 1, 1814; *National Intelligencer*, November 12, 1813.

11. Log of HMS *Dragon*, November 3, 1813.

12. George Pedlar to Robert Barrie, November 5, 1813, in Dudley, *Documentary History*, 2: 395.

13. Robert Barrie to John Warren, November 14, 1813, in Dudley, *Documentary History*, 2: 395–96.

14. Report of the Treasury Department, December 16, 1813, *American State Papers, Finance*, Senate, 13th Cong., 2nd sess., 2: 648.

15. Report of the Treasury Department, January 10, 1814, *American State Papers, Finance* [hereafter Treasury Report], 2: 649–50.

16. Albert Gallatin to James Madison, March 5, 1813, and April 6, 1813, James Madison Papers, Library of Congress, Manuscript Division, ser. 1 [hereafter Madison Papers].

17. U.S. Department of Commerce, *Historical Statistics of the United States from Colonial Times to 1970*, pt. 2, p. 1115.

18. Treasury Report, January 10, 1814.

19. Gene Allen Smith, *The Slaves' Gamble: Choosing Sides in the War of 1812* (New York: Palgrave Macmillan, 2013), 96.

20. Robert Barrie to John Warren, November 16, 1813, in Dudley, *Documentary History*, 2: 396.

21. Smith, *Slaves' Gamble*, 94–95; Ball, *Adventures*, 348–54.

22. Henry Adams, *History of the United States of America during the Administrations of Jefferson and Madison* (Chicago: University of Chicago Press, 1967), 7: 44; Borneman, *1812*, 252–56.

23. James Madison to John Armstrong, September 8, 1813, Madison Papers, ser. 3.

24. Albert Gallatin to James Madison, April 16, 1813, Madison Papers, ser. 3.

25. Alexander Cochrane, *The Fighting Cochranes* (London: Quiller Press, 1983), 141–48.

26. Ibid.

27. Ibid., 311.

28. Alexander Cochrane to Robert Dundas, Viscount Melville, March 25, 1814, Correspondence and Papers of Admiral the Honorable Alexander Forrester Inglis Cochrane Royal Navy, Library of Congress, Manuscript Division [hereafter Cochrane Papers].

29. Cochrane, *Fighting Cochranes*, 237–39.

30. Ibid., 245–48.

31. Robert Stewart Lord Castlereagh, *Memoirs and Correspondence of Viscount Castlereagh, Second Marquess of Londonderry* (London: William Shoberl, 1848–51), 9: 34–35.

32. Alexander Cochrane to George Cockburn, April 28, 1814, Cockburn Papers.

33. Alexander Cochrane to Robert Dundas, Viscount Melville, March 10, 1814, Cochrane Papers.

34. Ibid.

35. Alexander Cochrane to Earl Henry Bathurst, March 25, 1814, Cochrane Papers.

36. George Prevost to Alexander Cochrane, May 17, 1814, Cochrane Papers.

37. Alexander Cochrane to Earl Henry Bathurst, July 1, 1814, Cochrane Papers.

38. Alexander Cochrane to George Cockburn, July 1, 1814, Cochrane Papers.

39. Henry Goulburn to John Croker, March 18, 1813, Cochrane Papers.

40. Walter Lord, *By Dawn's Early Light* (New York: W. W. Norton, 1972), 37–38; Anthony S. Pitch, *The Burning of Washington: The British Invasion of 1814* (Annapolis, Md.: Naval Institute Press, 1998), 21.

41. Earl Henry Bathurst to Alexander Cochrane, May 20, 1814, Cochrane Papers.

42. Ibid.

43. Alexander Cochrane proclamation, April 2, 1814, Cochrane Papers.

44. Smith, *Slaves' Gamble*, 93.

45. James Madison to John Armstrong, May 20, 1814, Madison Papers, ser. 3.

Chapter 11. Sloops, Frigates, and Galleys

1. Charles Morris, *Autobiography of Commodore Charles Morris, U.S. Navy* (Annapolis, Md.: Naval Institute Press, 2002), 68.

2. Howard I. Chapelle, *History of the American Sailing Navy* (New York: W. W. Norton, 1949), 233.

3. Morris, *Autobiography*, 71.

4. Charles Morris to William Jones, December 31, 1813, in Dudley, *Documentary History*, 2: 401.

5. Ibid., 2: 402.

6. Morris, *Autobiography*, 72.

7. Ibid.

8. Ibid.

9. Ibid.

10. For officers' reactions to Lawrence's death, see Morris, *Autobiography*; Alexander Slidell McKenzie, *The Life of Commodore Oliver Hazard Perry* (New York: Harper and Brothers, 1840); Cooper, *History of the Navy of the United States of America*; and Fletcher Pratt, *Preble's Boys* (New York: William Sloane, 1950), 155–56.

11. Charles Gordon to William Jones, October 12, 1813, in Dudley, *Documentary History*, 2: 388.

12. Ibid., 2: 387.

13. Charles Stewart to William Jones, October 18, 1813, in Dudley, *Documentary History*, 2: 370.

14. Benjamin Bryan to William Jones, November 13, 1813, in Dudley, *Documentary History*, 2: 394.

15. William Jones to Charles Gordon, October 28, 1813, in Dudley, *Documentary History*, 2: 393.

16. Charles Gordon to William Jones, December 3, 1813, in Dudley, *Documentary History*, 2: 398.

17. William Jones to Charles Gordon, January 5, 1814, in Michael J. Crawford, *Naval War of 1812: A Documentary History*, vol. 3 (Washington, D.C.: Naval Historical Center), 6.

18. Charles Gordon to William Jones, February 11, 1814, in Crawford, *Documentary History*, 3: 8.

19. Joseph Tarbell to William Jones, February 15, 1814, in Crawford, *Documentary History*, 3: 8.

20. Charles Gordon to William Jones, February 24, 1814, in Crawford, *Documentary History*, 3: 10.

21. William Jones to Charles Gordon, April 15, 1814, in Crawford, *Documentary History*, 3: 13.

22. Report of William Jones to Congress, February 6, 1813, *American State Papers, Naval Affairs*, 1: 285.

23. Mary Barney, *Biographical Memoir of Commodore Joshua Barney* (Boston: Gray and Bowen, 1832), 115–17; Louis Norton, *Joshua Barney: Hero of the Revolution and 1812* (Annapolis, Md.: Naval Institute Press, 2000), 78–80.

24. Biography of Joshua Barney from *Captain Barney's Victory over the* General Monk (Philadelphia, 1806); William Frederick Adams, *Joshua Barney, U.S.N* (Springfield, Mass., 1910); Mary Barney, *Biographical Memoir*; Hubert Footner, *Sailor of Fortune: The Life and Adventures of Commodore Barney, U.S.N.* (New York: Harper Brothers, 1940); Norton, *Joshua*

Barney; Ralph D. Paine, *Joshua Barney: A Forgotten Hero of Blue Water* (New York: Century, 1924).

25. Joshua Barney to William Jones, undated letter, in Dudley, *Documentary History*, 2: 463.

26. Samuel Smith to William Jones, June 10, 1813, in Dudley, *Documentary History*, 2: 148.

27. William Jones to Samuel Smith, June 17, 1813, in Dudley, *Documentary History*, 2: 149–50.

28. Paine, *Forgotten Hero*, 168–69.

29. William Jones to Joshua Barney, September 2, 1813, in Dudley, *Documentary History*, 2: 360.

30. Joshua Barney to William Jones, December 15, 1813, in Dudley, *Documentary History*, 2: 399.

31. Walter Lord, *By Dawn's Early Light* (New York: W. W. Norton, 1972), 26.

32. Joshua Barney to William Jones, December 17, 1813, in Dudley, *Documentary History*, 2: 399.

Chapter 12. Old Tricks

1. Scott, *Recollections*, 3: 178.

2. Robert Barrie to Eliza Clayton, March 14, 1814, in Crawford, *Documentary History*, 3: 18.

3. Alexander Cochrane to George Prevost, March 11, 1814, in Crawford, *Documentary History*, 3: 38.

4. Alexander Cochrane to George Cockburn, April 27, 1813, in Crawford, *Documentary History*, 3: 51–52.

5. Cockburn journal, April 27, 1814, Cockburn Papers.

6. George Cockburn to John Warren, April 18, 1814, Cockburn Papers.

7. George Cockburn to Alexander Cochrane, April 28, 1814, Cockburn Papers.

8. George Cockburn to Alexander Cochrane, April 29, 1814, Cockburn Papers.

9. George Cockburn to William Hammond, May 19, 1814, Cockburn Papers.

10. George Cockburn to John W. Croker, September 2, 1814, Cockburn Papers.

11. Smith, *Slaves' Gamble*, 112.

12. Cockburn to Cochrane, April 28, 1814; Scott, *Recollections*, 3: 119–20.

13. George Cockburn to Alexander Cochrane, May 10, 1814, Cockburn Papers.

14. Donald G. Shomette, *Flotilla: The Patuxent Naval Campaign in the War of 1812* (Baltimore: Johns Hopkins University Press, 2009), 65.

15. George Watts to George Cockburn, May 3, 1814, Cockburn Papers.

16. James Ross to George Cockburn, May 29, 1814, Cockburn Papers.

17. Ibid.

18. *The War* (newspaper), June 14, 1814.

19. Cockburn to Cochrane, April 29, 1814.

20. William Jones to Joshua Barney, April 18, 1814, Crawford, *Documentary History*, 3: 55.

21. Joshua Barney to William Jones, April 14, 1814, in Crawford, *Documentary History*, 3: 54.

22. Joshua Barney to William Jones, May 12, 1814, Letters of Captains to the Secretary of the Navy, NARA, RG 45, MR 148.

23. Joshua Barney to William Jones, January 14, 1814, in Crawford, *Documentary History*, 3: 33.

24. Barney to Jones, April 4, 1814.

25. Orders to Spence to send his men to the flotilla, William Jones to Robert Spence, April 4, 1814, in Crawford, *Documentary History*, 3: 25; condition of the sailors sent to the flotilla in Joshua Barney to William Jones, April 15, 1814, in Crawford, *Documentary History*, 3: 54.

26. Joshua Barney to William Jones, April 15, 1814, in Crawford, *Documentary History*, 3: 54.

27. Joshua Barney to William Jones, May 4, 1814, in Crawford, *Documentary History*, 3: 56–57.

28. Ibid.

29. Ibid.

30. Joshua Barney to William Jones, May 11, 1814, in Crawford, *Documentary History*, 3: 58.

31. Shomette, *Flotilla*, 66.

32. George Cockburn to Robert Barrie, May 31, 1814, Cockburn Papers.

33. Robert Barrie to George Cockburn, June 1, 1814, in Crawford, *Documentary History*, 3: 78.

34. Joshua Barney to William Jones, June 3, 1814, in Crawford, *Documentary History*, 3: 80.

35. Barrie to Cockburn, June 1, 1814.

36. Barney to Jones, June 3, 1814; Barrie to Cockburn, June 1, 1814.

37. Barney to Jones, June 3, 1804.

38. Barrie to Cockburn, June 1, 1814.

39. Barney to Jones, June 3, 1804.

40. Barrie to Cockburn, June 1, 1814.

41. George Cockburn to Robert Barrie, June 3, 1814, Cockburn Papers.

Chapter 13. Up a Creek

1. Joshua Barney to William Jones, June 3, 1813, in Crawford, *Documentary History*, 3: 81.

2. William Jones to Joshua Barney, June 6, 1814, in Crawford, *Documentary History*, 3: 82.
3. Robert Barrie to George Cockburn, June 3, 1814, Cockburn Papers.
4. Scott, *Recollections*, 3: 229–31.
5. Mary Barney, *Biographical Memoir*, 256.
6. George Cockburn to Robert Barrie, June 3, 1814, Cockburn Papers.
7. Robert Barrie to George Cockburn, June 11, 1814, in Crawford, *Documentary History*, 3: 89.
8. Ibid.
9. Ibid.
10. Mary Barney, *Biographical Memoir*, 257–58.
11. Joshua Barney to William Jones, June 11, 1814, in Crawford, *Documentary History*, 3: 88–89; Robert Barrie to George Cockburn, June 11, 1814, Cockburn Papers.
12. Mary Barney, *Biographical Memoir*, 258; Barrie to Cockburn, June 11, 1814.
13. Joshua Barney to William Jones, June 13, 1814, in Crawford, *Documentary History*, 3: 99.
14. Barrie to Cockburn, June 11, 1814.
15. Joshua Barney to William Jones, June 20, 1814, in Crawford, *Documentary History*, 3: 105.
16. Barney to Jones, June 13, 1814.
17. Barrie to Cockburn, June 11, 1814; Robert Barrie to George Cockburn, June 14, 1814, Cockburn Papers.
18. Charles Gordon to William Jones, June 12, 1814, in Crawford, *Documentary History*, 3: 91.
19. Ibid., 3: 92.
20. Charles Gordon to William Jones, June 29, 1814, in Crawford *Documentary* History, 3: 93.
21. Charles Gordon to William Jones, July 18, 1814, in Crawford, *Documentary History*, 3: 96.

Chapter 14. Fire on the Patuxent

1. Samuel Miller Papers, U.S. Marine Corps Museum, Quantico, Va.
2. Ibid.; Edwin N. McClellan, "History of the Marine Corps 1807 to 1812," *Marine Corps Gazette*, March 1923 (electronic version).
3. William Jones, "Condition of the Navy, and the Progress Made in Providing Materials and Building Ships, March 18, 1814," report to U.S. Senate, *American State Papers, Naval Affairs*, 1: 311–13.
4. William Jones to Franklin Wharton, June 10, 1814, in "Proceedings of Court of Enquiry into the Conduct of the Marines at St. Leonard's Creek, Case No. 169," NARA, RG 125, MR 273 [hereafter Miller Enquiry].

5. Edwin N. McClellan, *History of the U.S. Marine Corps* (Washington, D.C.: Marine Corps History Branch, 1925), ch. 10, p. 24.

6. Roster of Marines at St. Leonard and Bladensburg, Samuel Miller Papers.

7. William Jones to Joshua Barney, June 12, 1814, in Crawford, *Documentary History*, 3: 98.

8. Joshua Barney diary, quoted in Marine, *British Invasion*, 64–65.

9. Testimony of 1st Lt. Benjamin Richardson, Miller Enquiry.

10. Joshua Barney to William Jones, June 16, 1814, in Crawford, *Documentary History*, 3: 101–2.

11. Ibid.

12. Notes of Judge Advocate General, Miller Enquiry.

13. Robert Barrie to George Cockburn, June 19, 1814, Cockburn Papers.

14. Ibid.

15. Ibid.

16. Ibid.

17. Ibid.

18. *American and Commercial Daily Advertiser*, June 20, 1814.

19. *Maryland Republican*, June 25, 1814.

20. Mary Barney, *Biographical Memoir*, 258.

21. Barrie to Cockburn, June 19, 1814.

22. George Cockburn to Robert Barrie, June 19, 1814, Cockburn Papers.

23. Joshua Barney to William Jones, June 20, 1814, in Crawford, *Documentary History*, 3:104.

24. Testimony of 1st Lt. Benjamin Richardson, Miller Enquiry.

25. Ibid.

26. Ibid.

27. Barney to Jones, June 20, 1814.

28. William Jones to Joshua Barney, June 14, 1814, in Crawford, *Documentary History*, 3: 100.

29. Ibid.

30. Joshua Barney to William Jones, June 16, 1814, in Crawford, *Documentary History*, 3: 101.

31. William Jones to Joshua Barney, June 18, 1814, in Crawford, *Documentary History*, 3: 102.

32. Ibid.

33. Barney to Jones, June 20, 1814.

34. William Jones to Joshua Barney, June 20, 1814, in Crawford, *Documentary History*, 3: 107.

35. Barney to Jones, June 20, 1814.

36. William Jones to Joshua Barney, June 21, 1814, in Crawford, *Documentary History*, 3: 109.

37. McClellan, *Marine Corps History*, ch. 11, p. 5. In 1834 Congress enacted legislation that placed the Marine Corps firmly under the Department of the Navy.

Chapter 15. The Battle of St. Leonard Creek

1. Testimony of Col. Henry Carberry, Miller Enquiry.
2. Deposition of Commodore Joshua Barney, Miller Enquiry.
3. Ibid.; testimony of Col. Decius Wadsworth, Miller Enquiry.
4. Testimony of 1st Lt. Benjamin Richardson, Miller Enquiry.
5. John Geoghegan to Joshua Barney, July 14, 1814, in Crawford, *Documentary History*, 3: 125.
6. Deposition of Joshua Barney, Miller Enquiry.
7. Thomas Brown to George Cockburn, June 23, 1814, Cockburn Papers.
8. Ibid.
9. Geoghegan to Barney, July 14, 1814.
10. Ibid.
11. *National Intelligencer*, July 19, 1814, letter of officers, 38th U.S. Infantry.
12. Testimony of Col. Henry Carberry and Maj. George Keyser, Miller Enquiry.
13. Testimony of Capt. Alfred Grayson and 1st Lt. Benjamin Richardson, Miller Enquiry.
14. Ibid.
15. Ibid.
16. Geoghegan to Barney, July 14, 1814.
17. Log of HMS *Narcissus*, June 26, 1814.
18. Mary Barney, *Biographical Memoir*, 261.
19. *National Intelligencer*, July 29, 1814; Report of Col. Decius Wadsworth to Secretary of War John Armstrong, July 26, 1814, Miller Enquiry.
20. Ibid.
21. Testimony of Capt. Alfred Grayson, 1st Lt. Benjamin Richardson, and Lt. William Nicoll, Miller Enquiry; Samuel Miller to Franklin Wharton, June 27, 1814, published in the *National Intelligencer*, July 7, 1814.
22. Testimony of John Geoghegan, Miller Enquiry.
23. Mary Barney, *Biographical Memoir*, 261.
24. Ibid., 259.
25. Joshua Barney to Louis Barney, June 27, 1814, in Crawford, *Documentary History*, 3: 123.
26. Mary Barney, *Biographical Memoir*, 259.
27. Geoghegan to Barney, July 14, 1814.
28. *National Intelligencer*, July 2, 1814.
29. Miller to Wharton, June 27, 1814.

30. Mary Barney, *Biographical Memoir*, 260; J. Barney to L. Barney, June 27, 1814.
31. Miller to Wharton, June 27, 1814.
32. Testimony of Col. Henry Carberry, Miller Enquiry.
33. Testimony of Col. Decius Wadsworth, Col. Henry Carberry, and Maj. George Keyser, Miller Enquiry.
34. Testimony of Col. Henry Carberry and Capt. Alfred Grayson, Miller Enquiry.
35. Testimony of 1st Lt. Benjamin Richardson, Miller Enquiry.
36. Deposition of Joshua Barney, Miller Enquiry.
37. *National Intelligencer*, July 9, 1814.
38. Thomas Brown to George Cockburn, June 27, 1814, Cockburn Papers.
39. Testimony of Col. Decius Wadsworth and Capt. Alfred Grayson, Miller Enquiry.
40. Ibid.
41. Testimony of Capt. Alfred Grayson and 1st Lt. Benjamin Richardson, Miller Enquiry.
42. *National Intelligencer*, July 9, 1814; extract from T. P. Andrews journal, June 26, 1814.
43. Testimony of Capt. Thomas Carberry, Miller Enquiry.
44. Joshua Barney to William Jones, June 26, 1814, in Crawford, *Documentary History*, 3: 123; log of HMS *Loire*, June 26, 1814.
45. Brown to Cockburn, June 27, 1814.
46. J. Barney to L. Barney, June 27, 1814.
47. Ibid.; Brown to Cockburn, June 27, 1814.

Chapter 16. Retribution and Recrimination

1. *National Intelligencer*, July 1–10, 1814.
2. Decision of Board of Officers, Miller Enquiry.
3. Mary Barney, *Biographical Memoir*, 262.
4. Thomas E. King to Benjamin King, quoted in Shomette, *Flotilla*, 165.
5. Alexander Cochrane to George Cockburn, July 1, 1814, Cockburn Papers.
6. George Cockburn to Alexander Cochrane, July 17, 1814, Cockburn Papers.
7. Alexander Cochrane, General Order, July 18, 1814, Cochrane Papers.
8. George Cockburn to Robert Barrie, July 14, 1814; George Cockburn to Alexander Cochrane, July 17, 1814; George Cockburn to Alexander Cochrane, July 19 and 21, 1814, Cockburn Papers.
9. Cockburn journal, July 19, 1814, Cockburn Papers.
10. George Cockburn to Alexander Cochrane, July 21, 1814, Cockburn Papers.
11. Scott, *Recollections*, 3: 242–43.

12. Ibid, 3: 245–46.
13. Cyril Field, *Britain's Sea Soldiers: A History of the Royal Marines* (Liverpool: Lyceum Press, 1924), 1: 299.
14. Joseph Nourse to George Cockburn, July 23, 1814, Cockburn Papers.
15. Ibid.
16. Joshua Barney to William Jones, July 21, 1814, in Crawford, *Documentary History,* 3: 147.
17. Joshua Barney to William Jones, July 24, 1814, in Crawford, *Documentary History,* 3: 148.
18. Nourse to Cockburn, July 23, 1814.
19. Cockburn journal, July 29–30, 1814, Cockburn Papers; Alexander Stuart to John Armstrong, July 24, 1814, in Crawford, *Documentary History,* 3: 167.
20. Scott, *Recollections,* 3: 250.
21. Frederick Chamier, *Life of a Sailor* (New York: J. J. Porter, 1833), 201.
22. The Petitions and Accompanying Papers relating to an Act of Congress for the Relief of Stephen Henderson, U.S. Treasury Department, Records of Various Settlements, NARA, RG 70, folder 862 [Henderson Claim].
23. Ibid.
24. Scott, *Recollections,* 3: 254–55.
25. Ibid.
26. Ibid., 3: 256.
27. Cockburn journal, August 4, 1814, Cockburn Papers.
28. Deposition of Maj. Gen. Alexander Parker, Henderson Claim.
29. Scott, *Recollections,* 3: 258.
30. Ibid., 259.
31. Ibid.
32. Ibid.
33. Ibid., 260–61.
34. George Cockburn to Alexander Cochrane, August 8, 1814, Cockburn Papers.
35. George Cockburn to Alexander Cochrane, August 13, 1814, Cockburn Papers.
36. Field, *Sea Soldiers,* 1: 300.

Chapter 17. Prelude to Disaster

1. John S. Williams, *History on the Invasion of Washington* (New York: Harper and Brothers, 1857), 45–48.
2. Ibid., 48.
3. Ibid., 47.

4. Richard M. Johnson et al., Report of the Committee on the Capture of Washington, *American State Papers, Military Affairs* [hereafter Johnson Report], 1: 524–25.

5. Williams, *History on the Invasion of Washington*, 77.

6. Ibid., 43.

7. William Winder to John Armstrong, July 9, 1814, in Report of Brig. Gen. William H. Winder, Johnson Report, 568.

8. Williams, *History on the Invasion of Washington*, 65.

9. Scott, *Recollections*, 3: 282.

10. Ibid.

11. William Jones to Joshua Barney, August 19, 1814, in Crawford, *Documentary History*, 3: 185.

12. Joshua Barney to William Jones, August 20, 1814, in Crawford, *Documentary History*, 3: 186.

13. William Jones to Joshua Barney, August 20, 1814, in Crawford, *Documentary History*, 3: 187.

14. William Jones to David Porter, August 19, 1814, and William Jones to John Rodgers, August 19, 1814, in Crawford, *Documentary History*, 3: 199.

15. George Gleig, *Campaigns of the British Army at Washington and New Orleans* (London: John Murray, 1879), 54.

16. George Cockburn to Alexander Cochrane, August 22, 1814, Cockburn Papers.

17. Mary Barney, *Biographical Memoir*, 268.

18. Williams, *History on the Invasion of Washington*, 66.

19. Report of John Van Vess, Johnson Report, 581.

20. Johnson Report, 527.

21. James Monroe to James Madison, August 23, 1814, Johnson Report, 539.

22. Johnson Report, 527.

23. Winder, Johnson Report, 555.

24. Ibid.

25. James Monroe to William Jones, August 19, 1814, in Crawford, *Documentary History*, 3: 197.

26. Report of Lt. Col. Jacint Laval, Johnson Report, 570.

27. Gleig, *Campaigns of the British Army*, 57.

28. Winder, Johnson Report, 556.

29. Ibid.

30. Report of Capt. Benjamin Burch, Johnson Report, 574.

31. Ibid.

32. Report of Brig. Gen. Tobias E. Stansbury, Johnson Report, 561.

33. George Cockburn to Alexander Cochrane, August 23, 1814, Cockburn Papers.

Chapter 18. The Bladensburg Races

1. Report of Brig. Gen, Tobias Stansbury, Johnson Report, 561.
2. Gleig, *Campaigns of the British Army*, 63.
3. William Winder to John Armstrong, August 24, 1814, in *Documents Accompanying the Report of the Committee Appointed on the Twenty-Third of September Last to Inquire into the Causes and Particulars of the Invasion of the City of Washington by the British Forces in the Month of August, 1814* (Washington, D.C.: A and G Way Printers, 1814) [hereafter *Committee Inquiry*], 115.
4. Report of William Winder, *Committee Inquiry*, 117.
5. Report of Benjamin Burch, Johnson Report, 574.
6. Report of John Armstrong, *Committee Inquiry*, 80.
7. Winder, *Committee Inquiry*, 146.
8. Ibid.
9. Mary Barney, *Biographical Memoir*, 261.
10. Report of Joshua Barney, *Committee Inquiry*, 283.
11. Armstrong, *Committee Inquiry*, 81.
12. Ibid.
13. Stansbury, Johnson Report.
14. Ibid.
15. Ibid.
16. Report of James Monroe, Johnson Report, 537; Williams, *History on the Invasion of Washington*, 282.
17. Ibid.
18. Monroe, Johnson Report.
19. Stansbury, Johnson Report.
20. Gleig, *Campaigns of the British Army*, 65.
21. Report of Benjamin Burch, Johnson Report, 574.
22. Report of William H. Winder, August 27, 1814, *Committee Inquiry*, 548.
23. Stansbury, Johnson Report, 562.
24. Report of William Pinkney, Johnson Report, 573.
25. Report of Walter Smith, Johnson Report, 565.
26. Report of Richard Rush, Johnson Report, 542.
27. Gleig, *Campaigns of the British Army*, 66; Stansbury, Johnson Report, 562.
28. Gleig, *Campaigns of the British Army*.
29. Ibid.
30. Pinkney, Johnson Report.
31. Report of Joseph Sterrett, Johnson Report, 568.
32. Ibid.
33. Ibid.; Pinkney, Johnson Report.
34. Pinkney, Johnson Report.

35. Winder, *Committee Inquiry*, 134.
36. Stansbury, Johnson Report, 562.
37. Barney, *Committee Inquiry*, 262.
38. Mary Barney, *Biographical Memoir*, 265.
39. Ball, *Fifty Years in Chains*, 468.
40. Report of Walter Smith, Johnson Report, 565.
41. Report of Col. Jacint Laval, *Committee Inquiry*, 239.
42. Smith, Johnson Report, 566.
43. Barney, Johnson Report, 263.
44. Gleig, *Campaigns of the British Army*, 67.
45. Samuel Miller to David Henshaw, December 24, 1843, Samuel Miller Papers.
46. Barney, Johnson Report, 263.
47. Anthony S. Pitch, *The Burning of Washington: The British Invasion of 1814* (Annapolis, Md.: Naval Institute Press, 1998), 83.
48. Mary Barney, *Biographical Memoir*, 266–67; Scott, *Recollections*, 291.
49. Mary Barney, *Biographical Memoir*, 268; Scott, *Naval Recollections*, 292.
50. Winder, *Committee Inquiry*, 169.
51. Report of Hanson Catlett, Johnson Report, 586.
52. Winder, *Committee Inquiry*, 168.

Chapter 19. Fire and Ruin

1. Scott, *Recollections*, 3: 295.
2. Pitch, *Burning of Washington*, 87–88.
3. Thomas Tingey to William Jones, August 27, 1814, in Crawford, *Documentary History*, 3: 215.
4. William Jones, memorandum, August 24, 1814, in Crawford, *Documentary History*, 3: 215.
5. Mordecai Booth to Thomas Tingey, August 24, 1814, in Crawford, *Documentary History*, 3: 210.
6. Gleig, *Campaigns of the British Army*, 68.
7. Scott, *Recollections*, 3: 296.
8. Ibid., 301.
9. Report of Thomas Tingey, Johnson Report, 578.
10. Scott, *Recollections*, 3: 301.
11. Ibid., 304.
12. Ibid., 305.
13. Ibid., 305–6; Pitch, *Burning of Washington*, 137–38.
14. Scott, *Recollections*, 3: 308.
15. Williams, *History on the Invasion of Washington*, 268–69; Pitch, *Burning of Washington*, 138–39.

16. Scott, *Recollections*, 3: 313.
17. Edward Delaval Hungerford Elers Napier, *The Life and Correspondence of Admiral Sir Charles Napier* (London: Hurst and Blankett, 1862), 78.
18. Ibid., 79.
19. Ibid., 80.
20. James Gordon to Alexander Cochrane, September 9, 1814, Cochrane Papers.
21. Report of John Morton, November 4, 1814, Johnson Report, 587.
22. Ibid.
23. William Winder to Samuel Dyson, August 24, 1814, in Williams, *History on the Invasion of Washington*, 272.
24. Samuel Dyson to John Armstrong, August 29, 1814, Johnson Report, 588.
25. Gordon to Cochrane, September 9, 1814.
26. Napier, *Life and Correspondence*, 80.
27. Ibid.
28. General Orders, Tenth Military District, November 17, 1814, Johnson Report, 588.
29. William Jones to John Rodgers, August 29, 1814, in Crawford, *Documentary History*, 3: 243.
30. Ibid.
31. William Jones to Oliver Hazard Perry, August 29, 1814, in Crawford, *Documentary History*, 3: 244.
32. William Jones to David Porter, August 29, 1814, in Crawford, *Documentary History*, 3: 244.
33. David Porter to William Jones, September 7, 1814, in Crawford, *Documentary History*, 3: 251–52; Oliver Hazard Perry to William Jones, September 3, 1814, in Crawford, *Documentary History*, 3: 248; John Rodgers to William Jones, September 3 and September 5, 1814, in Crawford, *Documentary History*, 3: 248–51.
34. Ibid.
35. Gordon to Cochrane, September 9, 1814.
36. Peter Parker to Alexander Cochrane, August 30, 1814, in Crawford, *Documentary History*, 3: 233.
37. Peter Parker to Alexander Cochrane, August 29, 1814, in Crawford, *Documentary History*, 3: 232.
38. Ibid.
39. Ibid.
40. Bills and Resolutions, 22nd Senate, 1st sess., March 9, 1832, S. Bill 141.
41. Chamier, *Life of a Sailor*, 1, 207.
42. Log of HMS *Menelaus*, August 30, 1814.
43. Edward F. Wright, *Maryland Militia: War of 1812* (Silver Spring, Md.: Family Line, 1979), 1, 38.

44. Philip Reed to Benjamin Chambers, September 3, 1814, in Crawford, *Documentary History*, 3: 235–36.
45. Chamier, *Life of a Sailor*, 1, 211.
46. Ibid.; Reed to Chambers, September 3, 1814.
47. Henry Crease to Alexander Cochrane, September 1, 1814, in Crawford, *Documentary History*, 3: 234–35.
48. Ibid.
49. Reed to Chambers, September 3, 1814; Maine, *British Invasion*, 122.

Chapter 20. Baltimore

1. Pitch, *Burning of Washington*, 183–84.
2. John Rodgers to William Jones, September 7, 1814, in Crawford, ed., *Documentary History*, 3: 286.
3. Samuel Smith to James Monroe, September 17, 1814, in Crawford, *Documentary History*, 3: 291.
4. John Rodgers to William Jones, September 23, 1814, in Crawford, *Documentary History*, 3: 300.
5. Ibid.; Pitch, *Burning of Washington*, 185.
6. Rodgers to Jones, September 23, 1814.
7. Gleig, *Campaigns of the British Army*, 93.
8. Ibid.
9. Arthur Brooke to Earl Bathurst, September 17, 1814, in Crawford, *Documentary History*, 3: 282.
10. Gleig, *Campaigns of the British Army*, 95.
11. Scott, *Recollections*, 3: 337.
12. Smith to Monroe, September 17, 1814.
13. Gleig, *Campaigns of the British Army*, 96.
14. Smith to Monroe, September 17, 1814.
15. Brooke to Bathurst, September 17, 1814, 3: 283.
16. James Williams, *Full and Correct Account of the Military Occurrences of the Late War between Britain and the United States* (London, 1818), 2: 321.
17. Brooke to Bathurst, September 17, 1814.
18. Alexander Cochrane to John Croker, September 17, 1814, in Crawford, *Documentary History*, 3: 287.
19. Lt. Henry Newcomb to John Rodgers, September 10–14, 1814, in Crawford, *Documentary History*, 3: 292–93.
20. Cochrane to Croker, September 17, 1814.
21. George Armistead to James Monroe, September 24, 1814, in Crawford, *Documentary History*, 3: 303.

22. Arthur Brooke to Alexander Cochrane, September 13, 1814, in Crawford, *Documentary History*, 3: 277.

23. Armistead to Monroe, September 24, 1814.

24. Ibid.

25. Solomon Rutter to John Rodgers, September 14, 1814, Rodgers Family Papers, Library of Congress, Manuscript Division.

26. Williams, *Full and Correct Account*, 2: 323.

27. Brook to Bathurst, September 17, 1814, 3: 284.

28. Ibid.

29. Scott, *Recollections*, 3: 344.

30. Alexander Cochrane to George Cockburn, September 13, 1814, in Crawford, *Documentary History*, 3: 277.

31. Scott, *Recollections*, 3: 345.

32. Arthur Brooke to Alexander Cochrane, September 14, 1814, in Crawford, *Documentary History*, 3: 278.

33. Alexander Cochrane to Charles Napier, September 13, 1814, in Crawford, *Documentary History*, 3: 278.

34. Elers Napier, *Charles Napier*, 1: 89–90.

35. Ibid.; Henry Newcomb to John Rodgers, September 18, 1814, Rodgers Family Papers.

36. Elers Napier, *Charles Napier*, 1: 91; Armistead to Monroe, September 24, 1814.

37. Ralph Eshelman, Scott Sheads, and Donald R. Hickey, *The War of 1812 in the Chesapeake: A Reference Guide to Historic Sites in Maryland, Virginia and the District of Columbia* (Baltimore: Johns Hopkins University Press, 2010), 345.

38. Robert G. Stewart, "The Battle of the Ice Mound, February 7, 1815," *Maryland Historical Magazine* 70, no. 4 (1975): 372–78; Eshelman et al., *The War of 1812 in the Chesapeake*, 149–50.

39. Elting, *Amateurs to Arms*, 285–93, 310–17.

40. Ibid.

41. Charles Gordon to Benjamin Crowninshield, February 15, 1815, in Crawford, *Documentary History*, 3: 365.

Bibliography

Primary Sources

American State Papers: Commerce and Navigation, vol. 1, 1789–1815

American State Papers: Finance, vol. 2, 1802–15

American State Papers: Foreign Relations, vol. 3, 1807–15

American State Papers: House Journal

American State Papers: Military Affairs, vol. 1, 1789–1819

American State Papers: Naval Affairs, vol. 1, 1794–1825

Annals of Congress

    Vol. 23, 12th Congress, 1st session, November 4, 1811, to March 9, 1812

    Vol. 24, 12th Congress, 1st session, March 9, 1812, to July 6, 1812

    Vol. 25, 12th Congress, 2nd session, November 2, 1812, to March 3, 1813

    Vol. 26, 13th Congress, 1st session, May 24, 1813, to February 16, 1814

    Vol. 27, 13th Congress, special session, February 16, 1814, to April 18, 1814

    Vol. 28, 13th Congress, 3rd session, September 19, 1814, to March 4, 1815

    Vol. 29, 14th Congress, 1st session, December 4, 1815, to April 30, 1816

Ball, Charles. *Fifty Years in Chains*. New York: Dover, 1970.

Barney, Mary. *Biographical Memoir of Commodore Joshua Barney*. Boston: Gray and Bowen, 1832.

Beatty, Henry. Henry Beatty Collection. Library of Congress, Manuscript Division.

Bryan Family Archives. Chestertown, Md. Stanley Quick Papers.

Chamier, Frederick. *Life of a Sailor*. New York: J. J. Porter, 1833.

Cochrane, Alexander Inglis. The Papers of Admiral Alexander I. Cochrane. Admiralty Letters to Admiral Sir John Borlase Warren, 1812–1814. Library of Congress, Manuscript Division.

———. The Papers of Sir Alexander Cochrane. Admiralty Letters Addressed to Admiral Sir John Borlase Warren and Delivered to Admiral Cochrane on His Assuming Command. Library of Congress, Manuscript Division.

Cockburn, George. The Papers of George Cockburn. Library of Congress, Manuscript Division.

Crabbe, Thomas. "Recollections of the Last War." *United States Nautical Magazine* 1 (1846): 341–44.

Crawford, Michael J., ed. *Naval War of 1812: A Documentary History*. Vol. 3. Washington, D.C.: Naval Historical Center, 1985.

Dudley, William S., ed. *Naval War of 1812: A Documentary History.* Vols. 1 and 2. Washington, D.C.: Naval Historical Center, 1985.

Exact and Authentic Narrative of the Events that Took Place in Baltimore the 27th and 28th of July Last, Carefully Collected from Some of the Eyewitnesses. Baltimore, Md., 1812.

Faulkner, James. James Faulkner Papers. Virginia Historical Society, Richmond, Va.

Field, Cyril. *Britain's Sea Soldiers: A History of the Royal Marines.* 3 vols. Liverpool: Lyceum Press, 1924.

Gordon, Charles. Charles Gordon Collection, Miscellaneous Papers. New York Public Library.

Harrison, Samuel A. Samuel A. Harrison Manuscript Collection. Maryland Historical Society, Baltimore, Md., MS 432.

Historical Register of the Army of the United States. Washington, D.C.: Government Printing Office, 1903.

Jones, Elias. *History of Dorchester County, Maryland.* Baltimore: Williams and Wilkins, 1902.

Letters of Captains to the Secretary of the Navy. National Archives and Records Administration, Record Group 45.

Letters of Masters Commandants to the Secretary of the Navy. National Archives and Records Administration, Record Group 147.

Letters of the Secretary of the Navy to Junior Officers. National Archives and Records Administration, Record Group 45.

Lovell, William Stanhope. *Personal Narrative of Events, 1799–1815, with Anecdotes.* Second edition. London: William Allen, 1879.

Madison, Dolley. The Papers of Dolley Madison. University of Virginia Alderman Library Special Collections, Charlottesville, Va.

Madison, James. James Madison Papers. Library of Congress, Manuscript Division, series 1.

Maryland Governor and Council Letterbook, 1796–1818. Maryland State Archives, Annapolis.

Miller, Samuel. Samuel Miller Papers. Marine Corps History Division, Quantico, Va.

Morris, Charles. *Autobiography of Commodore Charles Morris.* Annapolis, Md.: Naval Institute Press, 2002.

Napier, Edward Delaval Hungerford Elers. *The Life and Correspondence of Admiral Sir Charles Napier.* 2 vols. London: Hurst and Blackett, 1862.

Napier, William F. P. *The Life and Opinions of General Sir Charles James Napier.* 4 vols. London: John Murray, 1857.

Nicholson, William. William Nicholson to Thomas Wright, August 13, 1813. Maryland Historical Society, Baltimore, War of 1812 Collection, MS 1846.

Number of Troops in the Last War with Great Britain. Letter for the President of the United States communicating information in relation to the number of troops in the service for the United States in the late war with Great Britain. 35th Congress, 1st session, Ex Doc. no. 72.

Petitions and Accompanying Documents Related to the Act of Congress for the Relief of Stephen Henderson. U.S. Treasury Department. Records of Miscellaneous Settlements, National Archives and Records Administration, Record Group 70, folder 862.

Pickering, Timothy. Timothy Pickering Papers. Massachusetts Historical Society, Boston.

Proceedings of Court of Enquiry into the Conduct of the Marines at St. Leonard's Creek, Case No. 169. National Archives and Records Administration, Record Group 125, microfilm roll 273.

Proceedings of the General Court Martial of Commodore James Barron, Captain Charles Gordon, Mr. William Hook and Captain John Hall of the United States Ship Chesapeake in June, 1808. Washington, D.C.: Jacob Gideon Jr., 1822.

Register of Officer Personnel United States Navy and Marine Corps and Ships' Data, 1801–1807. Washington, D.C.: Government Printing Office, 1945.

Report of the Committee Appointed on the Twenty-Third of September Last to Inquire into the Causes and Particulars of the Invasion of the City of Washington, by the British Forces in the Month of August, 1814. Washington, D.C.: A and G Way, 1814.

Report of the Select Committee of the House of Delegates in respect to the Defense of Craney Island. Richmond, Va., 1848.

Royal Navy Log Books. Photocopies in Stanley Quick Papers.

HMS *Acasta*
HMS *Albion*
HMS *Barrosa*
HMS *Diadem*
HMS *Dragon*
HMS *Jaseur*
HMS *Junon*
HMS *Loire*
HMS *Menelaus*
HMS *Mohawk*
HMS *Narcissus*
HMS *Plantagenet*
HMS *St. Lawrence*
HMS *San Domingo*
HMS *Sceptre*

Scott, James. *Recollections of a Naval Life*. 3 vols. London: Richard Bentley, 1834.

Stewart, Robert Lord Castlereagh. *Memoirs and Correspondence of Viscount Castlereagh, Second Marquess of Londonderry*. 12 vols. London: William Shoberl, 1848–51.

Warren, Adm. Sir John Borlase. Correspondence between Admiral Sir John Borlase Warren and Robert Dundas, Viscount Melville, First Lord of the Admiralty. National Maritime Museum, Greenwich, England, Unbound Manuscript Collection.

Secondary Sources

Adams, Henry. *History of the United States of America during the Administrations of Jefferson and Madison*. Chicago: University of Chicago Press, 1967.

Adams, Henry, and John R. Elting. *The War of 1812*. New York: Cooper Square Press, 1999.

Adams, William Frederick. *Joshua Barney, U.S.N.* Springfield, Mass., 1910.

Barney, William L. *Captain Barney's Victory over the* General Monk. Philadelphia, 1806.

Berube, Claude, and John Rodgaard. *A Call to the Sea: Captain Charles Stewart of the USS* Constitution. Washington, D.C.: Potomac Books, 2005.

Borneman, Walter R. *1812: The War That Forged a Nation*. New York: HarperCollins, 2004.

Butler, Stuart Lee. *A Guide to Virginia Militia Units in the War of 1812*. Athens, Ga.: New Papyrus Publishing, 1988.

Calderhead, William L. "A Strange Career in a Young Navy: Captain Charles Gordon, 1778–1816." *Maryland Historical Magazine* 72, no. 3 (1972): 373–86.

Carson, William F. "Norfolk and Anglo-American Relations, 1805–1815." Master's thesis, Old Dominion University, Norfolk, Va.

Chapelle, Howard I. *History of the American Sailing Navy*. New York: W. W. Norton, 1949.

Cochrane, Alexander. *The Fighting Cochranes*. London: Quiller Press, 1983.

Cooper, James Fenimore. *History of the Navy of the United States*. 3 vols. New York: Singer and Townsend, 1856.

Cullum, George Washington. *Register of Officers and Graduates of the U.S. Military Academy at West Point, from March 16, 1802 to January 1, 1850*. New York: J. F. Trow, 1850.

Daughan, George C. *If by Sea: The Forging of the American Navy—from the American Revolution to the War of 1812*. New York: Basic Books, 2008.

De Kay, James T. *The Battle of Stonington: Torpedoes, Submarines and Rockets in the War of 1812*. Annapolis, Md.: Naval Institute Press, 1990.

Dictionary of National Biography. London: Smith, Elder, and Company, 1908–9.

Elting, John R. *Amateurs to Arms: A Military History of the War of 1812*. Chapel Hill, N.C.: Algonquin Books, 1991.

Eshelman, Ralph E. *Maryland's Largest Naval Engagement: The Battle of St. Leonard's Creek, 1814, Calvert County, Maryland*. St. Leonard, Md.: Friends of Jefferson-Patterson Park and Museum, 2005.

Footner, Hubert. *Sailor of Fortune: The Life and Adventures of Commodore Barney, U.S.N.* New York: Harper Brothers, 1940.

Fulton, Robert. *Torpedo War and Submarine Explosions*. New York: William Elliott, 1910.

George, Christopher T. *Terror on the Chesapeake: The War of 1812 on the Bay*. Shippensburg, Pa.: White Maine Books, 2000.

Gleaves, Albert. *James Lawrence*. New York: G. P. Putnam and Sons, 1904.

Ingersoll, Charles J. *Historical Sketch of the Second War between the United States of America and Great Britain*. 2 vols. Philadelphia: Lea and Blanchard, 1845.

Ingraham, Edward Duncan. *A Sketch of the Events which Preceded the Capture of Washington by the British*. Philadelphia: Carey and Hart, 1829.

Jacobs, James R., and Glenn Tucker. *The War of 1812: A Compact History*. New York: Hawthorne Books, 1969.

James, William. *The Naval History of Great Britain from the Declaration of War by France in 1793 to the Accession of George IV*. 6 vols. London: R. Bentley, 1878.

Johnston, George. *History of Cecil County, Maryland*. Elkton, Md., 1881.

Lambert, Andrew. *Admirals*. London: Faber and Faber, 2009.

——. *The Challenge: Britain against America in the War of 1812*. London: Faber and Faber, 2013.

——, gen. ed. *War at Sea in the Age of Sail*. New York: Collins, 2005.

Lavery, Brian. *Nelson's Navy: The Ships, Men and Organization, 1793–1815*. Annapolis, Md.: Naval Institute Press, 1987.

Lord, Walter. *By Dawn's Early Light*. New York: W. W. Norton, 1972.

Maclay, Edgar Stanton. *A History of American Privateers*. New York: D. Appleton and Company, 1899.

Marine, William H. *The British Invasion of Maryland, 1812–1815*. Baltimore, Md.: Society of the War of 1812 in Maryland, 1913.

Marshall, John. *Royal Naval Biography; or Memoirs of the Services of All the Flag Officers, Superannuated Rear Admirals, Retired Captains, Post Captains and Commanders*. London: Longman, Rees, Orme, Brown, and Green, 1829.

McKenzie, Alexander Slidell. *The Life of Commodore Oliver Hazard Perry.* New York: Harper and Brothers, 1840.

Morales, Lisa R. *The Financial History of the War of 1812.* Denton: University of North Texas Press, 2009.

Muller, Charles G. *The Darkest Day, 1814: The Washington-Baltimore Campaign.* Philadelphia: J. B. Lippincott, 1963.

Nicolas, Paul Harris. *Historical Record of the Royal Marine Forces.* London: Thomas and William Boone, 1845.

Norton, Louis. *Joshua Barney, Hero of the Revolution and 1812.* Annapolis, Md.: Naval Institute Press, 2000.

Pack, James. *The Man Who Burned the White House: Admiral Sir George Cockburn, 1772–1853.* Annapolis, Md.: Naval Institute Press, 1987.

Paine, Ralph D. *Joshua Barney: A Forgotten Hero of Blue Water.* New York: Century, 1924.

Peterson, Harold L. *The Book of the Continental Soldier.* Harrisburg, Pa.: Stackpole, 1968.

Petrie, Donald A. *The Prize Game: Lawful Looting on the High Seas in the Days of Fighting Sail.* New York: Berkeley Books, 1999.

Pitch, Anthony S. *The Burning of Washington: The British Invasion of 1814.* Annapolis, Md.: Naval Institute Press, 1998.

Powell, William H. *List of Officers of the Army of the United States from 1779 to 1900, Embracing a Register of All Appointments by the President of the United States in the Volunteer Service during the Civil War, and of Volunteer Officers in the Service of the United States, June 1, 1900.* New York: L. R. Hamersly, 1900.

Reid, Chipp. *Intrepid Sailors: The Legacy of Preble's Boys and the Tripoli Campaign.* Annapolis, Md.: Naval Institute Press, 2012.

Scharf, Thomas J. *Chronicles of Baltimore.* Baltimore: Turnbull Brothers, 1874.

Shomette, Donald G. *Flotilla: The Patuxent Naval Campaign in the War of 1812.* Baltimore: Johns Hopkins University Press, 2009.

Smith, Gene Allen. *The Slaves' Gamble: Choosing Sides in the War of 1812.* New York: Palgrave Macmillan, 2013.

Thomlinson, Everett T. *The War of 1812.* New York: Silver Burdett and Company, 1906.

Tilghman, Oswald. *History of Talbot County, Maryland, 1661–1861.* 2 vols. Baltimore: Williams and Wilkins, 1915.

Trow, Charles E. *The Old Shipmasters of Salem, with Mention of Eminent Merchants.* New York: G. P. Putnam and Sons, 1905.

U.S. Department of Commerce. *Historical Statistics of the United States from Colonial Times to 1970.* Part 2.

Williams, James. *Full and Correct Account of the Military Occurrences of the Late War between Britain and the United States.* London, 1818.

Williams, John S. *A History on the Invasion and Capture of Washington.* New York: Harper and Brothers, 1857.

Wirth, Robert, and Thomas Pinder. Unpublished Research for Wells-McComma VFW Post, Edgemore, Md.

Wright, F. Edward. *Maryland Militia, War of 1812.* 7 vols. Silver Spring, Md.: Family Line, 1979.

INDEX

About the Author

The late Dr. Stanley Quick served on active duty in the U.S. Navy from 1944 to 1947 before working for many years as a naval architect and civilian engineer. First with Edo Corporation and later with Target Rock Corporation, he conceived and developed helicopter, airship, and ship-towed sonar systems. He then went to Fairchild Republic Corporation, where he directed all proposal, research, and development activities of electric-powered rotary-wing aircraft. In 1963, a year after receiving his PhD from Brooklyn Polytechnic, he began his career with Westinghouse Electric Corporation. Following his retirement from Westinghouse in 1985, Dr. Quick formed his own business entity, Man-Tech Associates, Inc., as a consulting firm in management and technical programs. In his retirement he developed a passion for Maryland's Eastern Shore and the War of 1812, meticulously researching and writing what would eventually become *Lion in the Bay*. He died in 2008 and is survived by his wife of forty years, Marian.

About the Editor

Chipp Reid is an award-winning reporter and editor, a licensed ship captain, a historian, and a Marine Corps veteran. He has covered the wars in Iraq and Afghanistan as well as baseball, international soccer, and international piracy. Reid now works in Washington, D.C., and lives in Annapolis, Md., with his two dogs. His 2012 book *Intrepid Sailors: The Legacy of Preble's Boys and the Tripoli Campaign* (Naval Institute Press) was named a "Notable Naval Book of 012" by *Proceedings* magazine.

The Naval Institute Press is the book-publishing arm of the U.S. Naval Institute, a private, nonprofit, membership society for sea service professionals and others who share an interest in naval and maritime affairs. Established in 1873 at the U.S. Naval Academy in Annapolis, Maryland, where its offices remain today, the Naval Institute has members worldwide.

Members of the Naval Institute support the education programs of the society and receive the influential monthly magazine *Proceedings* or the colorful bimonthly magazine *Naval History* and discounts on fine nautical prints and on ship and aircraft photos. They also have access to the transcripts of the Institute's Oral History Program and get discounted admission to any of the Institute-sponsored seminars offered around the country.

The Naval Institute's book-publishing program, begun in 1898 with basic guides to naval practices, has broadened its scope to include books of more general interest. Now the Naval Institute Press publishes about seventy titles each year, ranging from how-to books on boating and navigation to battle histories, biographies, ship and aircraft guides, and novels. Institute members receive significant discounts on the Press's more than eight hundred books in print.

Full-time students are eligible for special half-price membership rates. Life memberships are also available.

For a free catalog describing Naval Institute Press books currently available, and for further information about joining the U.S. Naval Institute, please write to:

Member Services
U.S. Naval Institute
291 Wood Road
Annapolis, MD 21402-5034
Telephone: (800) 233-8764
Fax: (410) 571-1703
Web address: www.usni.org